S0-BKO-929

TEXAS

THE ALAMO, Shrine of Texas liberty, site of the battle of the Alamo in 1836 in which all 187 defending Texas soldiers were killed in one of the major battles of the Texas revolution.

— Photo courtesy the San Antonio Convention and Visitors Bureau

Archie P.
McDONALD

EAKIN PRESS AUSTIN, TEXAS

This history of Texas originally appeared in the *Dallas Times Herald* and their cooperation for this edition is gratefully acknowledged.

FIRST EDITION

Published in the United States of America
By Eakin Press, P.O. Box 23066, Austin, Texas 78735

ISBN 0-89015-388-4

FOR JUDY
And other "professional" Texans

THE STATE CAPITOL, built of native pink granite from nearby Burnet County.

CONTENTS

PALO DURO CANYON — Splendid scenery, rich in historical and geological significance makes Palo Duro Canyon the most celebrated attraction in the Texas panhandle near Amarillo. The best known formation is The Lighthouse, a tower carved out of solid rock by millions of years of erosion.

INTRODUCTION

Texas. Land. The two words seem to have the same meaning. Before the people came, before some of its rivers became political boundaries or transportation arteries or needed bridging, before its skies rumbled with sonic booms or glistened with the reflection of sunlight on the aluminum of mechanical birds, before great cities grew from the stimulus of cattle, crops, and oil, before the words of men on deeds and documents made it "private" and precious, before humans gave it their values and morals, Texas was just land.

The land changed constantly from the beginning. Wind and water change the three hundred and seventy mile coast daily, sometimes in hurricane season dramatically. The lighter soils, particularly of the western regions, blow in the summer sun; in the winters freezing water forces large rocks into smaller portions. Singly and in combination, these forces of nature build, rearrange, destroy, and build again. Geological action lifts the land and the seas recede; erosion lowers it and the sea returns, each time leaving deposits of animal and vegetable life to gather, fossilize, occasionally to transform itself into a black liquid which would be much valued by people in a distant future.

People have changed the land most of all. They have come as invaders and conquerors, for no human life is known to have originated here as in Africa, Asia, and Europe. And the people always came in struggle, running from climactic changes, food supply problems, other human enemies, or forces unimaginable to modern peoples. In later periods they came running to Texas' abundant and inexpensive land, alternately offered by friendly governments or in spite of unfriendly ones, running to fertile soils, milder winter climates, or to economic opportunities unavailable elsewhere. But always they have changed the land.

The first invaders doubtless regarded the land as empty, save for mastadons, sloths, and other huge animals they hunted with spears. Later invaders, still hunters, wandered the prairies and stream beds ever vigilant for their daily food and for others who might take it from them. Their concept of the land remained broad. No individual owned it as it was owned by the group, and it supplied the group's needs through the individual. The most recent invaders, Europeans mostly, assumed the land could belong to them in both collective and individual ways. Their kings or presidents presided over the dividing, rewarding their followers with land and its bounty just for being there, for service to the government, in settlement of debt to people and corporations.

These latter invaders changed the land most of all. They used the plow to break the land, and wood and wire to parcel its access and its use from others of their kind. And in a later age, they used mechanical monsters to remove it or move it about as they wanted. These people came to live together in such density that they built their houses higher than wider until they reached hundreds of feet into the sky. Their search for food, although still provided by the land, then centered on storehouses where they paid money earned elsewhere for their larder, even paying others to prepare the food for their use. Without realizing it at first—and glorying in the achievement when they did realize it—these people created a gigantic network of interindependence. No longer did all men hunt or pray, and all women preside in the lodge; now one labored and one managed and some did this or that for money to hire what they could not or would not do for themselves. No longer was the land a direct giver of food and sustenance, yet it grew constantly more valuable to them, a value based more on proximity to their daily activities than to its productivity, unless productivity is measured in minerals, especially oil. So Texas became more than land; it became people.

People have lived on the land of Texas for thousands of years, but until four hundred and fifty years ago, their sameness remains their distinction. The Paleo-Americans, who were first, and the American Indians who followed them, followed the same nomadic lifestyle and remained in cycles of their separate stock. The Europeans and their progeny came from a Babel of different cultures, countries, and religions, and developed into seemingly countless varieties from their own chemistry. When their numbers were sufficient — when they equalled the number of cattle — some say the people and not land became Texas. For them, centers of learning and medical healing and trade developed, some for profit and some for service. For them altars of pleasure, Astrodomes and Texas Stadiums and Cotton Bowls and concert halls appeared, all for profit, yet all serving the people's need for diversion. For the people, shrines of worship multiplied and became electronically pervasive, mostly for service, sometimes for profit. For them great business houses and stores and exchanges were erected, some housed in shiny buildings that reflected the sun, some covered in domes or enclosed within long, rectangular malls, some standing in individual independence, totally for profit, but also providing service.

For all these peoples, these nearly 15,000,000 inhabiters of the land — now nearly ninety percent of them living above the soil in high rises or on concrete slabs — the land is no longer close, no longer a clear source of their support. Symbols have changed as well. The hunter, bearing spear or bow and arrow, symbolizes the first invaders. For early Europeans and their farmer and rancher descendants, a man kneeling, running the soil through his fingers to feel its wetness or its dryness — it is never in between — to draw strength from its nutrients, and to know the progressive surge when it is *his* land, symbolized the middling time. But for the modern Texan, no single symbol will suffice. The modern Texan may find his meaning in an oil derrick or a windmill, in a ribbon of highway or a city street, in an armadillo or a mechanical bull, in a longneck or a longhorn, in designer cowboy costumes or three-piece business suits; in fact, in anything, so long as it is personal and new.

Modern Texans are still invaders, still possessers, still cowboyish and extractive in their attitudes, and they still feel for the land, even long for it, especially on weekends. They have come to terms with the land; they know what part of it they own and generally who cwns the rest of it. They use it, sometimes abuse it, but they expect it to be there always, parent-like in dependability. It still calls them — us — for we have yet to achieve the land's full potential for us.

BOOKS PUBLISHED BY ARCHIE P. McDONALD

By Early Candlelight, The Story of Old Milam. Masonic Home Press; Fort Worth, 1967.

Hurrah for Texas! The Diary of Adolphus Sterne. Texian Press: Waco, 1969.

The Mexican War: Crisis for American Democracy. D. C. Heath: Boston, 1969.

Fighting Men, The Western Military Heritage. Kendall-Hunt: Dubuque, Iowa, 1970.

Make Me a Map of the Valley: The Journal of Jedediah Hotchkiss, 1862-1865. Southern Methodist University Press: Dallas, 1974.

Recollections of a Long Life. Blue-Gray Press: Nashville, 1974.

First United Methodist Church, San Augustine, Texas, 1837-1976. Henington Publishing Co.: Wolf City, 1976.

Travis. Pemberton Press: Austin, 1977.

Eastern Texas History. Jenkins Publishing Company: Austin, 1978.

Nacogdoches: Wilderness Outpost to Modern City, 1779-1979. Eakin Press: Austin, 1980.

On This Day of New Beginnings: Selected Inaugural Addresses of Texas Governors. Texas State Library: Austin, 1979.

The Texas Heritage. Forum Press: St. Louis, 1980.

The Old Stone Fort. Texas State Historical Association: Austin, 1981.

The Texas Republic. American Book Company: Boston, 1981.

The Trail to San Jacinto. American Book Company, Boston: 1981.

Texas: A Sesquicentennial Presentation. Published by the DALLAS TIMES-HERALD, March, 1982.

ABOUT THE AUTHOR

Archie P. McDonald is Professor of History at Stephen F. Austin State University in Nacogdoches, Texas. He is a specialist in the fields of Texas history and the American Civil War.

McDonald received his primary and secondary education in Texas schools, his Bachelor of Science degree from Lamar University in Beaumont, his Master of Arts degree from Rice University in Houston, and his doctorate from Louisiana State University. His dissertation on Jedediah Hotchkiss, Stonewall Jackson's topographer, later published as *Make Me A Map of the Valley,* was a Civil War History Book Club selection, and was named to the *Civil War Times Illustrated's* list of the one hundred best books on the Civil War.

In addition to teaching and writing, McDonald serves as Executive Director of the East Texas Historical Association and as editor of its journal. He is also vice president of the Texas State Historical Association, Chairman of the Texas Committee for the Humanities, a member of the Advisory Board for the National Registry of the Texas Historical Commission, and a member of the Texas Sesquicentennial Commission.

LAND, the wide expanse of Texas is symbolized by this solitary windmill on this typical West Texas ranch.

1

Land And Early Invaders

Before there was a Texas, two hundred and fifty million years ago, in a time of the earth's development called the Pennsylvanian Age, mountains stretched northeasternly towards the present Red River from the area now called Big Bend on the Rio Grande. To the northeast, a shallow but lively sea covered the earth, and to the south and east dry land lay in what is now called the Gulf of Mexico. Life no longer present on this globe — strange reptiles, amphibians, vegetation unseen by any human — grew, flourished, and died.

Geologic action uplifted and drained the Permian Sea, the dry land became the continental shelf, and the waters of the sea covered it over. The mountains wore away in the wind, sediment covered and sealed the plant and animal life, and fresh earth washed down from more northerly areas to cover the sediments and provide soils for new life. Nearly 100 million years ago, in the Cretaceous Age, waters covered the eastern and western portions of Texas, and the dry land rose in the middle of the present map. It was a time of dinosaurs and other unfamiliar creatures, vegetarian and carnivorous. Again the swamps teemed with animal and plant life, and again geologic change captured the residue in pockets and with pressure and time, changed its substance into energy for the future.

Then the mountains came again. Not just in Texas, but in all the earth; the planet rearranged itself. Texas was pushed upward into nearly its present form, with a southeasterly slope and a drainage pattern that carried the rains and snows of the north and west to water the south and east, eventually to empty into the Gulf of Mexico. Within this last millennium, the basic features of modern Texas formed. Here merged all of the major geological forms of North America: the southern forest land, the central prairies, and the mountains.

As the earth cooled, warmed, and endured its constant change, even at a glacial pace, the western portions gradually became drier until desert conditions prevailed. This land remained fertile, even though it lacked life-giving moisture. The east, perhaps less fertile, retained its water, and thus could first support human life in greater numbers.

But there is much more to the earth of Texas than eastern and western portions. The Coastal Plain extends along the Gulf of Mexico from the Sabine River to present Corpus Christi, and moves inland for varying distances as much as two hundred miles. Its sandy soils are marshes in the lowest regions, but change to savannahs and timberland a few miles inland. Its salt grass has fed cattle for two centuries; its salt domes have produced oil from thousands of wells in the present century; and some of it has been used as rice fields or for row crops.

East Texas extends northward from the Coastal Plains along the Louisiana border, and is generally acknowledged as the area between the Sabine and Trinity Rivers as far north as the blacklands on the west and to the Red River directly north. The region's pine forests and hardwood stands are watered by the state's most generous rainfall, fifty-five inches annually in its wettest spots, and it has abundant animal and plant life. In the area just north of Beaumont, the Big Thicket Biological Preserve seeks to husband one of Texas' last vestiges of near-wilderness. The Thicket flora include such exotics as orchid, bay, and chinquapin, and its fauna counts reptiles, deer, armadillos, and innumerable ticks, among its many varieties.

East Texas developed the state's saw milling industry as early as 1816 near San Augustine and the state's first million dollar corporation, the Kirby Lumber Company, by the end of the nineteenth century. As a supplier of timber, the region participated in every phase of industrial development from railroads — supplying cross ties, for example — to the building of Houston and Dallas skyscrapers and homes. Although cotton ruled in the central and northern portion of East Texas in *ante-bellum* and post-Civil War years, the area is now dominated by wood processing, mostly plywood and paper, and by cattle, broilers, watermelons, peas and other crops.

West and north of the Coastal Plain and East Texas lie the Central Texas Prairies. The Colorado River country is the western boundary, then it runs north to the Red River. The Central Prairies are punctuated by the Eastern Cross Timbers, in the Dallas-Fort Worth vicinity, and the Cross Timbers proper, situated to the west of Fort Worth. These aberrations have some trees, usually oaks and mesquite, which offers some relief to the eye from the rolling, open country which supports grains, cotton, livestock farming and features oil wells in the Wichita Falls area to the west.

The celebrated and beautiful Hill Country, claiming Austin as its eastern extremity, features a terrain which suggests young mountains, at least until the real thing is encountered in the Basin and Mountain country of the far western reaches of the state. Dotted with mountain cedar and juniper, the Hill Country is good land for sheep, goats, and cattle, and its capital (as well as the state's), Austin, supports an educational center and a variety of country musicians.

To the far south, the Rio Grande Valley is Texas' cornucopia. Nearly anything that can be grown in California's Imperial Valley or Florida's rich central plains will grow in the Rio Grande Valley, including the Ruby Red grapefruit and other citrus crops. The Valley serves as a "snowbird" rookery in winter and the Latin influence is also strong in the Valley's towns. The state's largest contemporary ranching enterprise, the King Ranch, spreads out northward from the fruit trees.

Just to the northwest of the Valley, the Edwards Plateau sprawls across the lower central area of the state. The Plateau claims San Antonio and San Angelo as principal cities. Neither is truly on the Plateau, yet both service its commercial needs. It leads the state, and the nation, in wool and mohair production. Much of the land has been lost to dryness, drought, and erosion, but when watered, it can provide good pasture land.

The Basin and Mountain Country, or the Trans-Pecos, looks more like Old or New Mexico than it does any other part of Texas. It nearly remained a part of the first and would have become a part of the second had not Major Robert S. Neighbors established El Paso County in 1850 and called it Texas. This is true mountain and desert country, fit mostly for livestock and those who can stand the sun. Its principal city, El Paso, and its twin, Ciudad Juarez, wrap around the Franklin Mountains and gaze across a mud puddle in amazing international tranquility.

The High Plains is separated from the lower country by an escarpment called the Cap Rock. The true High Plains, whether called High around Amarillo or South around Lubbock, has become the row crop capital of the state. In the 19th century, East Texas played that role while Comanches roamed these western plains. Afterwards came the farmers and the miracle of the underground rain sucked to the surface by windmills, and the cotton culture moved to the fertile lands of the west. Maize, corn, and other crops grow so abundantly that sometimes one cannot see the end of the rows from Highway 84. In recent years, feed lots, each containing literally thousands of cattle in the last phase of their service, have been located in the plains to take advantage of the grain; curiously, many of the cattle were born in east and central Texas and then trucked to the grain.

Texas' climate varies dramatically because of the state's dimensions. Winter's cold and snow are fairly plentiful in the Panhandle, as the northern plains are called. Here the annual growing season is less than 200 days. Below Austin, the season lasts nearly 300 days annually. Growing seasons expand along generally horizontal lines as one looks at a map of the state, but precipitation grade lines are almost vertical; thus Amarillo receives about the same amount as San Angelo, and west of the 98th meridian there is never enough. East of the meridian, Texarkana will receive about as much rain as Nacogdoches or Livingston, over two hundred miles to the south. Depending on how these lines intersect, different lifestyles, economies, and even cultures develop. The environment dictates, it sets the limits of development. Technology can sometimes alter this development — witness the windmill — but it cannot permanently change nature.

It is convenient to think of East Texas as an extension of the Old South. In racial attitudes and economy, this was once true. Now it is more New South, largely owned by timber corporations, with a generous representation of the petroleum industry, many with out-of-state management. And in myth, West Texas remains the land of the cowboy, although the West Texan is as often seen riding a tractor, a combine, or perhaps an oil field service truck.

Everywhere in Texas the constant factor is the sun. Its warming rays bathe all parts of the state and make it a productive area. Often the sun also gives Texas the nation's summer, and sometimes winter, temperature highs; from Maine to Oregon, weather watchers have heard of Presidio for such dubious honors. The sun browns, weathers, gives outdoor Texans reddish-brown countenances and bleached white foreheads, stores its energy for millions of years in subterranial petroleum or for a season in citrus, truck crops and beef; the sun is hidden behind enormous clouds sometimes, but more often Texans can find no clouds to protect them from its heat. The Holy Bible claims that the rain falls on the just and unjust alike. The sun is more fitting for Texas.

The land has always been here, the people are more recent. Just when the first humans arrived, and why they left their former dwelling place, is unknown. We may assume that no Chamber of Commerce advertised the advantages of plentiful space, sunny climate, abundant labor, low taxes, and a friendly business climate, the daily attractions for thousands of people in the present century. These Paleo-Americans, a Caucasoid group who inhabited the Central Plains of the United States and of Texas as much as 15,000 or more years ago, probably came because of adverse climactic changes in their beginning place, possibly because enemies drove them out, or perhaps because their food supply system altered with the coming of glaciers. All is speculation. Archeologists differ on the arrival date of the Paleo-Americans because of the paucity of the discovery sites and artifacts. They are generally agreed, however, that the Paleo-Americans dwelled mostly in Texas in the High Plains and that they were oriented by the Clovis and Folsum cultures, the Clovis culture being the earlier one, named for discoveries of fluted spear points at sites in eastern New Mexico.

These spear points have been found in conjunction with fossilized vertebrae of huge animals such as the now extinct mastadon. Many are discovered at such sites, indicating socialized action for the hunt. One Paleo-American and one elephant would have been a totally uneven match. Together,

Tonkawa Indian woman typical of the Indian peoples in Texas at the time of the arrival of the first Europeans.

— From Smithsonian Institute
Photo courtesy Kenneth F. Neighbours

several of them could evidently bring one of the great beasts down for all to feast upon. Spear points and human bones have been discovered near Abilene, Midland, Plainview, and in a dump at Lubbock. Farther to the east, near Malakoff on the Trinity River, recent discoveries of points and three head-shaped sculptures have been attributed to these people. Human bones called "Midland Minnie," for they are female bones, are the earliest skeletal remains discovered.

As speculative as any observation about the Paleo-Americans must remain, these people evidently migrated with some social organization and maturity as a culture. They stood erect and used weapons sufficient to kill large prey; they used fire, presumably for ceremony as well as function, they wore skin garments, and they could fashion tools and weapons from flint and stone.

And then they vanished. They departed as mysteriously as they had come, for the group still called Indians after Christopher Columbus' misappellation, knew nothing of them. At least the Indians' cultures bear no witness of having taken the land from these people or having ever seen them. Even these Indians' arrival remains nearly as mysterious.

The group of Mongolian-stock peoples known as American Indians migrated from their native regions thousands of years ago. Their state of development did not differ significantly by contemporary standards from that of tribal Europeans of the same age. They walked on glaciers and land from the Siberian coast via the Bering Strait to the mainland of North America. Later they could use outrigger vessels to navigate the narrow passage between the continents. They fanned out across North and South America and generally lost whatever political, economic or social unity they may have once had.

Numbering only a million or so throughout the total land mass north of present Mexico at the time of European discovery, they had so accommodated to the environment and divided into small bands that for centuries they hardly recognized other Indians as their own kind. Most, regardless of tribe or clan, called themselves merely "the people," as distinguished from other natural phenomena. Once a group became separated, within a short time they lost the skill of oral communication with other groups as they developed new words or new meanings for old words, although most Indians generally retained the ability to communicate with one another by hand signals.

Across the land they developed into three major groups, the Forest Dwellers, the most prosperous because they lived on lands which provided the most natural foods, plant or animal; the Plains Indians, a nomadic group that lived in animal skins and constantly pursued the animals that produced them, as a source of food; and the Inter-mountain Seed Gatherers, the poorest of Indians because they found the poorest land for their food supply. They ate anything, literally, that would sustain life. All three of these groups, reflecting their geography, are represented in Texas. Until the coming of the Europeans, Texas Indians remained on the periphery of greater Indian Civilizations. To the east the Mound Builders reached greater sophistication, and to the south the Inca, Mayas and Aztecs achieved even more. Texas Indians, even the forest people called Caddo, lived a more primitive existence.

The East Texas Caddo belonged to a larger confederacy of Indians, one wing called Caddo and including peoples in Texas, Louisiana, and Arkansas, and another called the Hasinai group in the Angelina and Neches River areas to the south. Tribal or clan names included the Nacogdoche, the Naconiche, and the Natchtoche. Their villages stretched along creeks and rivers, rather than being clustered in true towns; the people lived in dome-shaped houses of stakes, twigs, mud, and plant life, layered up to a point at the top. The Caddoes were weavers of reeds, which they used as rugs, baskets, and bedding. They gathered the produce of the forests, including small animals and plants, and they had come by the time of the Europeans to be harvesters of their own crops of corn. Of all Texas Indians, these were the traders. They established exchanges with Comanches, for instance, for the flint of the western regions which they traded forest foods and bois d'arc wood to acquire. And they were emotional. Unlike the fabled Indian who never shows emotion, Caddoes wept for every occasion from joy to grief.

To the south the Caddo blended with the Atakapas, hunters and fish gatherers, known by clan identification as Orcoquisacs and Bidais. Farther south and west of the Atakapa, and extending along the coast, dwelled the Karankawa. They roamed the forest's edge, the marsh land, even the seacoast for food. Because they lived in heavy mosquito country, they annointed their bodies with foul-smelling animal grease to ward off the pests. The Karankawas still practiced ritualistic cannabalism when the first Europeans encountered them in the sixteenth century.

In South Texas lived the real Indian farmers, the Tonkawas. Like all Texas Indians, the Tonkawas also hunted for food. South of the Tonkawas lived the diggers and grubbers, called Coahuiltecans. The land yielded little food and great effort was required to obtain what was there. Spiders, ants, and other indelicacies to the modern Texan's palate were their fare, when they could find them. In the mission phase of Spanish control, these Indians became cooperative with the missionaries, perhaps because they had the most to gain.

In the far west lived the Apaches. They arrived somewhat later than the other Indians, so they had to fight for territory. They seemed always to be fighting, for this was their only true socializing activity. Whether western (Chiracahua, Mescalero), or eastern (Lipan, Jicarillas), they dominated the West Texas area as the first fighters and hunters until the Comanches came down from their mountain domiciles, learned the horse culture from the Spanish, and became the lords of the plains. This transition made the Comanches, who eventually dominated the plains country and Central Texas, into the most feared of all Texas Indians. The Caddoes traded with the Comanches for flint, but they would run rather than fight them. Even Apaches had second thoughts about combat with Comanches. They also were the last Indians to resist the Anglo-Americans, continuing their raids until late in the nineteenth century in order to defend their lands from encroachment.

Although environment and resulting lifestyles differed, Texas Indians had much in common. Their societies are sometimes called a "cultural sink" between the richer cultures to the east, south and west, but this may be unfair. The Texas Indians reflected the diversity of their kind; unlike the Paleo-Americans who retained a cultural unity appropriate to their territory and numbers, American Indians occupied the entire hemisphere and were sometimes widely separated from each other. Most, however, understood effective, if primitive, and artful, if functional, ways to make tools from stone, bone, wood and reed. They developed the use of the atlatl, a spear-like weapon propelled with great accuracy by a grooved shaft, and later the bow and arrow, to great skillfulness. Most had domesticated dogs. By the time of European arrival in the New World, especially in Texas, most Indians practiced some form of agriculture. Indeed, American Indian husbandry has developed over half of the world's edible crops, including corn, potatoes, beans, squash, pumpkins and peanuts. Some Texas Indians grew and used tobacco and cotton as well. They accomplished this without the use of the horse as a draft animal or for anything else. When they did obtain horses many became expert in using them for hunting as well as fighting.

The beginnings of Indian life in Texas remain speculative, but the end of their way of life has been more positively documented. No European conqueror regarded the Indians as owners of the lands they used. When the Europeans came, they took what they wanted. The Spanish attempted to use the Indians as laborers until this proved unproductive; they tried to Christianize the Indians to salve their own national and individual consciences as long as it suited them, then abandoned them. The French were willing to trade with them so long as it proved profitable. But the English and their descendants merely wanted to remove them, by whatever means, from their way. Thus, cultures thousands of years in the making were crushed, absorbed, altered. And the Spanish came first to have their way.

The Spanish Arrive And Leave

Christopher Columbus, a Genoese sailing for the kingdom of Spain, sougth a water route to the riches of the East which would not require the services of Mediterranean middlemen. The route around Africa had already been proven, but that course required many months at sea. Columbus charted a daring route due west which was based on the generally accepted assumption that the earth was spherical rather than flat. He made two serious mistakes in his calculations and discoveries, however: he failed to realize how far he would have to sail, even if his theory proved correct, and he failed to understand the value of the lands he discovered that barred his all water route to India. In this failure he was not alone.

Columbus tried unsuccessfully for years to convince European monarchs to back his plan. Finally, King Ferdinand of Spain agreed to guarantee Columbus' finances and to grant him the authority to sail in the name of Spain. Ferdinand commissioned Columbus Admiral of the Ocean Sea and Captain-General of all the lands he discovered, surely one of the grandest awards ever given to any human. After a perilous journey marked by near mutiny, fear, and course changes that were made in order to follow migrating birds and mysterious lights, Columbus made landfall at Whatling's Island in the fall of 1492. He never realized, even on subsequent voyages, just how much land he had found.

Nevertheless, other Spaniards quickly followed to explore the land he had located. These Spaniards seemed uniquely

PRIEST, soldiers and Indians arriving at El Paso del Norte, today's El Paso, to establish the first towns of Texas and New Mexico. Drawing by Jose Cisneros.

— Photo courtesy Cleofas Calleros Estate from copy at Institute of Texan Cultures.

qualified to begin European settlement and exploitation of his New World at this time in their nation's history. Courageous, audacious, hungering for fame and fortune, and convinced that being Spanish was the ultimate in the human condition, they quickly ran over the Caribbean Islands as well as the other lands around the Gulf of Mexico. Within thirty years they had conquered not only the native people of those places, but those of Florida, the Mexican Coast, and a large part of South America.

Hernando Cortes, for example, landed at the Yucatan in 1519 and quickly disposed of the Aztec authority not only there but elsewhere in Mexico. Using firearms, dogs, horses, and intense rapacity, these Conquistadors vanquished large numbers of Indians. Almagro and Pizarro lived the same story among the Incas. And everywhere the Spanish went it seemed, they found Indians with gold and silver, precious metals that had no moneyed value for the natives but captured the bold Spaniard's heart and soul. For two hundred years they eagerly sought to find more; they would tolerate the company of priests or do without them, go as government agents or alone, to find gold or silver anywhere in the world. And that included Texas.

The first Spaniard — indeed the first European — to see Texas, Alonso Alvarez de Pineda, came on such a search. Pineda's commission came from the governor of Jamaica, and his route ran north along the Florida coast, then westward around the rim of the Gulf of Mexico or Tampico. When Pineda's four vessels reached the landfall of Cortes, they received a trespasser's welcome and quickly retreated to the mouth of the Rio Grande, called the Rio de las Palmas by the captain. They remained there from four to six weeks for repairs and outfitting while Pineda mapped, explored, and dreamed of returning to the land he called Amichel (the earliest European name for Texas) to plant a permanent colony. Pineda's report indicated that the natives were hospitable and that they told him tales, which he gullibly absorbed, about giants and pygmies inhabiting the land.

A year later a second expedition came to the area, this time under the command of Diego de Camargo. Camargo's three vessels brought soldiers, masons, and other craftsmen. They intended to build the colony Pineda had recommended. The Indians seemed friendly at first, but suddenly turned on Camargo and killed several of his men. The remainder hastily withdrew to Vera Cruz. Three years later in 1523, Jamaican governor Francisco Garay personally commanded a flotilla of sixteen ships bearing seven hundred soldiers sent to locate Camargo and firm up the rival claim to Cortes' plantation. He explored the Rio Grande for some distance, as well as the coastline, before deciding to abandon Amichel, or Texas, to its Indians and to head for Cortes' plantation. Garay's reception by Cortes included imprisonment, where he met Panfilo Narvaez. Narvaez learned of the Rio de las Palmas from Garay, and, when back in Spain in 1525, petitioned for a commission to return to plant a permanent colony. His request finally granted, Narvaez returned to plant and command the new province of Panuco-Victoria Garayana, which included the entire coast from Florida to the Rio Grande.

In 1528 Narvaez returned to Cuba, organized his soldiers and vessels, and moved northward to Florida. He made a landfall, then sent his ships up the coast for a rendezvous while he led a party of exploration along an inland route. This portion of his adventure was plagued by mosquitos, swamps, and hostile Indians; yet it may have been the happiest part. At the rendezvous point, Narvaez found no ships because they had despaired that he would reach that point and had returned to Cuba. After a time of desperation, the Spaniards built rafts and tried to float along the coast to Mexico and safety. Near Galveston — they called it Mulhado — a hurricane pounded their crude vessels into the surf. Nearly eighty men struggled ashore. By the next year, only fifteen remained; and when the incredible journey ended, only four had survived.

Alvar Nuñez Cabeza de Vaca, the expedition's treasurer, eventually led Captain Alonso de Castillo Maldonao, Andres Dorantes de Carranza, and Carranza's slave, a Moroccan called Estavanico, to Mexico after seven years of wandering in the wilderness. De Vaca's story starts in early November, 1528, at Galveston where the Spaniards found the Indians friendly and willing to trade but unwilling to let them leave. De Vaca performed a healing of some kind on an Indian, apparently a combination of crude medicine and faith healing—he reportedly removed an arrow from an Indian's chest — so he naturally constituted a valuable resource for any tribe. As his fame grew, so did his freedom; so the little band wandered about, visiting various clans and tribes, trading, performing his "miracles," and all the while heading toward Mexico.

First walking northwest, then south, probably twice twisting back from his original course, de Vaca eventually led his small group into northwestern Mexico where they happened upon a Spanish patrol. They were first mistaken for Indians, then considered crazy because of their tattered dress and unusual behavior. De Vaca eventually made their identity known and these scarecrows of Spanish explorers were taken to Mexico City where they received assistance, and from where de Vaca eventually returned to Spain. Naturally his hosts had an interest in the lands he had crossed. Did he see gold? No, he reported, but he had heard about gold from his Indian hosts-captors, whole cities made of it, in fact. Nothing could capture a Spaniard's interest quicker than such a prospect, and soon many were ready to go in search of these golden cities.

De Vaca had had enough adventure, but Estavanico remained to accompany an exploration headed by the priest Marcos de Niza. Like many with the Call, de Niza burned with the desire to preach the message of Christianity to the Indians. He gratefully accepted assignment to retrace a part of de Vaca's journey to learn the whereabouts of the golden cities. For de Niza, it was a pilgrimage. At a Zuni pueblo in southern Arizona called Cibola by the Spanish and Hawikuh by the Indians, he ended his search, although he did not enter the village. Probably he did not want to learn the truth. He hastened back to report a city glistening in the southwest sun; surely it must be made of gold.

Still unsure, however, Viceroy Mendoza authorized a more thorough and spectacular exploration under the command of Francisco Vasquez de Coronado, governor of Nueva Galicia, a man of wealth from the New World's gold but ever anxious for more. In 1540 Coronado, with de Niza as guide, led an *entrata* of several hundred soldiers, priests, Indians, and women on what proved to be a two-year journey. The slow-moving group required nearly five months to reach de Niza's "golden" city and the disappointing discovery that the pueblo was constructed of stones and mortar, commodities much more plentiful and far less valuable than gold. And the Zuni people were not disposed to welcome the Spanish. The Spanish prevailed, after a hard fight, but de Niza was sent back in disgrace when a thorough search still failed to locate gold in the village. He died soon afterward.

But Coronado persevered. He divided his force for a thorough search; one group discovered the Grand Canyon, another the pueblos of New Mexico. He wintered at the pueblo of Tiguex on the Rio Grande, and in the spring moved northeasterly across the Texas Panhandle to another canyon, probably the Palo Duro Canyon, whose red soil and layered crystal were called Spanish skirts after their likeness to the whirling petticoats of dancers. Then he struck due north through Oklahoma and into Kansas, searching for Quivira, the general name of the still illusive seven cities of gold. Coronado's scouts found only prairie; they observed grazing buffalo and thought that the land might be useful for cattle some day. But without gold, the land's vacantness did not attract them. They went home to Mexico with stories of the land's emptiness, and they doomed the Spanish empire to a negative attitude regarding Texas and the northern provinces that lasted as long as they claimed the lands. Occasionally other *entratas* came to reconfirm what Coronado had learned in the beginning, that there was no gold. It was always the same. So thereafter the land's only value to them remained negative. They did little with it except in response to others' interest, yet they would not let it go because it offered a cushion from alien and infidel influences, especially French and Anglo-Celtic influence.

Meanwhile, another Spanish explorer approached from the east. Hernando de Soto landed in Florida in 1539 on the first leg of a two-year journey of exploration that cut northward through the peninsula, then headed west across Alabama, Mississippi, Arkansas and Oklahoma. In the summer of 1541, de Soto headed southwestward for some distance, probably into northern Texas. There de Soto died, and command fell to Luis de Moscoso, who continued to lead the troupe south in an effort to reach Mexico. At "a broad river," probably the Trinity, they turned back to the Mississippi River, built boats, and drifted down river and along the coast to a Spanish settlement in northern Mexico. They had carried de Soto's body as far as the Mississippi River, where they buried it in the unmarkable waters to prevent Indians from discovering it. Like Coronado's *entratas,* de Soto's men sought gold. Finding none, they despaired, despite the oil seepages they passed, a kind of gold their technology could not yet appreciate, and despite the considerable significant observations of natural history and Indian lifestyles their journey could have enjoyed.

Another Spaniard, Juan de Onate, came to Texas in 1601 to check a third time for gold. Onate represented the crest of Spanish movement to the north. His arrival at Santa Fe in 1598 to establish a permanent settlement and command it with a commission from the Viceroy found its base in a series of missions, silver mines, and other outposts that stretched back to central Mexico. Still eager to discover gold, but now more experienced in dealing with the native peoples, Onate led an expedition across the Texas Panhandle and brought friendly Indians with him to help tranquilize hostiles should they be encountered. He planned to bring back Indians from the areas he visited, and he also brought along potential settlers for colonizing the new land. Some of them did stay, but more importantly their cattle and horses remained to found wild herds after these few early settlers had quit their posts. But Onate found no gold, so for a third time the Spanish failed to find the commodity which seemed to justify their expensive expeditions. Onate returned to Santa Fe, which in 1609 became the Spanish political capital of their northern provinces.

The next Spanish activity had a somewhat higher motive than earthly riches, and mystery played an important role in this next Texas venture. Jumanos Indians appeared one day in 1629 at a mission in Albuquerque and informed the priests that they had been commanded to go there by a Lady in Blue who had visited their village and instructed them in Christianity. They had accepted Christianity, they claimed, and had been sent to the mission for baptism. Father Juan de Salas received permission to return with the Jumanos to convert other Indians. Meanwhile the visiting Jumanos established trade contracts with the Spanish in New Mexico. When the party returned to Texas with Salas and Father Diego Leon, they found other Indians willing to be converted, who, like the Indians that had visited Albuquerque, were already instructed in Christianity. But they never saw the Lady in Blue. They heard so much about her, however, that they were convinced that her appearances had been bonafide.

When Salas and Leon returned to New Mexico the priests

informed their Father-Superior, Alonso de Benevides, of the miracle. Then, when he returned to Spain, Benevides heard of a young nun named Sister Maria Jesus de Agreda who sometimes experienced the miracle of transportation while in a catatonic trance. She reportedly visited with strange, painted peoples during these experiences, but he did not know where the visits occurred. Benevides became convinced that the events were real so he sent word back to New Mexico to continue the contacts with these "prepared" Indians. In 1632 a second visit to the Jumano country departed to remain six months in Texas, baptising converts and distributing presents to the Indians. When the Spanish finally came to East Texas, they learned that even some of the Indians in that region claimed to have seen the Lady in Blue.

Several other *entratas* were undertaken to Texas, partially based on the trade routes to the Jumanos. One, under Hernan Martin and Diego del Castillo, travelled as far as the Nueces River; another, under Diego de Guadalajara, came in 1654 to explore the Tejas country; in 1675, Father Juan Larios led a brief venture into the Edwards Plateau; and most significantly, in 1683 Juan Domingues de Mendoza, a member of the Guadalajara party, led an expedition with Father Nicholas Lopez to establish a mission. Since the mission Corpus Christi de Isleta, then in New Mexico, had been founded in the El Paso country only two years before, they judged the chances of success there to be good.

The spark for this last venture also came from the Jumanos; they requested the Spanish to help with a significant problem — the appearance of Apache Indians in their country. The Mendoza-Lopez party travelled to the San Saba River country and briefly established their mission, but they were soon driven away by successive attacks by the Apaches. After returning to New Mexico, Mendoza and Lopez gave glowing descriptions of the country's potential, perhaps exaggerating in their zeal to return with enough resources to control the Apaches. They did not receive permission to return to Texas. The reason was the discovery of Frenchmen on the Texas coast, where all Spanish attention and resources must then be concentrated.

French interest in the New World lagged behind that of Spain's because their nationalism developed along different paths in the two countries and because the French suffered from religious divisions. They had claims dating as early as the English and other European nations, claims that were well-defined by the sailings of Roberval, de Verrazano, and especially by Jacques Cartier in the St. Lawrence region. Finally, in 1608, Samuel de Champlain made a permanent plantation at Quebec, and from that post traders moved through the back-country of North America trapping when they had to do so, but trading with the Indians for furs when they could. Montreal, Detroit, St. Genevieve, St. Louis and finally New Orleans resulted from their efforts. Thus, the French were occupying the interior of the continent while the English were moving directly westward from the Atlantic coast, and the Spanish were pushing ever northward. Confrontations, of course, eventually became inevitable.

The first to bring French exploration to Spanish claims was Father Marquette and Louis and Joliet, who led the French south when they traveled down the Mississippi River as far as the Arkansas River, where they became convinced it emptied into the sea. In 1682, Rene Robert Cavelier, Sieur De LaSalle led an expedition all the way to the delta below present New Orleans, struck up the Fleur de Lis, and claimed the entire drainage pattern of the great river in the name of his sovereign, Louis. LaSalle then returned to France. But two years later he arrived back in the New World with a small flotilla, intending to make a permanent plantation at the mouth of the Mississippi River. LaSalle's mission packed its problems in France; dissention between LaSalle and his naval commander, Beaujeu, communicated to the rest of the company; LaSalle's cold nature made the rest of the settlers distrust him; and by the time they reached North America, mutiny loomed. Then they missed the mouth of the Mississippi, sailing on instead to Matagorda Bay, some 400 miles distant from their target. Storms, poor navigation, and a ship wreck received the credit, but it is possible that the mistaken landfall was deliberate. From there the French could push their claims deep into Spanish territory. Within a few years they would be making similar landings in the other direction, with the founding of Biloxi and Mobile.

LaSalle's company moved a short distance inland out of sight of passing Spanish vessels and erected a palisaded fortress of sorts which they named Fort St. Louis. Food was prob-

San Fernando Church, San Antonio, was established during the Spanish colonial period in 1731. Shown here is the church and plaza from a drawing by Arthur Schott.

ably plentiful, but they lacked the know-how to obtain it; mosquitos became an immediate problem; and the unfriendliness of the Karankawa Indians complicated matters further. After the departure of their remaining ship, the few Frenchmen at the fort felt completely stranded, and their dissention grew. LaSalle searched the countryside, finding the Brazos River and other delights, but no relief, no riches, and no friendly Indians to help out. Finally he proposed to leave the bulk of the company in the safety of the fort and strike off for the known French settlements in Illinois where aid could be obtained. He left in the company of a few men, and somewhere in East Texas the men mutinied and killed LaSalle, burying his body in an unmarked grave to hide their crime. They effectively hid it from future generations as well. As a result, half a dozen communities claim LaSalle's bones, and Navasota has even erected a statue of his presence there to hold down their assertion.

LaSalle's men scattered after killing their leader. Some of them returned to the fort, others apparently became feral, and seven of them, following a man named Joutel, finally made it to Illinois. Henri de Tonti then led an expedition from Illinois to find the fort, but it proved unsuccessful.

The Spanish were more persistent in their search. When Alonzo de Leon, governor of Coahuila, learned of the fort, he began a search that did not cease until he had found the French trespassers. Nearly a dozen expeditions, some by land and some by sea, searched the Texas countryside for the French settlement in the land, now sometimes called the New Philippines. Finally in April of 1689, de Leon found the remains of their fort and a few French in the hands of local Indians. From them, de Leon learned what had happened to the fort. After LaSalle had left, they had had no word for a long period of time. Finally, their situation worsened by an epidemic that was possibly small pox, the French had decided to make friends with the Indians. They gambled on the opening of the palisade gates. The Indians had come in peacefully enough, but had then suddenly turned on their hosts and killed as many of them as they could and burned the fort. The few who had escaped had been captured by other Indians. Some of these had gone insane, and de Leon left them to their fate, while he marched the others to Mexico in irons.

De Leon must have been pleased that the Indians had done

his work for him, for surely he would have treated the French similarly had he found them first. Now he wanted to put up a signpost for any other interlopers to see. So, in 1690, he returned to East Texas with Father Damien Massanet to erect a Spanish mission among the Caddo Indians. The Mission San Francisco de los Tejas, with a few soldiers stationed with it for defense, was situated near the Trinity River at the community of Weches. Later a second mission, Santissimo Nombre de Maria, was located on the Neches River. Only three days were required to erect the original log structure. At first the Caddoes demonstrated the usual curiosity at the colorful vestments and ritual of the church, but they found no firm faith in the Christianity of the priests. The priests soon quarrelled with the presidio's soldiers, the Indians wearied of providing the mission with food and having to find ways to evade the labor that the soldiers wanted them to do, so they just quit coming to the mission. Having fulfilled the initial desire of the political chieftain who had authorized the mission, the mission priests and soldiers were withdrawn within three years. Even in the absence of active Spanish settlement and activity, the fact that the mission had existed, however briefly, affirmed Spanish claims. This first mission in Texas proper (Isleta was not then in Texas or even thought to be within Texas until 1849) thus fulfilled Spanish goals, but other missions would soon follow, sometimes in response to French activity, sometimes because the priests, particularly the Franciscans, burned with desire to bring Christianity to the Indians.

The most successful aspect about this first mission was its name, San Francisco de los Tejas. Among the names then applied to the province by the Spanish was Neuvo Reyno de la Montana de Santander y Santillana, but fortunately Tejas or Texas, came into general use after 1690.

Spanish techniques for dealing with the native peoples in the New World had been developing for nearly two centuries. Unlike the French and English, the Spanish at least had a place for the Indians in their society. At first they divided the conquered land into units called *encomiendas* and distributed them among those who had taken it from the Indians. The *encomiendero* received four-fifths of the produce of the land as a pension and he received the labor of the Indians who lived on the land to make it productive. The remainder, or royal fifth, went to the government. The *encomiendero* was also required to provide religious instruction. From the beginning, some Spaniards, although not all, believed that this system constituted a form of slavery that violated Christian principles. For instance, Bartholomew de las Casas, argued that potential Christians should be freed of their forced labor and replaced by Africans. After 1502, the use of Negro slaves was increasingly practiced in the Gulf Islands and on the mainland to the south. It was necessary to do this to get any labor at all, because the Indians, for whatever reason, refused to accommodate themselves to the system as the Africans did. Instead, the Indians died by countless numbers. So the Spanish moved to the mission concept (mission here meaning an activity more than a place) to carry the message of salvation to the Indians of each new conquest or place of occupation. In this the government and the church were in complete partnership: the government wanted to use religion as a tranquilizer to "reduce" the territory of hostility and to begin productive agriculture and industry for the benefit of future Spanish settlement. The church needed the permission and support of the government to carry their message of salvation. The remainder of the Texas missions will fit this pattern, with first the government and then the church taking the lead, but always with both partners participating in the efforts.

The church led as planters of Spanish authority. A priest named Hidalgo wanted to return to Texas after the failure of San Francisco de las Tejas, but in the absence of French activity he could not convince Spanish authorities to mount an expedition. So Hidalgo trumped up French activity. Writing a totally unauthorized letter in 1710 to the French governor Sieur de Cadillac, the French magistrate in Louisiana, Hidalgo proposed a joint venture between the French and the Spanish to carry Christianity to the Texas Indians. Cadillac knew Hidalgo's invitation did not have government approval, but he used it as a convenient excuse. He dispatched Canadian-born Louis Juchereau de St. Denis to the region. In 1714 St. Denis moved up the Mississsippi and Red Rivers, then descended to Natchitoches where he cached some trading supplies. He then set out for the Spanish settlements, blazing what became the major part of the El Camino Real in Texas, and travelled all the way to the settlements on the Rio Grande without being troubled by a Spanish patrol or any other evidence of government authority.

St. Denis became a house guest of presidio commander Diego Ramon instead of being arrested as he should have been. He courted Ramon's granddaughter, Manuela Sanchez, apparently with sufficient success to anger another suitor, who reported St. Denis' presence to higher authorities in Mexico City. When his arrest order arrived, St. Denis journeyed under guard to the capital for an audience with the viceroy, whom he evidently convinced to return him to East Texas in the dual role of Indian trader and mission founder. Just who was using whom is not completely clear, but what resulted was renewed Spanish activity in East Texas, again in response to French activity. St. Denis returned to Ramon's residence at San Juan Bautista and married Manuela Sanchez, then, with her uncle Domingo Ramon, he returned to East Texas to found six missions and trading posts which proved commercially beneficial to himself and the French and politically and religiously advantageous to the Spanish.

This activity, of course, was in violation of Spanish law and policy. First St. Denis and Ramon rebuilt San Francisco de las Tejas, leaving Father Hidalgo, who had started the process, in charge. The expedition then moved eastward and founded Nuestra Senora de la Purisima Conception at a Caddo village in the eastern portion of present Nacogdoches County, Nuestra Senora de Guadalupe at the present city of Nacogdoches, and at a Nazone village to the north, near present Cushing, they built San Jose de los Nazonis. Heading east toward French outposts (including St. Denis' own cache at Natchitoches) the two founded Nuestra Senora de los Dolores at an Ais Indian Village near present San Augustine and San Miguel de Linarea at an Adaes Indian village at present Robiline, Louisiana. The latter was the eastern most Spanish mission, and probably the most successful.

Ramon also established the presidio Nuestra Senora de los Delores de los Tejas on the Neches River near the San Francisco de los Tejas mission. The Franciscan padre, Antonio Jesus de Margil, had charge of the ecclesiastical functions of the missions, and is remembered as the greatest of the mission founders in Texas. St. Denis then opened a lucrative trading business with the missions' Indians as well as with other area Indians, enriching himself and the French in the process, and exerting significant influence over the Indians. The missions had to depend on this trade because the French influence and indifference attracted few Indians to the catechism. St. Denis lived until 1744 and became a Chevalier by direct order of the French king. His real contribution lay in hastening the Spanish to take care of their investment in Texas, especially in the missions.

To shorten the supply line to the eastern missions and to boost the morale of the missionaries, Martin de Alarcon, new governor of Coahuila, and Father Antonio de San Buenaventura Olivares came in 1718 to establish a supply mission between the Rio Grande and East Texas. Father Olivares selected a site on the San Antonio River—so named because they reached the stream on St. Anthony's Day—and there erected San Antonio de Valero, named in honor of a marquis who sponsored their efforts. The mission became known to history as the Alamo in a later time. San Antonio de Valero had several advantages over the East Texas missions, including proximity to Mexico and its supplies, which it, in turn, processed for use in the eastern theatre. It enjoyed a more even climate; and Christian Indians were brought from Mexico as an attraction for local Indians to come into the mission. By 1721 a presidio, San Antonio de Bejar, joined the mission across the river, and by 1726 nearly 200 Europeans lived in the beginnings of a Spanish settlement to become known as San Antonio. A few Spaniards had also drifted into East Texas, some along the supply route and some via the French connection, but they lived usually in the countryside rather than at the missions.

Then the French activity called forth a third mission era. Near Los Adaes, as the most eastern mission was known, a French patrol under a Corporal Bondel showed up on a day in 1719 and took charge. As his men plundered the unprotected mission, a flock of chickens escaped and in the resulting clamor one of the priests escaped to report the French "invasion." In response, the viceroy appointed the Marquis de San Miguel de Aguayo to lead a force to East Texas to re-establish Spanish authority, another signpost for the French.

Aguayo reached San Antonio in March, 1720 and found most of the East Texas priests there where they had established themselves as the Mission San Jose y San Miguel de Aguayo in his honor. He secured the area near La Bahia del Espiritu Santo, as the Spanish called the site of Fort St. Louis, with a detachment, then pushed on to East Texas. Aguayo found the area unoccupied by the French or anyone else. He relocated the San Francisco mission on the Neches River, giving it the new name of San Francisco de los Neches. At the other sites he left new priests and supplies, and at Los Adaes, he constructed the Presidio Nuestra Senora del Pilar and left cannon and a hundred troops to hold the area. This show of force, coupled with lessened difficulties between the French and Spanish in Europe, calmed the situation in East Texas. Aguayo then returned to San Antonio, strengthened the presidio there, then moved on to La Bahia to found a permanent presidio, La Bahia de Loreto, and a mission called Nuestra Senora del Espiritu Santo de Zuniga, although both are commonly called La Bahia.

Aguayo left the Spanish missions in good condition. Four presidios and six missions functioned, and civil settlements operated at San Antonio and Los Adaes, but he suggested to higher authorities that more civilian personnel should be located in Texas to hold it in an even firmer grip. Some years later over 100 families were recruited from the Canary Islands for this purpose. Most did not make it all the way, but fifty-six persons were eventually relocated at San Antonio. Each head of household received the title of hidalgo and land for farming. The Canary Islanders created the first legally recognized civilian government in Texas, called the Villa San Fernando de Bexar. Eventually, it became the nexus of one of the nation's largest cities, and the heart of the city is still called La Villita.

Following the Aguayo expedition, things remained quiet for a time. The Spanish had rimmed Texas with evidence of their authority, including six missions in East Texas, one on the coast, one in the heartland, four presidios, settlements on the Rio Grande, and missions and civilian settlements in the New Mexican territory. But they had yet to make much headway in the vast interior or in the main territory between Texas and Mexico proper.

Jose de Escandon, a career officer in the Spanish service, provided the next movement in the process. Escandon received a commission in 1746 to fill in the settlement line along the Rio Grande to protect the main part of Mexico from either French or English penetration through Texas. Escandon selected likely sites for missions and towns along the river. His new province was called Nuevo Santander. In 1747 Escandon entered

Nuevo Santander as governor with 2,500 settlers, 750 soldiers, priests, and adequate supplies. Within seven years, he established twenty-three towns and fifteen missions, including Camargo and Reynosa, the first two towns, and Laredo and Dolores, the only two in Texas.

The pattern Escandon used to develop the area was born in Europe and shared by the Dutch in New York. Vast riparian, or river-front, grants were given to officials called *patrons,* who controlled the land and its people in authority second only to the governor's powers. The *patron's* people provided the labor for building, his priests supplied religious services for the people, and together they began towns. The *patron's* house was the seat of government, and eventually it became a city hall; the church lay to one side, his granaries and store houses filled in the other sides of a plaza. Around this nexus grew the town proper.

As years passed and other settlers came to live in these places, their houses or businesses were built behind these plaza-base structures as the town expanded. At first Escandon's territory stretched to San Antonio, although it was later reduced to the Neuces River. Here a cattle industry and a border culture known as *charro* were born, both with considerable impact on Texas.

Then, to fill in the heartland of Texas with more evidence of Spain, more missions were planted. The San Gabriel site was established by Father Mariano Francisco de los Dolores y Viana, a veteran of service in San Antonio and in the East Texas area. He had made friends with the Tonkawas and wanted to supply them with a mission. Now that his plan supplemented government policy, in 1748 Viana was permitted to found San Francisco Xavier de Horcasitas, with a presidio two miles distant. The next year San Ildefonso and Nuestra Senor de la Candelaria were also founded. The three missions struggled along until 1755 when they were removed to a site at the head of the San Marcos River near present New Braunfels, where they only operated briefly until permanently closed.

Next came missions for the Apaches. Pressure for these missions came mostly from a New Mexico mine owner, Pedro Romero de Terreros, who offered to help finance the mission in an effort to ease Apache troubles for himself. He also wanted his relative, Father Alonzo Giraldo de Terreros, in charge.

Spanish soldiers in Texas.
— Courtesy Institute of Texan Cultures

Father Terreros probably initiated the proposal, sparked from his earlier work with the Apaches at a mission in Mexico. In 1766, Father Terreros, with other priests, Christian Indians, and a group of soldiers under Colonel Diego Ortiz de Parilla, founded the Mission San Saba de la Santa Cruz on the San Saba River. At two miles distant, Parilla established the presidio San Luis de las Amarillas. But few Apaches came to the missions, and finally most of the Apaches left the area, apparently on a buffalo hunt.

A better reason for their departure, however, was the return of the Comanches to the area. The Comanches were not only uninterested in the Spanish mission, they proved overly hostile to their presence. In 1759 a large band attacked the mission, then moved on to the presidio. Parilla managed to escape to report the loss to authorities in San Antonio, who decided he should go back with 500 soldiers to re-establish Spanish authority. Parilla attacked the Indians at a Taovayas village but he was unsuccessful, partially because of the Indians' superior numbers and because they enjoyed French assistance. The French had already established trading connections in the area and delighted in helping the Indians eliminate the competition.

One last mission effort was made for the Apaches following Parilla's failure. The western survivors of mission activities fell back to a mission on the upper Neuces River called San Lorenzo de la Santa Cruz, and later established Nuestra Senora de la Candelaria del Cañon in 1762. Both were commonly called El Cañon, and both were singularly unsuccessful in attracting the Apaches.

Meanwhile, reorganization of established missions reflected still another change in Spanish aims. In 1749 the La Bahia mission moved from the Guadalupe River to a site on the lower San Antonio River, and the community which grew up around it became known as Goliad. A second mission, Nuestra Senor del Rosario, was erected some four miles distant from La Bahia to serve dissident Karankawas, and as a result of a different direction in Spanish policy, many of the East Texas missions were, at different times, relocated in the area of San Antonio until that community's missions numbered six. By the end of the century most of these had been secularized as parish churches.

A policy shift began in Europe at the completion of what

was known there as the Seven Year's War and elsewhere as the Great War for Empire (England) and the French and Indian War (American colonies). As a result of this war, with the Spanish and English on the same side, those powers eliminated France as a North American rival. By the Treaty of Paris, 1763, France surrendered her North American holdings to both, and thus England and Spain became neighbors at the Mississippi River. French settlements—New Orleans, St. Louis and St. Genevieve—dotted the river, but English settlement seemed then a comfortable distance away. So the Spanish estimate of Texas' value changed again to accommodate what seemed like a less threatening neighbor. The Spanish continued their efforts, known in American history as the Conspiracies, to create a new buffer state east of the Mississippi. Later, recognizing that they had lost their homogenous society by absorbing French territory, they for a time admitted American settlers on the condition that they become Spanish vassals and Roman Catholics. But in Texas, the decade after the Treaty of Paris was again a time of withdrawal.

To plan adequately for this shift, the Marquis de Rubi received a commission to visit all Spanish borderlands holdings from Texas to Baja in California. Accompanied by a cartographer named De la Flora, Inspector-General de Rubi travelled the breadth of the northern holdings. Ultimately he recommended to King Charles III what became known as the New Regulation of the Presidios when they were pronounced in 1772.

De Rubi's visit revealed considerable weaknesses in the Spanish mission-presidio system. Everywhere the missions were either in some danger from those they sought to serve, or they were ignored by them. Usually it was the latter. If possible, the presidios were in worse condition than the missions. Mostly their garrisons were composed of the dregs of the Spanish military personnel; often they included discipline cases. To make matters worse, the soldiers were exploited by ruthless officers who often embezzled funds allocated for the soldiers' food and other supplies. More seriously, neither missions nor presidios really gave the Spanish a secure hold on the territory.

The system can be visualized as a wheel, with the various missions as the extension of the spokes and San Antonio as the hub. De Rubi recommended that the missions on the periphery of Texas be abandoned and relocated in San Antonio; he suggested San Antonio should be developed as a center of Spanish political, economic, and military strength. The city would then become the farthest frontier in New Spain, while the Rio Grande line became the supply point and main holding place. The rest of Texas could be abandoned to the Indians. He also recommended that active war should be made on the Apaches in West Texas to keep them from harrassing Spanish settlers in northern Mexico. The rest of the Indians, de Rubi suggested, should be pacified by employing "French methods," that is, leaving them alone as Indians, but establishing trading posts in their villages. De Rubi's suggestions became law in 1772. Athanase de Mezieres, a Frenchman in high standing in the Bourbon court but well-experienced in dealing with North American Indians, became the principle Indian pacifier and trader for Spain, and Teodore de Croix drew the assignment of making war on the Apaches. De Mezieres proved more successful, even though his service was brief and ended before he even officially assumed the position. His methods, however, proved as successful as any employed by the Spanish in the New World. De Croix's efforts kept an uneasy peace with the Apaches that lasted until the end of the Spanish period, although they constantly threatened. The even more dreaded Comanches also posed a continuing problem.

The mainstream of de Rubi's recommendations lay in the eastern part of Texas. The new Texas governor, Juan Maria Vincente, the Baron de Ripperada, received the assignment to withdraw the missions and settlements in East Texas to new homes in San Antonio. He personally travelled to Los Adaes to oversee the process. About 500 people lived in the community, with perhaps an equal number scattered at other missions, presidios, and on isolated farms, ranches, and trading posts. When Ripperada informed them that they must leave their homes, the priests and soldiers left easily, some happily, but the settlers were disappointed and angered. But they knew that the only resistance to his armed might was flight. Some did, losing themselves in the forests. Most watched in horror as Ripperada's men stripped the presidios and missions of their furniture and livestock, forced the settlers to do the same, burned the buildings and even trampled crops to prevent the settlers from sneaking back.

Antonio Gil Y'Barbo, a rancher from the Lobinillo Creek

area with trading connections to New Orleans, emerged as the natural leader of the retreating settlers. Y'Barbo kept the wagons and the stock moving and gradually won the confidence and the sympathy of Ripperada. By the time they all reached San Antonio, the governor had agreed to endorse a petition to the central government in Mexico City that the Los Adaes people be allowed to return part of the way to their homes. They received permission to do so within a few months, but with qualifications. The Los Adaes settlers could come no closer to their former homes than one hundred leagues of Natchitoches, an inconvenient distance from the French influences which still existed there. In August of 1774, Y'Barbo led his group back along the San Antonio road to the Trinity River crossing, and there, on the west bank, established a new community which they named Bucareli in honor of the viceroy who had permitted them to leave San Antonio. The community lasted four years.

Comanche raids, to which they were more vulnerable on the west bank, plus annual spring floods, convinced them to move on east to the vicinity of the abandoned mission at Nacogdoches in the spring of 1779. They found the buildings of the mission Nuestra Senora de Guadalupe de los Nacogdoches still standing — probably the only Spanish structure then in East Texas following the work of Ripperada's crews — and they decided to remain there. Y'Barbo laid out a town, calling it Nacogdoches, and reported within a few months that he had moved the people to the new site. By late summer, he received confirmation that the authorities would tolerate his action, and in October he was commissioned Captain of Militia and Lieutenant-Governor of the pueblo of Nacogdoches, with full accountability as well as responsibility for his town.

Y'Barbo proved a good shepherd. He drafted a code of conduct for the community that demanded moral and lawful conduct of its citizens and visitors, with punishments ranging from death, years of service on Spanish galleys, to corporal chastisement. He erected a Stone House for trading and business purposes, and as he was the government, the building became a civic headquarters as well. Known to future Texans as the Stone Fort, it stood on the plaza of Nacogdoches until razed in 1902. Y'Barbo soon ran afoul of local traders who were determined to violate Spanish trading laws with French and American business houses along the Mississippi River, and he was himself accused of trading in contraband; a San Antonio court believed the charges and banished Y'Barbo from Nacogdoches. But his town remained, and despite numerous opportunities to wither away, flourishes in the modern period.

Much can be said for the methods of Y'Barbo and Jose Escandon. Spanish attempts to control Texas rarely included attempts to settle it. Bonafide citizens were permitted to live in the vicinity of the missions and presidios, and some even received generous land grants from the government. But except for the Canary Islanders at San Antonio, the government remained less interested in settling Texas than determined that the French and English would not do so. So their missionaries and soldiers and traders came in small numbers, did their best, and retreated to the more civilized society of Mexico. Escandon and Y'Barbo moved into their respective territories with individuals. They allowed each settler to work his own way in this New World, for his own well-being, albeit with severe restrictions on civic and religious regularity. And in the end, that way worked best in the environment of Texas. These last invaders came to the land itself, rather than as agents for church or state. They came to use it for themselves, and they came to stay.

The Spanish experience in Texas, which lingered until Mexican independence in the 1820s, has been termed a "successful failure." It was successful in that Spain left a permanent legacy in language, in religion, in the development of agricultural husbandry—especially in stock raising—and in the architecture of its missions. The major Hispanic influences would come later, remain close to the Rio Grande border for most of the nineteenth century, then sweep across the entire state in the present century. Spain failed to permanently claim the land, to really impact, much less control, the majority of its Indian population, or to keep it pure of other European occupation. So Spain eventually lost the land itself.

The 1774 withdrawal was a setting sun for Spanish efforts. Only the individual actions of men like Y'Barbo remained in most of Texas outside of San Antonio. Occasionally, the government sent military forces to the areas of Indian uprisings or Anglo invasions, but without knowing it then, their occupation of Texas was over. Already from the east the new waves of invaders, the Anglo-Celtics, were coming to have their way with the land.

A frontier Texan carrying a revolver and a double-barreled shotgun.

— Painting by Bruce Marshall, Photo courtesy Institute of Texan Cultures

3

Anglo-American Arrival in Texas

"Westward I go free!" In these feeling words Henry David Thoreau summed the spirit of nineteenth century America. This spirit — the restless, ceaseless, unquenchable desire to move west, to find a fresh start, to seize opportunity, to forget mistakes (or have others forget them), to build a nation, to manifest an individual expression or dream even yet unformed, or just to have something to do — is part of all the reasons for moving west. And each Anglo-Celtic invader's matrix of reasons was unique. Thoreau, and America, rejected the human and geographic restraints that barred the other points of the compass and cleaved to the west because there the restraints were at last invisible or imperceptible to expectation's star-filled eyes.

These restraints were real enough, for hostile Indians, dust, aridity, extremes of heat and cold, snakes, poisonous plants, and sheer space are all factors of reality, and even hope and faith may not be sufficient to overcome them. Ignorance of them, many migrating Americans found, did not provide a reprieve, but each barrier could be overcome by persistence; so in a cumulative victory, the Anglo-Celtic invader became a new man, an American. And some Americans became Texans.

The Texan-American or "super-American" experience, as some have called it, is but an extension of the general American frontier process. The process in Texas faced a slightly different factor: the presence of a well-established, if somewhat weak, pre-existing society. Here the frontier provided the familiar battle with nature, but it also involved Spanish — and then Mexican — society, a scattered French influence, and the most capable and determined Indians yet encountered. Some Americans were aware of the differences that this would make, but they did not realize how fiercely the Spanish and then the Mexicans would contest them for the land. One invader does not easily give way to a successor.

Most Spaniards, it is sometimes said, came to Texas and the rest of the New World pursuing the alliterative formula of "gold, glory, and gospel." For many Anglo-Celtics, this impetus might be better expressed as "running from" or "running to" with the appropriate object being supplied by the individual invader. Herein lay a great difference in the settlement methods of the two cultures.

Except for the Las Adaes settlers in East Texas and the Escandon settlers along the Rio Grande, nearly all Spaniards who had come to Texas since 1528 had done so by accident or fate, in which case they quickly left; or by *entrada*, mission, or presidio, and these left slowly. Few remained for an entire generation to plant permanent homes or businesses, and none did so because the government wished for them to do so, save the Canary Island settlers at San Antonio. The Spanish society in Texas, as it did everywhere in the colonies, reflected the government's desire to discover even more precious metals, to reduce the Indians to a manageable and tolerable status, and to squeeze some kind of produce from the land. But most of all, the Spanish wanted to prevent other peoples from taking the land from them.

On the other hand, the Anglo-Celts reflected the diffusions and confusions of their British parenthood. Their plantations appeared helter-skelter and diverse, sometimes reflecting but just as often differing from the homeland. Unlike the Spanish orthodoxy in religion and ethnic compulsion, Anglo-Celtic colonies produced seemingly infinite varieties of faiths and government forms. Political, social, and economic institutions developed amid bitter hardships, often without notice or concern, and sometimes in spite of that concern, for a British policy seeking to discourage a particular trade might only encourage it by making that business more profitable in the smuggling trade.

The British-European frontiersman who started out on the Atlantic coast thus metamorphized into an American. He had faced down challenges to his presence in North America from Indians, the Dutch and the French, and the environment; and, by the beginning of the nineteenth century, he appeared ready to take on the Spanish, whose claims lay in the American's path. Like a giant arrow pointed southwestward from the Atlantic seaboard, this new breed ricochetted along the Great Lakes, followed the river valleys of the continent's interior, and sped through lands once Indian or French, directly confronting the Spanish holdings north of the Rio Grande.

The Spanish could, of course, see the trouble coming. Since LaSalle had first threatened their authority in Texas in 1684, Spanish jealousy flamed each time a new French penetration or an Anglo-American appeared, with their own efforts to develop the territory reflecting the activities or threats of activities of these other powers in Texas.

By all rights, the Spanish should have enjoyed a period of calm following the conclusion of the Seven Years' War. By the Peace of Paris, 1763, Spain reaped the reward of about half of France's North American holdings for fighting on the winning side in this first truly international conflict. The treaty not only eliminated the French as a Mississippi Valley neighbor of theirs, but it also placed the English, who received the remainder of French holdings, as a distant neighbor. The two powers bordered on the Mississippi River, but Anglo settlement still lay mostly east of the Appalachian Mountains, while Spanish settlement, scattered in small clusters in Texas, almost stopped at the Rio Grande nearly a thousand miles away from the river.

This distance should have provided adequate insulation for both nations, but it failed to do so. For one thing, the Anglo-American migration kept moving past the Appalachian line. By 1790, some 277,000 of them had already made homes in the regions westward to the Mississippi River. And after 1783, they no longer represented the British, a familiar opponent, but thereafter became agents of a new, energetic, aggressive nation; they had already determined on a Manifest Destiny for themselves several generations before learning the name.

And things changed within Spain as well. In 1800, as a

result of the Napoleonic disturbances of Europe, France forced Spain to return its North American holdings lost in 1763. This increased American concern in this theatre, because the French were much more threatening to trading interests along the Mississippi. Efforts to purchase New Orleans to protect American back-country trade resulted instead in the startling purchase of all of the Louisiana Territory in 1803. This acquisition produced a giant step westward toward the boundary between the United States and the Spanish territory in the Southwest, but seemingly neither power knew exactly just how big a step.

The Jefferson administration preferred to believe that Louisiana extended to the Rio Grande, but it would probably have accepted the Brazos River and been thankful for it. The Spanish, of course, thought the line was surely much farther east, holding out for the Arroyo Hondo, a tributary of the Red River. The conflict was not settled until 1819, and in the meanwhile the Americans, sometimes covertly and sometimes openly, encouraged their citizens to penetrate the disputed land. Most required little encouragement—they were ready to move west.

After nearly 250 years of controlling Texas, Spain, particularly through the government of New Spain, should have been holding that territory in a firmer control. It defended Florida, the Gulf coastal rim, and the New Mexican territory adequately. Texas eluded their grip if not their grasp because of the French, the Indians, and perhaps because of their own lack of attention. New Spain's 7 million population more than doubled that of the infant United States; her mineral wealth, within the limits of contemporary technology, exceeded that of the Americans; and her society shone with a sophistication that greatly eclipsed that of the cruder Americans. But their strength was more apparent than real. When the house was shaken by turmoil in Spain itself, republicans emerged in New Spain to turn that land into Mexico, and the contagious disease of republicanism swept away all mainland Spanish colonies within twenty-five years.

Under such conditions the Americans helped themselves by occupying Spanish territory at every opportunity. And sometimes the Spanish helped them. For example, in 1776, Don Francisco Bouligny, who commanded the upper Louisiana, known as Missouri, proposed the admission of Americans to his territory. This proposal recognized the fact that ethnic solidarity had already been lost in that area by the presence of so many French people who lived along the Mississippi River from St. Louis all the way to New Orleans. These had come under Spanish control by the Peace of Paris, but Bouligny knew they would never become Spanish.

So, he suggested, why not bring in Americans and turn them into Spanish vassals with the promise of abundant and inexpensive land? They would need only to swear allegiance to the Spanish government and become Roman Catholics. Governor Galvez, Bouligny's superior, agreed even to the point of winking at the religious requirements because of his own affiliation with Freemasonry. Both officials were motivated by their official charge to develop the country economically, and to hold the line against the British, and then later against the Americans. They thought that they would be more likely to succeed with Americans-become-Spaniards than with attempting to keep the Anglos out.

The American movement for independence provided a steady stream of takers for this scheme, including those who refused to participate in the war, loyalists, and finally the veterans, all looking for land and a new start. The Spanish accepted them all, helping some find land in the Amite River area. During the Articles of Confederation period, Galvez's successor, Miro, even authorized Spanish agents to solicit more American settlers.

A significant change in the method of settlement occurred in the 1790s when Colonel William Morgan of New Jersey obtained the first *empresarial* grant given to an American by the Spanish. Morgan obtained a large block of land in the southeast section of Missouri that he could offer to Americans for settlement under the same conditions of political and religious affiliation as the previous settlers. Morgan received total authority and total responsibility; as far as the Spanish officials were concerned, they dealt only with him. Morgan soon disappointed them by permitting a somewhat more democratic arrangement within his colony: he allowed them to elect him as their representative to the Spanish.

Still, the idea seemed to work. One who observed that it did was Moses Austin, himself a migrant to the upper regions of Missouri. He would later remember the Morgan example when he wanted to settle families in Texas. But such methods, called a Conspiracy in American history, failed to hold the land for the Spanish because the United States proved too strong and because the apparently potent Spanish empire collapsed from its own weakness. America's strength lay in its still flexible institutions; Spanish weakness, in the same area, resulted in their downfall. So the American came. And, after the retrocession of the border area to the French—and, in turn, its sale to the United States—they came uninvited.

The term *filibuster* is often used to identify such men as Philip Nolan, Aaron Burr, Augustus Magee and James Long, the best known of the type. The word elided from the English term "freebooter," for which the French used "boucanier," and the Spanish employed the more direct "piratas." It refers to a type of adventurer who came for personal gain, but who seemed also to bear a quasi-governmental status. Inevitably when such men proclaimed their empires, they seemed to help their parent government, and their empires seemed destined to come under the eventual control of the parental government.

The first important *filibuster,* Philip Nolan, came to Texas several times as a mustanger beginning in the 1790s. He captured horses in the central Texas plains, green-broke them, then trailed them to the Mississippi River country to sell to the Americans. Nolan's fictional namesake in the Edward Everett Hale story achieved greater fame, and his life also lasted longer. Nolan's activities, of course, were known to the Spanish authorities, who even tolerated them a while.

But when Spanish agents reported that Nolan spent too much time with American frontier military commander General James Wilkinson, that he even visited Thomas Jefferson, they became alarmed. So Governor Juan Bautista de Elguezabal ordered Nolan's arrest after several trips to Texas. Nolan resisted. Killed in a fight, his ears were sent to the governor as proof of his death. The survivors in Nolan's party were taken to the Stone Fort at Nacogdoches for a brief period, then moved to Mexico under guard. They languished in prison for an extended period while their case was ignored, finally learning that their penalty for trespass would be decimation — one in ten would be killed — and the remainder would receive ten years imprisonment at hard labor. Only nine had survived.

Old Stone Fort in Nacogdoches where survivors of Phillip Nolan were taken after fight in which Nolan, an American filibuster, was killed.

When men threw dice for the lowest number, Ephraim Blackburn lost.

Another, Peter Ellis Bean, became a true survivor. The revolutionary General Jose Maria Morelos was causing the Spanish government much trouble then, so Bean convinced his captors to allow him to fight with them against the revolutionaries. As soon as he was released from prison Bean defected to Morelos, then convinced that gentleman to send him to New Orleans for military supplies. While Bean did send the supplies, he of course did not return with them. Later, however, he did return to Mexico and became an officer in both the Spanish and Mexican services.

Aaron Burr, United States presidential and New York gubernatorial hopeful and unhappy Vice President under Thomas Jefferson, also added tension to the border area. Following his falling out with Jefferson, Burr spent a great deal of time with Wilkinson in the Old Southwest. Burr's intentions are difficult to determine because Wilkinson accused Burr of treason before his plans really developed. Wilkinson claimed that Burr intended to take part of Louisiana or Mississippi for a personal empire. Burr was known to have enlisted men and stored military supplies for some kind of adventure, but at his trial he was acquitted because of the narrow interpretation of what constituted treason by Chief Justice John Marshall. Much later, following the successful Texas revolution from Mexico, Burr claimed that his intentions were to do something of the kind in Texas during the Spanish regime.

Meanwhile, many law abiding Americans made their way onto Spanish lands. In 1804 the census indicated sixty-eight foreigners lived at Nacogdoches. Many of these were Americans who had not bothered to take out Spanish citizenship, although some had done so. James Dill, originally from Pennsylvania, moved there in 1793 to trade with the Indians; later he became *alcalde*. William Barr and Peter Samuel Davenport also operated a mercantile trade in Nacogdoches. Edward Quick acquired property on the site of present San Augustine in 1801. Other Anglo settlements were located on the Ouachita and Red rivers.

The Spanish doubted the sincerity of such invaders as William Dunbar and George Hunter, who explored the Arkansas country in 1804-05, and of Dr. Peter Custis who came to the

Red River country with an expedition from Fort Adams in early 1806. When the party attempted to open trade negotiations with the Coushatta Indians, some of the Indians informed Spanish authorities of their presence. A Spanish patrol under Francisco Viana located the party and chased them from Texas.

Such activities as those of Nolan and Burr caused tensions to rise between the Spanish and American military commanders within the disputed territory, and sometimes the American Commander, James Wilkinson, deliberately encouraged such tension. He is often accused of being a double-agent, a man who lined his own pockets from both sides by alternately creating or calming the situation. Serving his American bosses, Wilkinson in 1807 dispatched a force under Zebulon Pike to scout the Arkansas River country.

After following the river for several hundred miles, Pike turned southward toward Santa Fe, where his troops were captured by Spanish troops. Unlike Nolan's men, Pike's uniformed soldiers could claim that they were lost, so the Spanish accepted this charitable interpretation and treated Pike's men to a tour of Mexico on their way back to the United States. Pike's report, complete with maps smuggled out in the linings of his coat, revealed that the Spanish society's glitter really masked weakness, and that their territory would be taken easily. However, his characterization of the far west as a "great desert" also discouraged interest in taking the country for some, and it even held up American settlement there after it became United States territory.

In November 1806 Wilkinson met with Colonel Simon de Herrera, this time both of them on a mission to dampen tensions over the disputed territory. The resulting agreement created a Neutral Ground between the Sabine River and the Arroyo Hondo, a tributary of the Red River. Both pledged to prevent clashes by not patrolling the area or permitting settlement there. Neither could really stop individuals from moving into the area, where total lack of military or other law enforcement provided a haven for the lawless of both societies. Each side occasionally sent expeditions into the Neutral Ground on justified policing missions.

One such mission was led by Lieutenant Augustus Magee, a graduate of West Point. Magee did his work well, and in the course of his duties learned much about the territory and the people. Later, when he became disgruntled over his failure to receive promotion to captain, Magee fell in with a Spaniard-turned-Mexican nationalist named Bernardo Gutierrez de Lara. Gutierrez had come to American territory as an agent of the revolutionary Father Hidalgo, who published his *grito*, or cry for Mexican independence, in 1810. In San Antonio an insurgent party overthrew the government authorities, but Juan Zambrano led a counter-revolutionary movement there which restored royalist authority and separated Gutierrez, then in Louisiana, from Hidalgo. In 1811 the priest was captured and later executed at Chihauhua City.

Gutierrez had come to the United States to find help for Hidalgo among the Americans; now he looked to them to fight for him in an effort to regain his lands and perhaps add to his holdings. Gutierrez visited with Dr. John Sibley at Natchitoches; eventually he even visited in Washington and Philadelphia, seeking to arouse American interest in moving onto Spanish territory. He hoped they would do the fighting while he would reconstruct an independent government in Texas. The United States government would not do this for him, of course, but many private citizens showed interest, some even with money and supplies, and others with their services. Gutierrez returned to New Orleans where he met with William Shaler, a consular officer, and Shaler put him in touch with Magee at Natchitoches. Shaler is probably the one who persuaded Magee to join with Gutierrez in a scheme to invade Texas in June, 1812.

The Magee-Gutierrez partnership was shaky from the first. Magee led the military forces, called the Army of the North, with the rank of Colonel; Gutierrez proposed the civilian government they hoped to establish. Magee recruited among old Neutral Ground enemies who were willing to participate on promises of forty dollars a month pay and large land settlements from the new government. In August the several-hundred-strong army of this pretender republic crossed the Sabine River and easily took Nacogdoches from a small Spanish garrison; the civilians offered no resistance at all. Many joined with Magee; others cooperated, although some later correctly claimed that they had had little choice. After taking Nacogdoches, Magee commanded over 800 men. He posted his green flag on the Stone House and used the building as a headquarters. There type was set for the first newspaper to be published in Texas, the *Gaceta de Texas,* or *Texas Gazette,* by a Philadelphia printer named A. Mower who accompanied the expedition. The newspaper was little more than a propaganda sheet for the political movement, but it made journalistic history in Texas.

It was also in Nacogdoches that the partners proclaimed Texas free from Spain on April 6, 1813, the first such declaration of independence in Texas. Afterwards, Gutierrez began asserting more control. He persuaded Magee to move on to La Bahia, or Goliad, where 1,500 Spanish troops were stationed under Jose Antonio Saucedo. Magee flanked the Spanish garrison, captured their position, then released the men. Saucedo and his men moved briefly to San Antonio, then returned with reinforcements to besiege the Army of the North, which had stalled on the rich supplies of the Spanish. Magee's mental and physical condition may have deteriorated during this delay—Gutierrez later claimed that Magee committed suicide—and he died there. Samuel Kemper, a competent officer, assumed command. When the Spanish attempted to attack shortly after Magee's death, Kemper's command had little difficulty in defeating them. He then pursued the retreating Spanish soldiers to San Antonio, where he destroyed the last stronghold of royal forces in Texas.

Gutierrez demanded full control of the venture in San Antonio. His new republic, it seemed, would have little place for Kemper and the few honorable men in the command who had come for free land. So Kemper resigned and returned to Louisiana, only to be replaced briefly by Reuben Ross. When a new Spanish force under Ignacia Elizondo arrived, Ross advised against a fight, so Gutierrez replaced him with Henry Perry, a daredevil adventurer who would fight anything. Perry defeated Elizondo in an action known as the Battle of the Alazan. Then Jose Alvarez de Toledo arrived from Natchitoches after conferring with Shaler, and intimidated Gutierrez into surrendering the civilian authority in the as yet un-established republic. Now commanded by Perry and Toledo, a true cut-throat element reigned in a venture that had begun with higher, if no more legal, motives.

Gutierrez wisely left before a more potent Spanish force under General Joaquin de Arredondo arrived. Arredondo drew

Perry into battle at the Medina River in the summer of 1813, where he killed nearly all of the Americans who remained to fight. Many fled back to East Texas and Louisiana. Arredondo moved on to San Antonio where he arrested and killed everyone who had cooperated with the Americans, and threatened the same for those at La Bahia and Nacogdoches. The latter community's citizens, Americans as well as Spaniards, vanished. One of Arredondo's cadet officers, Antonio Lopez de Santa Anna, learned from his Spanish general a lesson he later attempted to employ in 1836 during the Texas Revolution: the best way to end trouble with trespassers is to kill them.

The Magee-Gutierrez expedition and its dreams of empire in an independent Texas proved a failure. But it encouraged the hopes of many who still longed for an independent Texas and an independent Mexico, and many of its participants returned later to make both a reality.

Individual Americans continued to make their way to Spanish lands in Texas following the failure of Magee, but the next major filibustering expedition came after the United States had renounced all claims to the lands beyond the Sabine River by the Adams-Onis Treaty of 1819. These negotiations resulted from an invasion of Spanish Florida in 1817 by Tennessee militia commander Andrew Jackson, who was pursuing renegade Indians. For years Florida's Indians had raided American settlements, then hastily retreated to the protection of the Spanish territory. Jackson ignored the boundary, pursued these Indians until he caught and fought them. And without civilian trial, he also hanged two British subjects whom he accused of stirring up the Indians.

An international incident resulted which placed both the Spanish and the British in opposition to the United States. Secretary of State John Quincy Adams advocated, and President James Monroe accepted, a tough policy toward these nations: they told the British to keep their agents out of Florida, and the Spanish to police their Indians or the United States would do whatever was necessary to preserve its own interests. The British chose to drop the matter to protect their growing friendship with the United States in other areas, and the Spanish reluctantly but finally admitted that they could not control Florida.

In negotiations between Adams and Spanish minister Luis

de Onis, the two nations agreed to the cession of Florida to the United States in return for $7 million, giving the latter country not only the peninsula itself, but for the first time, control of the Gulf coast all the way to Spanish territory in Texas. Also the Adams-Onis Treaty of 1819 attempted to "permanently" settle the boundary between the two nations in Texas. The boundary line ran along the west bank of the Sabine River to the 32nd parallel, then directly north to the Red River and along its bank to the 100th meridian, then up that line to the Arkansas River headwaters, then due north to the 42nd parallel, and along that line to the Pacific Ocean. In the northern regions this agreement simply ignored already pre-existing British, American, and Russian claims. And in the lower regions, the treaty angered southern Americans who coveted the lands beyond the Sabine River as expansion territory for their agricultural economy and lifestyle, including African slavery.

Protest meetings raged through the South, but especially along the Mississippi line. At Natchez, Dr. James Long received the endorsement of one such meeting to lead an expedition into Texas to declare it independent and therefore available for southern American cultural and political expansion, despite the treaty with Spain. Offers to help Long guide it came in, including one from Bernardo Gutierrez de Lara.

Dr. Long led an expedition of about 120 men across the Sabine River to Nacogdoches in June, 1819. Within a short time, he occupied the Stone Fort, proclaimed Texas independent, and recruited another 200 men. Long travelled to Galveston to confer with the pirate Jean Lafitte, whom he hoped to enlist in the scheme to make Texas free. Lafitte already operated as freely as he wanted in the Gulf waters on a live-and-let-live basis with the Spanish government, so he refused. Without Lafitte's help, and lacking sufficient supplies, Long returned via Nacogdoches to Mississippi then moved on to New Orleans, where he conferred with Mexican liberals seeking someone to fight the Spanish for them. One, Jose Felix Trespalacios, helped Long plan an invasion of Texas at Bolivar, a coastal point just to the east of Galveston, which would guarantee a supply line.

Long's second expedition arrived at Point Bolivar in April of 1820 with a large force and his young bride, Jane, and her servant girl Kian. Long and Trespalacios soon parted, and

Long took a small force to capture La Bahia. He succeeded at first, but soon a larger Spanish army arrived and captured Long, who was then taken to Mexico and executed. Jane Long decided to remain at Bolivar after the remaining "Patriot" army, as Long's men were called, decided to return to New Orleans. She and her slave wintered there, surviving on fish and what other seafoods they could obtain, and using a cannon to keep curious Karankawa Indians from coming near them. When she learned of Long's fate, Jane Long rode horseback to Mexico in an effort to have her husband's murderers punished. Unsuccessful in the attempt, she returned to Mississippi but eventually resettled in Texas and became known as the Mother of Texas.

Jean Lafitte, although not a true filibuster, was but one of several others who sojourned in Texas in the twilight of Spanish control. For example, Louis-Michel Aury, a French naval officer and later privateer, prowled the Gulf until he and New Orleans associates established a rebel port at Galveston. Jose Manuel de Herrera, a Mexican rebel, had also settled at Galveston and proclaimed the island an independent republic in 1816. Francisco Xavier Mina also operated in and out of Texas during these years until captured and executed in 1817.

Spanish authorities continued to repulse such invaders as long as they remained in authority, but their day drew quickly to a close after the disposal of Long's last expedition. Spain's hold over all of Mexico was weakened by persistent nationalist movements—such as that of the padre Hidalgo—and because of the Napoleonic disturbances in Europe, especially those within Spain itself after Napoleon forced his brother upon the Spanish as their king. The Spanish-Mexican clergy, large landowners, and other vested interests feared the reforms and changes which the new order might require. The revolution resurfaced and smoldered under the leadership of Jose Maria Morelos and Vicente Guerrero.

By the end of the Napoleonic Era in Europe, it appeared that the restored Spanish monarchy under King Ferdinand might regain sufficient strength to hold onto New Spain. Viceroy Juan Ruiz Apodaca in 1819 even reported that no additional troops would be required to do the job. But further liberal changes that Ferdinand accepted under a liberal constitution alarmed conservatives in New Spain, who then determined that only independence could sustain their way of life and secure their hold on the church and land ownership.

So upper classes joined in support of Augustine de Iturbide; and that leader, in concert with the near-liberal Guerrero, issued the Plan of Iguala in February, 1821, proclaiming Mexico free from Spain. They planned for a Catholic nation, racial equality, and secured land titles. In August the last viceroy, Juan O'Donoju, recognized the Independence of Mexico with Iturbide as chief executive. Thereafter, the administration of Texas affairs, although remaining somewhat confused, would come exclusively from Mexico. And many new American invaders came to make those affairs even more troublesome for the Mexican nation than they had ever been for the Spanish.

Land hunger, not easily satisfied at United States prices and terms, drew hundreds of settlers to Texas when the lands were opened to settlement by the new Mexican government under the empresarial system. Moses Austin and his son Stephen Fuller Austin led the way. Although the settlements on the Red River at Pecan Point and Jonesborough preceded the Austins' activity, they were then regarded as a part of the Arkansas Territory.

Moses Austin followed the frontier all his life. Born in Connecticut, he joined his brother in business in Philadelphia and later in Virginia, operating mercantile establishments and later engaging in lead mining. Austin moved to the Missouri territory in 1798 while the Spanish still controlled it. He established the village of Potosi and again followed the mining and mercantile trades. His son, Stephen F. Austin, born in Virginia and educated in Kentucky, worked with his father in the Missouri enterprises. He also served in the militia, the territory legislature, and was appointed a territorial judge.

The Panic of 1819 eliminated the Austins' financial resources, especially following the failure of the Bank of St. Louis in which they had invested heavily to bolster the sagging local economy. Stephen Austin then left for New Orleans to study law, perhaps hoping to make his way in that profession; but Moses Austin remembered the experience of William Morgan and looked to Spanish Texas for the solution to his financial problems. He travelled to San Antonio to request permission from Governor Antonio de Martinez to establish a colony of 300 families in Texas. Martinez turned Austin down un-

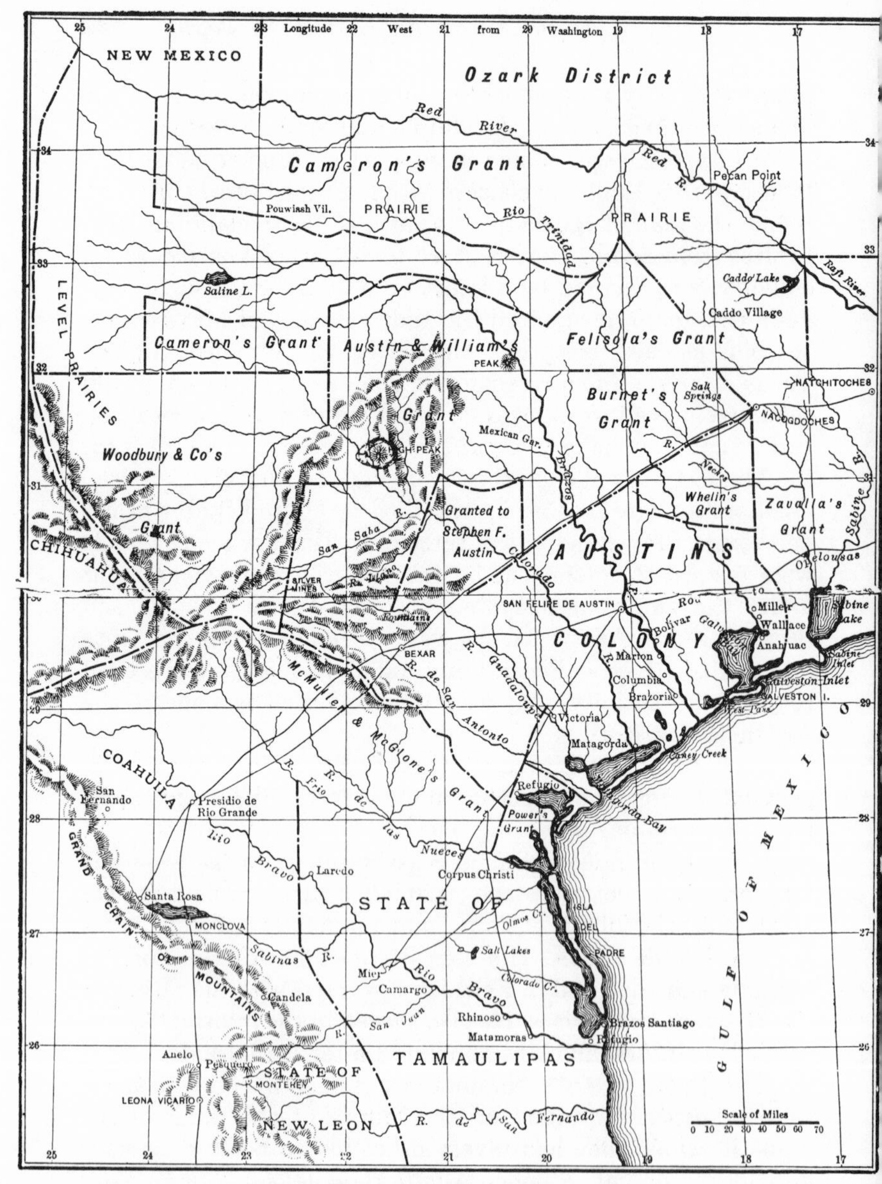

AUSTIN'S MAP OF 1835.

til an old friend from Missouri, the Baron de Bastrop, vouched for Austin's good record and former Spanish citizenship. Martinez then agreed to the venture, which also received endorsement by a board of supervisors of the provincial deputation at Monterrey. Moses Austin died soon after returning to Louisiana, but the project was assumed, as a death-bed promise, by Stephen Austin. He had taken little interest in his father's scheme until then; afterward, it became an obsession.

Austin visited San Antonio in the summer of 1821 to confirm the inheritance of his father's commission. Martinez recognized Austin's rights and told him to explore the country and to locate his colony. News of the venture reached Natchitoches before Austin returned there, and he found over one hundred letters from interested parties. Austin's New Orleans law teacher, partner and friend, Joseph Hawkins, helped him purchase *The Lively*, a schooner, to ferry supplies. Austin dispatched it with eighteen settlers for a rendezvous at the mouth of the Colorado River.

He himself returned to Texas by an overland route to find the first settler, Andrew Robinson, already at the Brazos River. Shortly afterward, Robert and Joseph Kuykendahl, Daniel Gilliland, Thomas Boatright, and Jared E. Groce, the latter with a train of fifty wagons and ninety slaves, arrived. They established plantations and started settlements. Austin went to the mouth of the Colorado to meet *The Lively,* but it was not there; he moved to the Brazos and learned that the vessel had arrived sometime earlier, and despairing of meeting Austin, had returned to New Orleans. This incident only began his troubles.

Visiting San Antonio, Austin learned from Martinez that the Mexican government would not recognize his grant because it had been approved by the Spanish. He travelled to Monterrey and eventually to Mexico City to see what he could do about the situation, leaving Josiah Bell in charge of the colony. Austin spent over a year unraveling the complexities of Mexican politics. Iturbide had become emporer by the action of a trumped up mob demanding that he be given the office. Iturbide had assumed the position and dismissed the Congress, but not before the Congress had passed the General Colonization Law of January 4, 1823, which authorized Austin's colony. Iturbide agreed to Austin's scheme as well. But in March, Iturbide was forced to abdicate. A new Congress approved Austin's claim again, then voided the Colonization Law, making his the only land grant issued under its provisions.

Austin was made totally responsible to the government for his colonists' actions. They had to be or become Roman Catholic, be hard working, and be able to present certificates of good conduct from their former places of residence. Finally, in August, 1823, with the Baron de Bastrop as the government's land agent, Austin began to issue land titles to his settlers. By the summer of 1824, he had issued 272 titles, with twenty-five remaining titles of this original grant being issued in the late 1820s, making a total of 297 grants. This group of grantees is known as "The Old Three Hundred."

Austin selected the site of his colony well. The Brazos and Colorado rivers, the two most navigable streams in Texas, cut his lands into three approximately equal segments. In addition, his land was freer from timber than the area to the east, thus requiring less labor for clearing; yet it received more rainfall than the land to the west. The Indians in his area, mostly Karankawas, occasionally posed problems, but they were easier to deal with than the Comanches or Apaches. By law, each colonial family received one *labor* (la-bor), 177 acres, of land if they farmed, and one *sitio,* a square league, or 4, 428 acres, if they were ranchers. On such terms, most testified that they were ranchers. Few ever paid Austin his agent's fee of twelve-and-a-half cents per acre; some could not because cash remained a scarce commodity in colonial Texas, and some refused to do so because they figured that the nearly 40,000 acres he received from the government made him rich enough. In cash, however, he remained poor for the remainder of his life.

The Mexican Congress enacted another general colonization law in 1824. This legislation turned over to the state government the administration of all land alienation and colonization. It provided, however, that the state laws conform to general constitutional provisions, that foreigners should not settle near the coast or international boundaries, and that all who received land become citizens. Another act passed on May 7, 1824, combined Texas and Coahuila as one state until Texas' population grew to sufficient size to justify separation.

Thus the state legislature meeting at Saltillo had charge of land affairs in Texas. The Coahuila-Texas Colonization Law, passed in 1825, created the empresarial system for colonization. Land could be obtained by individuals, but if settlers worked through an empresario, they also received that officer's assistance in settlement and representation. An empresario's contract lasted six years. He received compensation by means of a fee paid by the settler, and by personal land grants from the government. Between 1825 and the revocation of this system by the Law of April 6, 1830, some twenty-five empresarial contracts were issued. Under the program Austin obtained a contract to settle another 500 families on his original lands, another in 1827 to settle 100 families on the Colorado River immediately to the north of his original grant, and still a third grant in 1828 to settle 300 families in an area between the Lavaca and San Jacinto Rivers. Stephen F. Austin settled a total of 1,200 families, with a population of over 4,000 people on his four grants.

In 1825 Green DeWitt received a grant to settle 400 families between the Lavaca and Guadalupe rivers, and Gonzales became his principal town. Toward the coast from De Witt, Martin de Leon obtained a grant, and because of Indian problems in 1826, many of DeWitt's people moved down river to de Leon's lands. Arthur Wavell received a grant along the Red River in the northeast corner of Texas, although his associate Ben Milam actually located the settlers there. Sterling Robertson obtained a grant just to the north of Austin's original grant, and quickly became involved in a bitter dispute with Austin. In South Texas, grants were obtained by James Power and James Hewetson and by John McMullen and James McGloin, who attempted to attract direct European immigration. But they settled few families.

The most troublesome contract was East Texas. There Haden Edwards obtained lands with Nacogdoches as a capital, but because his grant contained settlers with grants dating from early Spanish occupation, he experienced difficulty in proving out claims. This ultimately resulted in a brief and unsuccessful declaration of independence for a Fredonia Republic, but even Austin helped Mexican authorities put down the Edwards revolt. Later Edwards' lands were given in three grants to David G. Burnet, Joseph Vehlein, and Lorenzo de Zavala, who turned their lands over to a land speculation company called the Galveston Bay and Texas Land Company to solicit settlers in the United States. Finally, Drs. John Charles Beales and James Grant, physicians, obtained a contract to settle European immigrants between the Rio Grande and the Nueces Rivers, but they had little success.

The Robertson grant left the bitterest legacy among the Americans. Robertson really fronted for the Texas Association of Nashville, and apparently he made little progress in attracting and settling families. Before the Law of April 6, 1830, became effective, Samuel Mays Williams, in partnership with Austin, sought to obtain Robertson's land to settle over 800 families. The Mexican governor first forfeited Robertson's colony and gave it to Austin and Williams, but then reversed the ruling and returned it to Robertson when he showed that he had settled over 100 families on the land. Austin and Williams later regained the land after the passage of the Land Law in 1830. Bitterness between the families lingered for decades.

Life in this colonial period can be characterized as isolated. Austin's capital, San Felipe de Austin, remained the largest center of Anglos. It was second only to San Antonio in total population, but it could not be called even a real town. A few log structures in the middle of nowhere is a better description. Yet settlers came to his colony, attracted by the inexpensive land. Some walked; some rode horseback with their wordly goods in saddle bags; some trudged beside wagons laden with supplies, seeds, and hopes for the future; others came by coastal vessels from New Orleans.

Jared Groce's wealth was unique for Austin's colonists. Most were poor, even by American standards of the time; they lacked capital, cash, or credit. Shelter posed a constant problem. The one-room cabin dominated, made of logs if available, and of anything else that was handy such as rocks, stones, or mud-on-stakes, when they were not available. As settlers became established, some built second adjacent cabins bonded by a common roof, in the southern American style. Such breezeway or dog-run houses became common in Texas. Furnishings could only be called functional; home-made was in vogue. Cross sections of logs became chairs and tables; bamboo reeds were fashioned as forks or carved into spoons; corn husks or moss became mattress ticking, gourds were dippers or drinking vessels, and so forth.

Food in its natural state abounded in small and large ani-

Stephen F. Austin issuing deeds at San Felipe de Austin. From mural in Southern Pacific Railroad Station in Houston.

mals and fishes; in season, berries or nuts were plentiful; bees provided honey as a food sweetner and preservative; in time, field crops and gardens supplemented such fare from the hunt and the fishing trip. In addition, hunting also provided clothing for deer hides could be fashioned by a frontiersman or his wife into very suitable wearing apparel that lasted almost indefinitely.

Because of the restricted, monotonous diets, early Texans did not enjoy good health. Even when their communities became established, their food remained seasonal; that is, they had plenty of green foods in the warmer months and few in the winter, because their only method of preserving meats or vegetables was by drying or salting. If a physician's care was available for injury or sickness, it might be worse than none at all since anyone could advertise himself as a doctor. And even the best of them sometimes prescribed laxatives to treat diarrhea, bleeding to relieve a variety of problems, and none of them had yet learned what a germ was.

In matters of faith, all had agreed to worship as Roman Catholics. Father Michael Muldoon, allegedly a somewhat alcoholic priest evidently banished to Texas to serve the Americans, performed baptisms without much catechism, and most Texans continued to be either non-believers or Protestants of some kind. As early as 1832, Samuel Doak McMahon operated a Methodist Sunday School in East Texas, and William Stevenson wandered East Texas preaching from a Methodist pulpit. Baptists Joseph E. Bays and Thomas J. Pilgrim preached in their own ways with relative freedom, and Cumberland Presbyterian Sumner Bacon did the same.

There was no system of education in colonial Texas, although a public school had existed in San Antonio for a time under the Spanish, and Nacogdoches, San Augustine, and Jonesborough also had schools. Usually sons learned from their fathers how to earn a living and daughters learned from their mothers how to keep house. Most immigrants were functionally literate, but often their children could not make the same boast.

Farming and trading were colonial Texas' chief enterprises. Cane was grown along the rivers, especially the Brazos, while some cotton was also cultivated. The inevitable corn to feed livestock and man also grew here. Trade centers, if they could be called that, existed in small form in most empresarial grants and could be called developed at San Felipe and Nacogdoches. No banks or credit institutions existed to help expansion, and a chronic lack of cash reduced most exchanges to barter. Most Texans remained dependent on trade from the United States for staples.

Colonialism in Texas offered the settlers a hard life, but one that promised much in the future. For the moment, these last invaders remained guests in a land where the hosts first welcomed them, then grew fearful of their growing numbers. But these invaders had come to stay, no matter what.

The Texas Revolution

"Take care of my little boy. If the country should be saved I may make him a splendid fortune. But if this country should be lost and I should perish, he will have nothing but the proud recollection that he is the son of a man who died for his country." This passage from the second most quoted letter written from the Alamo by William Barret Travis captures the spirit of the Texas Revolution.

Travis represents much of the Texian cause in the clash of cultures, religions, political systems, and ethnic identities which collided in the 1830s in Texas. Born in South Carolina, reared and maturing in Alabama, Travis migrated to Texas in his twenty-first year and in the first year of the clash between Mexican authorities and American settlers. Young, ambitious, acquisitive, and rash, Travis maneuvered himself into positions of leadership in a movement he did not create and, perhaps, did not understand; yet he led that movement as much as anyone before his death in the defense of the Alamo. Travis' life and the nature of his death symbolize the story of the Revolution.

William B. Travis had arrived in Texas just in time to see the result of the first decade of legalized Anglo-Mexican cohabitation of Texas. Like other Americans who had preceded him as migrants, he accepted the requirements for citizenship and religious regularity required by the colonization law. His generation of Americans could easily remember the causes and concerns of the American Revolution from Great Britain; they were as fresh as first or second generation memories.

Col. William Barrett Travis migrated to Texas from South Carolina when he was twenty-one years old. He fought in the Alamo, and was among the first Texans to be killed in the Texas revolution.

— Portrait by H. P. McArdlis

Although the Americans had come from a centralized government, many of them had resented the government's power. Their concept of citizenship and natural rights lay rooted in centuries of development, beginning at Runnymeade with the Magna Carta and punctuated with the Roundhead revolution in 1640, the Glorious Revolution of 1688, and their own Declaration of Independence in 1776. Their fathers had dealt with the issues of Salutary Neglect, taxation without adequate or proper representation, and sudden and arbitrary exercises of power by a central government; and the memory of their previous response remained in their consciousness.

When the Americans came to Texas, few expected to have to deal with these problems themselves. They were migrating to a country which ostensibly operated under the liberal, decentralized Constitution of 1824, a document which theoretically created the kind of government in which many of the Americans believed, the kind many had wanted for the United States, the kind that Thomas Jefferson had championed, the kind that John Calhoun would soon call for again in the United States.

When the Anglos arrived in Texas, they accepted the citizenship change and the church requirements because these surface obligations caused little inconvenience. They came for inexpensive or free land, and such requirements were well worth the price of an oath. They came to develop the land, not meddle in national politics, and most made sincere efforts to be peaceful, law abiding Mexicans. Stephen F. Austin remained the premier example of this effort; he succeeded in becoming "Estaban" F. Austin, the way he signed most of his correspondence in Texas until 1835.

But some could not make the adjustment. They regarded the lack of development of the land as a mark of Mexican indolence; they believed themselves superior to their hosts, whom they saw as lazy and unachieving. And, most conceitedly, they expected the Mexicans to agree with them. Many felt as Israelis might have believed in the late 1940s when their nation was created in Palestine where the land had been under the Palestinians for centuries and had remained underdeveloped, that it was because of some innate weakness of the owners.

Like their Spanish predecessors, some Mexicans suspected every Anglo of plotting to steal Texas from them. Nolan, Magee and Long planted that seed of suspicion. More than a decade of Americans behaving themselves could have convinced the Mexico City leadership that these Anglo colonists were not in a conspiracy with the United States government to take Mexican lands from them; but it did not work out that way, for they suspected all Anglos of this desire, from Washington, D. C., to San Felipe de Austin. Unfortunately, there were plenty of incidents in the decade of the 1820s which a paranoia-like imagination could easily accommodate to that scenerio. So by 1830, peoples in both camps eyed the others suspiciously; they over-reacted to statements and acts of the other side; and within six years they had become bitter enemies.

Part of the problem lay in their differing concepts of citizenship. The Anglo political experience was participatory; they were accustomed to voting their leaders into office and accepting a loss at the polls with only gritted teeth. They petitioned their government as equals of its leadership, and expected their petitions to be answered if not honored. Their concept of governmental power was inductive; such power came from the people and was delegated to a constitutional government that was run for a limited time by elected officials.

The Mexican background, on the other hand, saw power as mostly deductive; that is, power belonged to God, then to the King; each had representatives who exercised power in the name of their chief and both had absolute authority. Even after the Mexican Republic was established, these old concepts remained essentially unchanged because so many contenders for power in the system were willing to go outside the constitutional provisions for change to achieve more power. The Anglos were unaccustomed to sudden and arbitrary changes of power, to the use of the military to enforce civilian policy, or to cowed acceptance of these things when they occurred. And finally, the Americans mostly settled in the eastern part of Texas, where there were very few Mexicans *except* military officials, and, where, for their part, the Mexican leadership, liberal and conservative, regarded the increasing Anglo population in Texas as a threat. Yet the Anglos did give the Mexican leaders bonafide problems. The Fredonia Rebellion at Nacogdoches is a good example.

In 1825, Haden Edwards received an empresarial grant to the lands around Nacogdoches and extending down the Trinity, Neches, Angelina, and Sabine rivers. Edwards had aided Austin in the negotiations which resulted in the Constitution of 1824 and the Colonization Law of 1825 in Mexico City and Saltillo. Like all empresarios, Edwards knew that preexisting Spanish or Mexican land grants must be excluded from his area. But since his lands included the largest number of Spanish and Mexican inhabitants of any empresarial grant, he had the greatest problems. Edwards did not know how to locate these claims, because, unlike the Anglo tradition of Court House deed registration, most Hispanic grants were represented only by an original document in the hands of the recipients. Many of these had become lost in the forced migration of 1772, or in house fires, Indian raids, or through carelessness.

So Edwards posted a notice at the Stone Fort in Nacogdoches to inform all prior claimants that they would have to come to him and prove ownership of all lands within his grant, or they would be assumed to be his and could be sold to new settlers. Naturally this irritated the older settlers, many of whom were Anglos, and they protested to government officials in San Antonio and Saltillo. Then Edwards became involved in an election for *alcalde* of Nacogdoches; he backed his son-in-law, Chicester Chaplain, while the older settlers supported Samuel Norris. Chaplain was declared the winner but Norris' supporters protested to the governor at San Antonio, who reversed the results and ordered Norris to fill the position.

Edwards' brother Benjamin administered the colonies' affairs in May, 1826, while the empresario travelled to the United States to recruit more settlers. In correspondence with Stephen F. Austin, Benjamin Edwards complained of mistreatment by Mexican officials in these matters, and Austin cautioned Edwards against offending the government. Naturally, Austin was concerned for his own situation and feared that Edwards would anger the Mexicans against all Americans, but Edwards continued to complain and posted more notices for the older settlers to prove ownership or lose their land. Again, they complained, and on June 3, 1826, authorities in Mexico City ordered the Edwards grant forfeited.

Governor Victor Blanco delayed the execution of the order until October, but when he received a letter from Edwards which he characterized as "sarcastic" and "disrespectful," Blanco voided the grant and ordered the Edwards brothers to leave Texas. Instead, Benjamin Edwards proclaimed their grant area as the free state of Fredonia. A bond was made with the local Cherokee Indians who had recently come to Texas from the United States, having received permission from the Mexican government to assume lands in East Texas. They also had had difficulties with the government in obtaining titles; so, following the leadership of John Hunter and Richard Fields, some of the Cherokees joined the Edwards brothers in the Fredonia movement. On December 16, 1826, the Fredonia Republic flew its red and white flag, symbolizing the Anglo and Indian alliance. It proclaimed Independence, Liberty and Justice in bold letters along with signatures of several of the supporters of this pretender government.

When news of these events reached Mexican authorities, Lt. Col. Mateo Ahumada, principal military commander of Texas, moved his 110 infantrymen and twenty dragoons to San Felipe. Austin agreed to join Ahumada and enlisted some of his settlers to suppress the Rebellion to show their own legality. By the time this force reached Nacogdoches in late December, the Fredonia Republic had collapsed. Knowing that the military authorities were on their way, most of the supporters fled into the wilderness, and the Edwards brothers returned to the safety of Louisiana. The Indians later executed Fields and Hunter for involving them in the scheme. Ahumada was able to report that his mission had been accomplished without a shot being fired.

The Fredonia movement, despite its peaceful ending, alarmed many Mexican officials of the potential for trouble from the growing Anglo population, and events within their own capital alarmed them still more about the intentions of the United States government. Since the signing of the Adams-Onis Treaty in 1819 many Americans had worked to undo its denial of westward expansion. When John Quincy Adams became president in March, 1825, he attempted to shore up western support for his administration by making a show of attempting to move the boundary farther west. Americans sometimes offered the excuse that inaccurate maps employed in the negotiation had used the name of Sabine in referring to the Brazos River two hundred miles to the west, and that this was where they had thought the real boundary would be. Adams, who knew better and was only trying to gain support in the west, appointed Joel Poinsett as the United States' first minister to Mexico and instructed his new agent to offer the Mexicans $1 million for Texas.

Poinsett proved quickly that he lacked diplomatic skills. In an address before a public gathering in Mexico City, he informed the general populace of his mission before it had been decided by the authorities. Then he meddled in internal affairs by helping in the founding of York Rite Masonry as a competitive organization to the Scottish Rite variety already operating in Mexico where it served as a safe and secret meeting place for conservatives. Poinsett hoped to provide the liberals with a similar vehicle, thus helping his cause, but he only made matters worse. Poinsett operated under the impression that Adams really wanted to purchase Texas. Later, Andrew Jackson—who really did want to acquire Texas—used Poinsett and Anthony Butler, his own man, to continue the offer; and he even increased the price to $5 million. But the results were the same; no sale, plus increased suspicions of American intentions with regard to Texas. In the end Poinsett's only positive contribution was the importation of the beautiful plant which shares his name.

With the Fredonia Rebellion as hard evidence of Anglo perfidity, and the Poinsett mission to feed their suspicions, a heady Mexican nationalism with an anti-Anglo bias began to grip many Hispanic leaders. Manuel Mier y Teran, Don Jose Maria Tornel, and Don Lucas Alaman conducted an investigation of the Anglos' colonies in Texas, and found what they wanted to find: that the Anglos outnumbered the Mexicans by a 10 to 1 margin in Texas, and that the Mexicans were likely to have been assigned an inferior station in life. They also found that the Anglo population grew by the thousands each year. These leaders determined to stem the tide and contol the Americans more closely.

In 1829 Alaman pursuaded President Vicente Guerrero to proclaim an end of slavery in Mexico. The Texans knew that this was intended for them alone since only the Anglos there held slaves. Then these leaders pushed the Law of April 6, 1830 through the Mexican Congress. This legislation, intended to suppress a crisis that did not then exist, stopped further Anglo colonization in Texas and restored such matters to the central government from the states, which had exercised these powers

Portrait of David Crockett, hero of the Alamo.

under the Constitution of 1824. Further importation of African slaves was also proscribed. To bolster the Mexican population, convicts would be relocated in Texas; and to further dilute the Anglo solidarity, efforts would be made to encourage direct European immigration. In addition, investigators would be stationed in Texas to monitor events and watch for conspiracies.

Nearly all Texas Anglos resented these measures. They had to prove their good citizenship for admission, but would now have convict neighbors. They recognized the stopping of immigration and slave importation as a deliberate effort to keep them in a minority and weakened status. As American frontiersmen, they resented any interference with their freedom of movement. They believed that only continued immigration could enable them to prosper in Texas. They resented the customs collection, even though their exemption from such collections was due to end within a year anyway. Each side misunderstood the other: the Mexicans were moving to head off a movement which did not exist, and the Americans allowed their resentment to confirm their prejudice about unworthiness of their host nation to govern them.

The Americans were concerned about the rapid and unconstitutional changes in Mexican politics. President Vicente Guerrero failed in his bid for re-election, but refused to relinquish the government to the victor, Gomez Pedraza. Anastacio Bustamante then overthrew Guerrero and gave Pedraza his post, but the Americans knew that the orderly constitutional process which they expected from their United States experiences had not been honored. Later, when Bustamante and Antonio Lopes de Santa Anna warred against each other for leadership, they knew that the time of the *caudillo,* or charismatic leader, had come to them, perhaps without knowing the label for it.

The American's first expression of resentment came as Mexican troops deployed in Texas early in 1831. General Manuel Mier y Teran, commander of the northern provinces, including Texas, stationed Colonel Jose de las Piedras with 350 men at Nacogdoches. Captain John Davis Bradburn, an adventurer Kentuckian-turned-Mexican, commanded 150 soldiers at Anahuac, and Colonel Don Domingo de Ugartechea had over one hundred men at Velasco. Bradburn was the first to provoke anger among the Americans. He established his post at

Anahuac and quickly decreed that all ships clearing the Texas coast must first receive authorization from his headquarters at Anahuac and settle tax accounts with customs collector John Fisher, a Serbian exile who had become a Mexican citizen, stationed at Galveston. Most ship captains ignored Bradburn's order, one difficult to enforce anyway, rather than make an overland journey from the Brazos or Colorado rivers, to obtain clearance papers. But they were angered by the order just the same.

Then Bradburn became involved in a dispute with the state government of Coahuila y Texas. Governor Jose Maria Letona, reopened lands in Texas to Anglo settlement. Letona sent Francisco Madero, general land commissioner, to issue titles to Americans already in Texas. Madero had already authorized the settlement of Liberty before Bradburn learned of his activities. He ordered Madero to cease, and when the officer refused, Bradburn arrested Madero and his surveyor, Jose Maria Carbajal, and annulled the charter for the town of Liberty. This angered the Americans who depended on Madero as their only hope for land titles after the Law of April 6, 1830. They also accused Bradburn of using their slaves for his own purposes, of appropriating their supplies without compensation, and of the arbitrary arrest of some of the Americans.

This last charge referred to the arrest of William B. Travis, an attorney for William T. Logan of Louisiana. Logan had appeared at Anahuac in the spring of 1832 seeking runaway slaves who were being sheltered by Bradburn. Bradburn refused to release the slaves without proper proof of ownership, and Logan engaged Travis to press the case while he returned for ownership papers. Before leaving, Logan threatened Bradburn that he would return with armed aid should the papers prove insufficient. This alarmed Bradburn, and he nervously awaited the return of the Louisianian.

To annoy Bradburn, Travis secretly sent a note claiming that Logan was at hand with an armed force. When patrols failed to locate these men, Bradburn had Travis arrested, and when Patrick Jack, Travis' law partner, protested, he too was arrested. William Jack was also threatened with arrest should he continue the argument. Instead, he hastened to San Felipe for aid. Finding Austin away from his headquarters, Jack had little difficulty raising over 150 men, including John Austin from Brazoria. This force gathered at Anahuac to demand the surrender of the Americans, whom Bradburn threatened to send to Mexico for military trial. They captured a Mexican patrol and proposed an exchange, but Bradburn convinced the Anglos to release his men first, then he refused to release Travis and Jack.

The Americans withdrew to Turtle Bayou and drew up a set of resolutions which pledged their continued support to the Constitution of 1824 and their resentment of those who had set it aside, including Bradburn. John Austin returned to Brazoria to obtain a cannon for the more forceful statement of their case. Colonel Piedras, however, learned of the disturbances and hurried to Anahuac. He heard the Anglo version first, and although his sympathy lay with Bradburn, to avoid further trouble, Piedras discharged that officer and ordered the release of the prisoners.

When Piedras returned to his post at Nacogdoches, he precipiated trouble for himself by ordering all the settlers in his district to turn in their guns at Nacogdoches. In late July, they arrived — and turned their guns *on* Piedras. Most of the Americans in the Battle of Nacogdoches came from the Ayish Bayou country. They arrived on the eastern flank of town at the home of Adolphus Sterne, who showed them how to move around Piedras' soldiers at the Stone Fort and at his Cartel by a route along Lanana Creek. Then, from the west and north, they attacked both positions. Only two or three Nacogdoches citizens joined the fight, which lasted until dark. During the night, Piedras attempted to escape, but was caught the next day at the Angelina River near the residence of Joseph Durst, and another fight occurred. Piedras finally surrendered, and his command was escorted to San Antonio.

Meanwhile, John Austin obtained the cannon at Brazoria but had to fight his way past Ugartechea at Velasco. In that action ten Texans and five Mexicans were killed, but Ugartechea was forced to surrender and move his troops to Matamoros. So in the summer of 1832, all Mexican troops in Texas sent by the central government to enforce their new regulations were pushed out of the area.

Events in Mexico then favored the Texans. Santa Anna was just then making his first push for power with an armed insurrection. Santanista commander Jose Antonio Mexia suggested to Jose Mariano Guerra, commander of the opposing Bustamante forces, that they declare a truce to deal with the Anglo insurgents. Guerra agreed, so Mexia led several hundred troops to Texas to investigate the disturbances.

Stephen F. Austin convinced Mexia that the Texans were on his side, the side of states' rights and opposition to central authority, which was Mexia's and Santa Anna's position in the immediate struggle, and that all Texans remained loyal to their pledges of Mexican citizenship. Santa Anna was not a sincere states' righter, but Mexia was; so he accepted this explanation, and following a party at Brazoria where he was the honored guest, he returned to the fight in Mexico confident that the Texans were for Santa Anna. And they were, at least to the degree that he represented the states' rights position.

Santa Anna had become a national political figure following his heroic defense of Tampico during the last Spanish attempt to reclaim Mexico. As a national hero, a status partially earned by the loss of a leg in the battle, he commanded the support of many in Mexico as he alternated between liberalism and conservatism, centralism and states' rights, jockeying always for a better position to further his personal goal of absolute control. This maneuvering had brought him into opposition to Bustamante in 1832. Then, in 1833, he won the Presidency of Mexico in national elections by favoring liberalism and reform. Texans generally supported these moves, and were grateful that Mexia had accepted their pledges of loyalty. They were really in no position to face an armed force of any real strength.

Santa Anna allowed his vice-president, Gomez Farias, to assume an acting presidency in April, 1833, to put reforms of the Roman Catholic Church and the army into force. Santa Anna believed that these reforms would bring about a reaction which he could lead to assume absolute control. Without knowing Santa Anna's game, the Texans nonetheless felt uneasy with the causes of the 1832 disturbances left unresolved. So on August 22 the *ayuntamiento,* or council, of San Felipe, issued a call for all districts to send delegates to a convention at that town on October 1.

Sixteen districts sent fifty-eight delegates, who elected Austin as their president. They voted to petition the federal and state governments for repeal of the Law of April 6, 1830, to exempt them from taxes for three more years, to issue more land titles, to create more *ayuntamientos,* and to provide for schools, postal services, trial by jury of peers in their own territory, and above all, separation from Coahuila as a state of the Mexican union.

These resolutions did not get past the political chief at San Antonio, who returned them with the scolding reproach that the meeting was unauthorized. Again there was misunderstanding. The Americans were asking for separate status like they had known in the United States territories, not for independence. To the Mexican officials, who saw it in the light of the recent disturbances, it looked like the familiar *grito,* or cry of revolution in the classic Latin pattern. This first rebuff did not deter the Texans. They tried again with another convention the following year.

In the meantime committees of safety and vigilance, reflecting a need to remain close together for mutual reassurance, came into existence to keep the colonists informed of communications with government officials. The Central Committee of Safety and Correspondence called the second convention in January, 1833 when it became obvious that Santa Anna would become the new president of Mexico. The convention would again meet in San Felipe on April 1. This time Austin was bypassed as presiding officer in favor of William H. Wharton, a more militant individual. Again, the convention asked for the repeal of the restrictive immigration laws, relief from the customs, and separation from Coahuila. This time they prepared a proposed constitution so the Mexicans could see their purpose, with Sam Houston chairing the committee that wrote the constitution.

Now they asked Austin to deliver the petition to Mexico City. As usual, he forgot their earlier snub and accepted the task as a way he could be of service. The Americans had prepared the constitution because that was the way it was done in the United States. As territories readied themselves for statehood in the American union, this was one of the things they did, and the Congress simply accepted the new state or deferred consideration to a later date. But to the suspicious Mexican officials, it looked like the *pronunciamento,* or the second stage of revolution.

Austin arrived in Mexico City on July 18 and learned that

Col. Travis depicted at his last sword thrust from a painting by artist Connerly of the battle of the Alamo.

— Courtesy Daughters of the Republic of Texas

Santa Anna again had left Gomez Farias in charge while he rested at Vera Cruz. Austin attempted to deal with the acting president, but got nowhere. The reaction to Farias' reform movements gave him plenty to do, and he had little time for the troublesome Texan. Their few meetings were cordial but unproductive. In desperation, Austin tried to be candid with Farias. He told him that the Texans might as well be given their independence because they were already behaving as if they were independent. Candor was taken as a threat by Farias, and the two argued bitterly. Afterward, Austin wrote an ill-advised letter to the members of the *ayuntamiento* at San Antonio urging them to go ahead with plans to establish a separate state; perhaps he though that Farias could be better influenced by a working example. When Austin's letter reached San Antonio, the authorities then turned it over to central officials.

Meanwhile, Santa Anna returned to the capital and Austin visited with the President just before he departed for Texas. The meeting ran smoothly; Santa Anna agreed to most of Austin's requests, including the repeal of the prohibition on immigration, and promised to work for improved mail service and trial by jury. He claimed that the Texas population hardly numbered enough for efficient separate operation, and this argument was something an American could understand since the United States had a minimum population requirement.

Santa Anna also told Austin that he intended to send more soldiers to Texas to aid with defense against Indian attacks. This should have alarmed Austin, because the government had rarely shown such concern before. He left the capital in early December and made it as far as Saltillo on January 3, where he stopped to visit with state officials. There soldiers awaited him. Austin's letter to San Antonio had reached the capital just after his departure, and Farias had ordered his arrest. Austin was returned to Mexico City and held incommunicado at the Prison of the Inquisition. He could not learn the specific charges or move his case to trial.

News of Austin's arrest quieted Texas. No one wanted to be the cause of his suffering or death from their own rash acts. In fact, things became so quiet that Austin finally thought he had been forgotten by his fellow Texans. Learning of this, Peter W. Grayson and Spencer H. Jack raised funds and petitions in his behalf and they finally secured Austin's release from the prison by Christmas Day, 1834. Austin remained in Mexico City until the following summer under a kind of house arrest, then was permitted to return to Texas under the provisions of a general amnesty proclamation. He was never charged or tried for a crime, yet he spent eighteen months under arrest.

While Austin remained incarcerated, affairs in Texas seemed to improve. Immigration from the United States was restored and continued steadily. The government divided the area into three administrative departments for more efficient operation, including Bexar, San Felipe, and Nacogdoches. English was recognized as an official language; religious regularity was relaxed; and the judicial procedures were revised. Texas received three deputies of the twelve slots in the state congress. Most Texans managed to remain aloof, and a few even condemned illegal or questionable practices which might involve them in arguments with the government. Land speculators mostly did this, often perpetrating frauds against the government to obtain additional land.

Texas also stayed clear of an argument which raged in 1833 and 1834 over the location of the state capital. The legislature of Coahuila y Texas wanted to move the official seat of government to Monclova and the central government wanted it to remain at Saltillo. Santa Anna sided with those who wanted the capital to remain in Saltillo, and sent his brother-in-law, General Martin Perfecto de Cos, with troops to enforce his view. Governor Agustin Viesca, representing the states' rights position, tried to flee to Bexar with the government archives, but Cos arrested him and helped Rafael Eca y Musquiz become governor in his place. Musquiz then moved the capital back to Saltillo. Most Texans could not have cared less where the capital was located, but they did resent the arbitrary use of central power.

In 1835, the issue of centralism versus states' rights came closer to home. In January of that year Santa Anna sent a detachment of soldiers under Captain Antonio Tenorio to Anahuac to enforce the custom laws. In a dispute which ensued with a local merchant, Andrew Briscoe, one Texan was wounded and Briscoe and DeWitt C. Harris were arrested for refusing to allow the search of a box filled with rocks and intended for ballast on a ship. The Mexican soldiers thought that the box contained smugled goods, and they became frightened when a third party walked up on the tense scene. They opened fire, and things were never the same again in Texas.

Cos, learning of this incident in Anahuac, sent a courier to Tenorio directing him to stand firm. The courier was intercepted at San Felipe on June 21, and this is also how the Texans learned of Viesca's arrest. Resistance fever seized a group of rash Texans. They met secretly, elected J. B. Miller, political chief of the Brazos, to preside, and authorized William B. Travis to organize a body of men to drive Tenorio from Texas. Travis was selected because of his knowledge of Anahuac and possibly because of his involvment in the disturbance there in 1832.

Travis led approximately twenty-five men to Anahuac by barge in late June. He stopped by Harrisburg to inform David G. Burnet of his mission, then continued to Anahuac where the citizens greeted him with dread and concern: they feared, rightly, a renewal of conflict. Travis demanded the immediate surrender of Tenorio's garrison. The Mexican soldiers took to the woods near Fort Anahuac, and Tenorio surrendered them later that evening.

The next day, Travis sent the Mexicans ahead to Brazoria under guard. They arrived in time to find a July 4 celebration under way. Curiously, the guards were treated with disdain and Tenorio and his men became honored guests. This reaction to the affair was common; in Texas the Peace group feared that Travis' raid would draw more soldiers and cause more trouble. They condemned him with resolutions and apologies to the Mexican government; even Miller wrote a letter of apology to General Cos.

But Cos would not accept their contrition. He demanded the surrender of "Juliano" Travis and other "outlaws" for their treason. He also wanted Lorenzo de Zavala, an exiled opponent of Santa Anna, arrested. Moreover, he wanted these criminals turned over to him by their own people for military trial. This was more than the Texans would do. The Committee of Correspondence buzzed with rumors of Cos' threats to come to Texas with iron hobbles for all uncooperative Texans.

Into this circumstances Stephen F. Austin returned from Mexico. War or peace was literally in his hands when he rose to speak to a gathering at San Felipe on September 19. His statement cast the die: "War is our only recourse. There is no other remedy. We must defend our rights ourselves and our country by force of arms."

Increasingly the Committee of Safety called for a consultation of delegates from all the Anglo communities to decide what should be done. This movement began at Mina (Bastrop), and soon was endorsed by every community. Following a call from Columbia, all committees agreed to a meeting on October 15 at Washington on the Brazos River. Before they could meet, however, the Mexican military provided the spark of revolution at Gonzales, often called the Lexington of the Texas Revolution.

Colonel Ugartechea, commander at San Antonio, sent a patrol to Gonzales to confiscate a six-pound cannon originally provided to empresario Green DeWitt for Indian defense. Alcalde Andrew Ponton assumed it was an attempt to weaken the Americans, so he hid the cannon and demanded a written request for the piece from Ugartechea. While the patrol returned for this order, Ponton alarmed the countryside. Nearly 160 Texans hurried to Gonzales to defend the cannon, and they elected Colonel J. H. Moore as their spokesman and leader.

Ugartechea sent Lieutenant Francisco Castaneda with 100 troops to fetch the cannon, and when this force reached the Guadalupe River opposite Gonzales on September 29, they saw an armed camp of Americans. On October 2, Moore crossed the river with the cannon loaded and, flying a flag with a picture of a cannon and the words "COME AND TAKE IT" painted on it, opened fire on the startled Mexican troops, who hurriedly retreated to San Antonio.

Meanwhile, some of the Americans under Captain George M. Collinsworth of Matagorda, who had heard of the threat at Gonzales and moved toward that town, learned at Victoria that Cos, who had recently landed at Copano and occupied Goliad, had departed for San Antonio. So Collinsworth diverted his command from the route to Gonzales to capture Goliad.

More men arrived at Gonzales, but now there was nothing to do. The sentiment quickly grew that they should go on to San Antonio for a showdown with Cos, but they lacked leadership. On October 12 Austin arrived and became the general by common consent, and he agreed to lead the "army" where it intended to go anyway. Austin, for all his services to Texas in

Battle of San Jacinto from painting by Bruce Marshall.

— Courtesy the Institute of Texan Cultures

various capacities, was not a military man. Still, his men were willing, an important factor in warfare, and they were unafraid of the 1,200 or so men Cos had under his command.

As the Texans neared San Antonio, an advance under James Bowie and James W. Fannin was attacked near Mission Concepcion by Mexican cavalrymen. After the skirmish, the Mexican cavalry retreated into San Antonio and a month-long seige of the city began. Austin remained with the army for nearly the whole month, although the Consultation, which was finally held at San Felipe instead of Washington, designated him to go to the United States for help. Before he left his men fought the quixotic Grass Fight, a raid on a supposedly paymaster's train headed into San Antonio, that turned out to be only foragers seeking grass for the Mexican cavalry horses.

Additional men drifted into camp, but many also left, as farmers had to return to their homes to prepare for the winter. Following Austin's departure on November 25, Edward Burleson was elected to command and for over a week he continued the seige and watched more men leave. On December 4 he determined to withdraw to winter quarters at Goliad. Hearing of this decision Ben Milam challenged volunteers to go with him into battle in the city. Milam was encouraged to attack after learning from a captured Mexican courier that Cos' army was demoralized and ready to surrender.

The assault began on December 5th. For three days cannon fire held the Texans at bay; then the fighting became a house-to-house assault. Milam was killed on the third day and replaced by Francis W. Johnson, who led the men on to take Cos' surrender on December 9. Cos forfeited all money, weapons, and supplies in the city and promised to leave Texas and never return. His troops filed out of San Antonio toward the Rio Grande shortly afterward.

Meanwhile, the Texans began to assemble a political organization out of a chaotic situation. Before the Consultation could meet, the Committee of Public Safety at San Felipe organized the Permanent Council with R. R. Royall of Matagorda as president. Despite this group's auspicious name it lasted only three weeks, or until the Consultation replaced it. In that short time the Permanent Council sent supplies and volunteers to the army, commissioned privateers, established a tentative postal system, and sent Thomas F. McKinney to the United States to borrow funds and to raise troops.

The Consultation met on November 3 after moving to San Felipe in hopes of raising a quorum. Most of the natural leaders were at San Antonio and reluctant to leave the forces there lest they be called cowardly. Finally, by a vote of the soldiers, some were released and their arrival at San Felipe helped the Consultation get started.

The Consultation consisted of fifty-five delegates from twelve municipalities. Branch T. Archer was elected president. For a while the delegates argued over their goal: should they strike for independence or claim that they were fighting for the restoration of the states' rights Constitution of 1824, and separate statehood within the Mexican union? The majority finally decided on the latter course. But they also agreed that they would have to fight hard against the central government in power to achieve their goal.

So they asked Archer, Wharton, and Austin, who was still with the volunteer soldiers at San Antonio, to go to the United States for financial aid and volunteers; they authorized the raising of an army and appointed Sam Houston as its commander; and they appointed Henry Smith and James Robinson as governor and lieutenant governor of a provisional government. These officers were to serve with the assistance of a council composed of Consultation members. The Consultation adjourned on November 14 but provided that it would reassemble on March 1, 1836 unless Smith called them into session earlier. The provisional government soon paralysed itself with contention. Smith quarrelled with the Council, which in turn impeached him and recognized Robinson as the governor; then Smith attempted to function without the Council, thus giving Texans two governments. Neither was effective.

The Matamoros scheme is a good example of their ineffectiveness. Following the victory at San Antonio, Dr. James Grant convinced Johnson to lead his volunteers against Mexican troops at Matamoros. Grant wanted the Texans to regain his lands that had been confiscated by Santa Anna, and he promised them booty for their trouble. Johnson first demurred, then agreed, and then the Council approved the plan. Johnson and Grant stripped San Antonio of most of the supplies and left. At San Patricio, long before he arrived at their goal, Johnson again had second thoughts and informed the Council that the scheme was a mistake.

The Council then named Colonel James W. Fannin to lead another expedition using troops gathering at Goliad, mostly from the United States. But Houston was trying to get the troops at Goliad and other places, including the force still under Johnson, to obey him instead. Both Fannin and Johnson refused to accept Houston's leadership, but they delayed their movement to Matamoros. Houston resolved the problem of leadership by taking leave of the army until March 1 when the Consultation was due to meet again. But his work was done well, for neither commander ever attacked Matamoros.

Meanwhile, Houston travelled to East Texas and negotiated a treaty with Cherokee chief Philip Bowles which kept the Indians from taking advantage of the American-Mexican troubles. The treaty was signed in Adolphus Sterne's parlor in Nacogdoches, with a free mulatto, William Goyens, assisting Houston as an interpreter.

Santa Anna decided in late October that the time had come for him to punish the Texans. Fresh from crushing a revolt in Zacateches, he decided that the time was ripe to assume full control of all of Mexico. The Texans' unexecuted plans for an attack on Matamoros was all the excuse he needed. He sent General Jose Urrea with 1,500 cavalrymen to Matamoros on January 25, 1836 to hold that place, then to march into Texas and take Refugio and Goliad.

On February 16, Santa Anna crossed the Rio Grande with General Joaquin Ramirez y Sesma's command. With over 6,000 troops in Texas, he intended to eliminate every American from the area as he had seen General Arredondo do in 1813. Santa Anna promised his countrymen that this would be his mission, and headed straight to San Antonio to avenge Cos' loss and to redeem his promise.

The Texans in San Antonio were not prepared for such an army. Having lost most of their manpower and supplies to the Johnson-Grant expedition in December, J.C. Neill, who was left in command, complained bitterly to Governor Smith that the city could not be defended. On January 17 James Bowie arrived at San Antonio with orders from Houston to destroy the place if it could not be defended. Bowie intended to do so, but never got the job done.

Meanwhile, William B. Travis, recruiting officer for the provisional government, was ordered to raise one hundred men and lead them to relieve San Antonio. Travis could raise only twenty-nine men, and he virtually begged Smith not to make him go, not from cowardice, but from embarrassment at having recruited so few men. But he went anyway, and within a few days after his arrival on Janury 30, found himself in command when Neill quit because of a family illness. Travis assumed command of the regular troops, but the volunteers under Bowie refused to accept him as their commander as well. Travis and Bowie worked out an inefficient dual command structure, but injury and illness soon forced Bowie to leave the decisions to Travis anyway.

Travis tried to ready San Antonio's defense; he fortified the old San Antonio de Valero mission compound, now usually called the Alamo, with the aid of engineer Green B. Jamison; supplies were moved to the fort when they could be found; and he sent letters by courier to Fannin, Johnson, and everyone else, begging them to come to the Alamo to fight against Santa Anna. He welcomed the arrival of David Crockett, late of Tennessee, and in Texas to reclaim a lost political career in the United States by taking part in the Texas war.

Santa Anna reached San Antonio on February 23. Two scouts, Dr. John Sutherland and John W. Smith, sounded the alarm, and then were soon on their way to Gonzales to tell that community the news and to ask for help. Travis' letter reached Fannin and that officer started for San Antonio, then turned back. On the 24th, Travis' letter to fellow Texans and "all Americans in the world" claiming that he intended to fight to the death in defense of his position, left in the saddle bag of John W. Smith. Travis still hoped for reinforcements, but each passing day brought none until the entire male population of Gonzales, thirty-five men, slipped through the Mexican lines on March 1.

For twelve days the Mexicans bombarded the Alamo compound. On the morning of March 6, wave after wave of assault troops stormed the Alamo's walls until they had killed all but seven of the defenders; those seven, including David Crockett, were executed after they attempted to surrender. Travis died early in the assault, trying to work a cannon; Bowie was slain as he fought from his sick bed. A few non-combatants, mostly women, children and a black slave, were spared.

While Santa Anna finished burning the corpses of the slain

Rare photo of Jim Bowie, co-commander with Col. Travis of the Texans who fought in the Alamo.

— Courtesy Daughters of the Republic of Texas

Texans, and sent Mrs. Suzanna Dickenson, widow of artillerist Almeron Dickenson, to Gonzales with word of the Alamo's fall, Urrea was taking care of Fannin at Goliad. On his way to Goliad, Urrea had surprised and killed Johnson's troops at San Patricio and another group under Grant some miles away, then headed for Goliad, where Fannin had retired after turning back from San Antonio. Mostly through Fannin's inept leadership, Urrea captured nearly 500 men with only a skirmish after Fannin was caught in the open with no protective cover. His troops, mostly recent arrivals from the United States, were then executed. Now future Texans had their battle cry: Remember the Alamo! Remember Goliad!

On March 1, the quarrelling between Smith and the Council ceased when the Consultation recommenced at Washington-on-the-Brazos; within two weeks this body declared independence from Mexico, reappointed Houston to lead the army, wrote a constitution for a new republic, and selected officers for an *ad interim* government. David G. Burnet was to serve as President, with Lorenzo de Zavala as Vice-President. Samual P. Carson became Secretary of State, Bailey Hardeman became Secretary of the Treasury, Thomas J. Rusk accepted the post of War Secretary, and David Thomas became Attorney General.

Houston left for Gonzales on March 11 to raise troops to relieve San Antonio. Ironically, the Alamo's defenders never knew that independence had been declared on March 2, four days before their deaths; and the convention's fifty-nine delegates did not know the fate of the Alamo until after their adjournment on March 7. When Houston arrived at Gonzales he reported 374 men already there, as usual too late for the action and not knowing what to do. They reportedly had not heard the signal cannon from the Alamo since the sixth day of the month. He sent Erastus "Deaf" Smith to reconnoiter, and Smith found Mrs. Dickenson on the road to Gonzales bearing the grim news. When the new widows of Gonzales learned the fate of their men, their grief fixed a permanent and unpleasant picture in the mind of every man there.

Houston ordered Gonzales burned and retreated toward the Colorado River, evidently planning to make a stand there. He arrived at Burnham's Ferry on the Colorado River and crossed just ahead of Santa Anna's scouts. Then Houston learned of

Fannin's defeat, so he retreated again to the Brazos River. With his retreat, and the news of the Alamo and of Goliad, the civilians fled in wild abandon, a frightful experience known as the Runaway Scrape. Meals were left on tables, corn abandoned in the crib, furniture too heavy to move was left, sometimes on the roadside. Streams swollen from spring rains made crossings difficult, and the roads became quagmires.

Burnet wrote Houston to urge him to turn and fight Santa Anna. Instead Houston remained on the Brazos River at Groce's plantation for nearly two weeks, drilling his men and trying to raise more. At San Antonio Santa Anna divided his force into three groups to pursue Houston's army. He sent Urrea on a southern, coastal route from Goliad to capture the Burnet government at Columbia if possible and to destroy all towns along the way; Sesma drew the center, in direct pursuit of Houston, while General Antonio Gaona was sent up the Nacogdoches road to destroy the settlements there. Before reaching Nacogdoches, however, Gaona received orders to join Sesma.

Santa Anna followed Houston's path to the Brazos River, sometimes with Sesma and sometimes with a smaller body. When he reached the river and saw it was defended by only a company under Moseley Baker who had, incidentally, received the assignment from Houston after flatly refusing to retreat another inch — Santa Anna decided that Houston had headed north and east, trying to escape to the safety of the United States.

He also learned that Burnet was then in Harrisburg, a short distance away; so with 500 men he moved south along the river, crossed into the lower regions, and tried to capture Burnet. But the Texas president escaped by ship to Galveston. When Houston learned on April 12 that Santa Anna had separated himself from his main force, Houston started down the Brazos River, then crossed with the assistance of the steamship *Yellowstone.* He also received the "Twin Sisters," two cannons sent by the citizens of Cincinnati to help in the war for Texas independence.

When the army headed due east, many felt they were still in retreat since they were going straight to Harrisburg and Lynch's Ferry on the San Jacinto River, an avenue of escape to Louisiana. But Houston had decided, as he revealed in a letter written on April 18, to fight Santa Anna while the Mexican leader was separated from his main command. As the lead of his troops reached a fork in the road, one way leading to the ferry and Louisiana and the other to Harrisburg, Buffalo Bayou, and San Jacinto, Houston gave no order. The lead split the fork, then some of the men turned south and the advance hastened back into position. Generations have wondered if Houston was thus led to battle by his men, or had allowed them to seem to make a decision he had already determined so they would fight all the more. It seems clear that he had come to fight, and it also seems clear that the men needed no such encouragement now.

On the afternoon of April 20 the Texans were positioned with the bayou to their back, the river on their left, and the Mexican force directly in front, a mile away across a rolling plain. An afternoon skirmish proved indecisive. Cos arrived with 500 reinforcements for Santa Anna during the night, giving him a larger force. In the early afternoon of April 21, following a council of war held that morning, Houston led about 700 men across the plain, shouting for his men to hold their fire, yet encouraging them to move faster. The Texans struck the Mexican line just seconds after the "Twin Sisters" opened a hole, and streamed through to slay the surprised Mexicans. The battle lasted but eighteen minutes, but the carnage lasted for hours afterwards.

The Texans lost two men in the action and seven of their thirty wounded died later. The Mexicans lost about 600 men, and had over 700 captured, including Santa Anna, who was apprehended on April 22 after attempting to flee back to the Brazos River where the main body of his force was commanded by General Vicente Filisola. Houston was badly wounded in the ankle during the battle and he hemorrhaged severely. But when Santa Anna was brought before him the next day, he protected the Mexican president as a great prize. Dead, Santa Anna would be of little use; alive, he represented Mexico to Houston. Although Houston was forced to go to New Orleans for medical attention, interim President David G. Burnet, who remained critical of Houston's leadership, assumed the job of negotiating with Santa Anna and protecting him from the angry Texans who remembered the Alamo and Goliad.

Filisola and the remaining Mexican commanders surprisingly obeyed Santa Anna's orders to return to Mexico. With over 5,000 men in Texas, they would have had little difficulty in finishing what Santa Anna's poor judgment had prevented him from doing. On May 14, Burnet and Santa Anna signed the Treaty of Velasco, named for the coastal town where it was negotiated. Santa Anna recognized the independence of Texas, ended hostilities, and promised to work for a commercial treaty between Mexico and Texas.

In a secret passage he also recognized the Rio Grande as the boundary, the first time in Texas history that this river was so regarded. The Mexican government naturally repudiated all these concessions, but Texans regarded them as permanent as if they were engraved in stone. Santa Anna would, of course, have conceded anything to save his life, and under international law such concessions are not considered binding on nations.

Burnet had some difficulty keeping the Mexican president alive. He tried to send Santa Anna to Vera Cruz but mutinous soldiers stormed the ship before it could sail and refused to allow him to leave. The problem would be left for the new government of the republic when it organized in September. But Burnet had other troubles with the army; he asked Mirabeau B. Lamar, a recent arrival from Georgia and a gallant veteran of San Jacinto, to replace Thomas J. Rusk, who had taken over the field command following Houston's departure; but the men refused to follow Lamar. This too he would leave to the new government.

After the Treaty of Velasco, many Texans believed that the war and troubles with Mexico were over. Others knew better. They had a declaration of independence and at least one important Mexican politician who had acknowledged it; they had successfully defended their homes against invasion, although they enjoyed a good deal of good luck and poor judgment on the part of the opponent; and they had a plan for a new government which would give them an independent republic. These invaders felt that they had come to possess the land at last.

5

The Texas Republic

"The Republic of Texas is no more . . . ." The conclusion of President Anson Jones' valedictory on February 19, 1846, remains one of the really memorable statements of Texas' public men. Even modern Texans respond to its claim of uniqueness for Texas among the United States, for it reminds us that once there was a time of true independence for Texas, albeit one troubled, financially destitute, and beset with enemies in Mexico and within, but still a Republic that was free, at least in the belief that the Texans controlled their own destiny. Unlike the Camelot of myth, that Republic of Texas did exist. Its days few, its troubles real, its problems many, this Republican era claims a mighty portion of every Texan's memory of the history of his state.

The Republic was conceived in war. In the midst of the military activities of the revolution, and as a part of the revolution itself, delegates at Washington-on-the-Brazos met to proclaim Texas free of Mexico, and they stayed in the cold and damp of the late winter to draft a constitution and to launch their new government. George Childress, a recent arrival from Tennessee, headed a committee and personally wrote the Declaration of Independence that the convention adopted on March 2. This declaration strongly resembled the 1776 document adopted at Philadelphia by the American revolutionists. The Texans settled the matter of a constitution much more speedily than did their predecessors, who required thirteen years to produce a constitution that would finally establish a

President Sam Houston, first president of the Republic of Texas.

— Courtesy Texas State Capitol

real national government. The Texas convention wrote its constitution in only fifteen days. Adopted on March 17, it endured until adaptations were made necessary by Texas' admission as a state of the American union.

The Republic's constitution, like their Declaration of Independence, reflected the United States experience. Its first article divided the branches of government into legislative, executive, and judicial departments and prescribed the functions for each as well as the qualifications for those who would fill government offices. The Republic's government was unitary by nature, rather than federal. It called for a president and a vice-president, a bi-cameral legislative structure, and a judiciary structure headed by a supreme court. Article I described the electoral process for obtaining membership in the Congress, and methods of legislative procedure. The Second article identified the powers of the Congress, including the authority to levy and collect taxes, regulate commerce, coin money, establish post offices, declare war, maintain an army and navy or militia, and make "all laws deemed necessary and proper" to carry these into effect.

Perhaps in memory of the failures of the emergency government under Henry Smith during the Revolution, Article Three restricted the first president to a two-year term, and extended subsequent presidential terms to three years without the privilege of immediate succession. Other articles created a Supreme Court, identified specific presidential powers, and established an *ad interim* government to guide the country until the permanent government could be established. The constitution also established a Declaration of Rights. One curious article barred "Ministers of the gospel . . . or priests of any denomination" from service in any executive or legislative office.

Richard Ellis, a delegate from Red River and president of the Convention, led the fifty-eight delegates in signing the document. Following the Constitution's direction, the Convention named David Gouvereur Burnet as president and Lorenzo de Zavala as vice-president of the *ad interim* government. Samual Price Carson became Secretary of State, Thomas Jefferson Rusk became Secretary of War, Bailey Hardeman was named to the Treasury post, and Robert Potter, David Thomas and John Rice Jones received appointment to the navy, attorney general's office and as postmaster general. Only Potter and Jones served for very long, with six men serving within as many months at the War post.

The new government faced overwhelming problems. When Burnet assumed office, the main Mexican army was at San Antonio and various other detachments were even nearer. Burnet had to move his government to Harrisburg and later to Galveston to avoid capture by Santa Anna's troops. The Convention had named Sam Houston to head its military force and Houston had duly organized the men who had gathered at Gonzales into a fighting force, then led them eastward, away from the Mexican army. Santa Anna followed, confident that its victories at the Alamo and at Goliad would be repeated. But Houston's small force defeated the Mexican president's advance at San Jacinto and captured Santa Anna himself. Leaderless, the remaining Mexican forces eventually obeyed his orders to General Vicente Filisola to lead them back south to Mexico.

With the Mexican regular forces gone from Texas, and still holding Santa Anna prisoner, Burnet could move more deliberately to establish the regular government of the Republic. He negotiated the Treaty of Velasco with Santa Anna, and both men signed the document on May 14, calling for Santa Anna to pledge to bring the war to an end and never again to renew it. He also agreed to order his troops to withdraw from Texas, to honor life and property during the withdrawal, and to release all Texas prisoners. In a secret portion, Santa Anna further agreed to work for treaties of commerce between the two countries and to secure the acceptance of all his agreements in Mexico, including the Rio Grande as a boundary between the two Republics. For his part, Burnet agreed to release Santa Anna unharmed. Neither negotiator could really guarantee his agreement, and both sides violated most of these provisions. But the treaty is significant in at least two respects: it demonstrates that Burnet was trying to get on with the business of establishing the Republic; and it enabled Texans thereafter to regard the lands all the way to the Rio Grande as their rightful legacy of the Revolution.

Burnet struggled with the problems of finance, Indians, immigration, and foreign recognition — all without the assistance of a Congress, courts, or an established administrative structure. His government also had to move about a great deal, creating an image of instability. From Galveston Burnet first took the government to the San Jacinto battlefield, then to Velasco, and finally to Columbia. His nation was destitute. The Runaway Scrape, that fearful flight of civilians before the advance of Santa Anna's army, had left much of the people's material wealth abandoned or lost. Crops went unplanted, work undone. The refugees slowly returned to find many of their homes plundered and their personal property stolen. Money did not really exist; and even food was scarce. The population of Texas was also sparse — only 30,000 Anglo-Americans and an estimated 22,000 Mexicans, Indians, and Negroes.

But many others were on the way to help rebuild Texas. The lure of adventure, the expectation of land as a reward, and the promises of Texas recruiters in the United States attracted a flood of Americans to Texas. Burnet did not know what to do with these people. Newly arrived, expectant, without the battles of the Revolution to requite their ardor, and perhaps without the respect earned by its leaders in those days, these men refused to accept military discipline or even direction from Burnet. For example, Burnet tried to send Santa Anna home in early June, 1836, perhaps to save the Mexican leader from assassination, but some of Burnet's rebellious soldiers removed him from the Texas schooner *Invincible* before it could sail. In further defiance, the army refused to accept Secretary of War Rusk's leadership; then under the influence of Thomas Jefferson Green, they also rejected Mirabeau B. Lamar, whom Burnet asked to replace Rusk.

Burnet knew that the fabric of Texas would soon break by such stress, so on July 23 he issued a proclamation which called for general elections on the first Monday in September, three months ahead of the plan of the March Convention. The election would select all constitutional officers, ratify the constitution and respond to a resolution concerning annexation to the United States.

It seemed as if no one wanted to run for the presidency except Henry Smith at first. Then Stephen F. Austin, home from seeking money and men in the United States, entered the race. Others wanted Rusk or Branch T. Archer to run. Rusk refused, but Archer did not stop his friends from advancing his cause. Then Sam Houston let it be publically circulated that he would accept the will of the electorate just eleven days before the election. Houston won by a landslide. He received 5,119 votes to Smith's 743, while Austin received only 587 votes. Mirabeau B. Lamar won election to the vice-presidency, and both the constitutional ratification and the referendum favoring annexation to the United States, somewhat contradictorally, passed handily.

Houston assembled many leaders of Texas' various political and personal factions within the framework of his administration. Stephen F. Austin, whose devotion to Texas remained unquestioned, accepted appointment as Secretary of State; Henry Smith became Secretary of the Treasury, and despite his lack of popularity, worked to solve problems of finance which were the Republic's greatest concern; Thomas J. Rusk headed the War Department; James Pinckney Henderson became Attorney General; and S. Rhoads Fisher as Secretary of the Navy and Robert Barr as Postmaster-General completed the cabinet.

The First Congress of the Republic of Texas convened at Columbia. The Congress elected Ira Ingram as its Speaker of the House, and Mirabeau Lamar assumed his duties as presiding officer of the Senate. The Congress also selected James Collinsworth as Chief Justice of the Supreme Court, and lesser officers received appointments to complete the Republic's official roster.

President Houston faced many difficulties. The Mexican government still regarded Texas as part of its country, and even with the assumption of Texas independence, a state of war existed between the two governments. And even if they were separated, the two governments differed on a precise boundary between their jurisdictions, regardless of which of them prevailed. There was almost literally no money for the Texas government's necessary activities and little for the people's exchange of goods and services. Returning settlers faced the monumental task of rebuilding or restoring abandoned homes and businesses. And growing pressure from the military for some kind of activity created a danger of a potentially disastrous involvement with Mexican military forces.

The Republic's first president grappled with these problems, but most survived his administration. Houston attempted to follow a policy of rigid economy, especially in avoiding further military involvement with Mexico or the

David G. Burnett, a judge and president of the Republic of Texas. Engraving from Pictorial History of Texas.

— Courtesy Institute of Texan Cultures

Texas Indians because either would cost more money than the government could afford; the former might even jeopardize the Republic's precarious existence. He attempted to mollify the Indians by urging the Congress to honor the treaty with the Cherokees which he had negotiated during the Revolution, but the Congress refused. Furthermore, only three months after joining the government, Stephen F. Austin died of pneumonia on December 27, 1836, at the age of forty-three. He had developed a cold from working in the drafty, improperly heated capitol building at Columbia, and did not survive when the rapidly advancing disease developed into pneumonia.

Houston's first term as president ended in 1838. Ineligible for the succession, and perhaps reluctant to surrender the office, Houston's forces also lost the race to name his successor. Instead, the prize was captured by a man who had rapidly moved forward in Texas politics to become Houston's chief rival.

Mirabeau Bonaparte Lamar won the election in October, 1838. Houston's forces tried to enlist Thomas J. Rusk in the race, although the relationship between Houston and Rusk vacillated between support and rivalry. But Rusk declined, relieving even Lamar who had worried about his chances against the popular East Texan who lived in the section of the nation with the greatest number of votes. Free of this threat, Lamar announced his candidacy and quickly became the leader in the race. Houston's people then settled on Peter W. Grayson as their candidate, but Grayson committed suicide while on a trip to Tennessee. Stunned, they persuaded James Collinsworth to run, but he too took his own life while drunk by jumping from a ship at Galveston. Lamar won by virtual default, but he would most likely have been the choice of a majority of the voters anyway.

Mirabeau B. Lamar had come to Texas from Georgia following a career in education, newspaper publishing, and merchandising. He distinguished himself for bravery at the head of the cavalry unit at the battle at San Jacinto, and later received appointment as head of the entire army from Burnet, only to be rejected by the military. While Lamar served as vice-president under Houston, he became increasingly critical of the President's policies. Now president himself, Lamar determined on a much bolder course. But he first suffered a wound to his pride at his own inauguration. Lamar labored to prepare a ringing call for a different path in his inaugural address. The capitol was then located in the new city of Houston, and the city's namesake stole the show with nearly three hours of impromptu remarks. This so wearied the audience and angered Lamar that the new President handed his address to someone else to read and left in disgust. Then, as a Congressional representative from San Augustine, Houston continued to agitate Lamar with constant opposition from the floor of Congress throughout his administration.

In every respect, Lamar's attitudes were almost exactly opposite to Houston's. His attitude on finance was to spend, his policy on Mexico was to force recognition, and he believed that the Indians should be pushed back as Americans always had done. Despite the expense of such policies and the fact that his nation lacked the means of producing the necessary money, he dreamed of achieving Texas' goals with boldness, not with the conciliation which had marked Houston's term of office.

Ironically, the brash, bold Texan image so prevalent throughout the world is owed more to Lamar than to Houston, although most would imagine it to be just the opposite. The irony is the more noticeable because of the physical and intellectual differences between them. Despite numerous wounds and an apparent disregard for his health as witnessed by his well-known appetite for alcohol, Houston remained robust throughout his life, while Lamar suffered numerous physical ailments and such poor health that his absence from his capital was required on several occasions. Yet Lamar was the dreamer of bold action for Texas. He always wanted the Republic to do more than it was doing, perhaps more than it could do, to establish its independence, to gain recognition from foreign governments, and to put the economy and the educational system on a sound footing. Lamar's three-year presidency failed to achieve any of these to his satisfaction, although beginnings were made in all areas.

Houston returned to office following the election of 1841. There was really no contest since Lamar could not succeed himself, although David Burnet, who had served as Lamar's Vice-President and had acted as chief executive officer during Lamar's absences from the capitol, made a run for the office.

Houston won the election easily, and Edward Burleson, an old comrade in arms, was elected vice-president. Burleson really thought of himself, and acted, as an independent, despite being regarded as a Houston man.

Houston's return to office brought back a quieter approach to the Republic's problems. Houston recognized that the government's lack of money made this policy necessary, and he also believed that these problems could not be solved by the Republic at all. The only real course available to him in his view was to keep the problems from getting worse and to bide his time until the United States decided to annex Texas and assume responsibility for Texas' troubles.

Everywhere Houston reduced expenditures. Lamar's administration had spent or obligated $2.5 million; Houston's second term got by on about $500,000. Houston achieved this by leaving many things undone and shifting expenses to local agencies or making them voluntary. He recommended a fifty percent cut in pay for himself and for the Congress and other governmental offices. He nearly abandoned Indian policing except in response to specific raids, and even these were assigned to volunteer militiamen. He significantly reduced the size of the army to save even more; as a result of a dispute, he eliminated the Texas navy. And he worked hard, if quietly, to persuade the United States government to consider the annexation of Texas. As a result, the Republic's financial, international, and Indian problems did not grow significantly worse, and, mostly because of forces outside of Texas, the United States did move closer to the annexation decision by the conclusion of Houston's second term in 1844.

Houston's successor for the fourth and final administration of the Republic of Texas, Dr. Anson Jones, inherited all the aforementioned problems, but he also inherited a good chance to turn them over to the United States. Jones had served as Houston's secretary of state and was regarded as a Houston man, although he secretly resented the designation. Because he served as president at the time of the Republic's admission to the American Union, he claimed for himself the title "Architect of Annexation," and he deserves much credit for the consummation of this achievement.

Houston, Lamar, and, to a lesser degree, Jones, permanently stamped the history of the Republic of Texas and the re-

Mirabeau B. Lamar, the second president of Texas.

— Courtesy Library of Congress

mainder of Texas history with the force of their personalities; Houston's image is that of a bold leader, while his actual service seems otherwise; Lamar's mild manner hid a bold, perhaps even rash, steel-like determination; and Jones' coyness at just the right juncture helped Texas achieve admission to the United States.

All three grappled, with varying success, with the problems of their nation. For example, adequate revenue to fund necessary services is a problem for every government, and for those seeking to establish a new government, indebtedness is a constant, nagging, and sometimes insurmountable problem. Beginning with the General Council, and continuing through the Convention, the *ad interim* government, and the Republican phases, all Texas governments faced the lethal combination of mounting expenditures and insufficient revenues. And when the Republic became a state of the American union, the debt was still there.

The story of the efforts of these governments to find a solution to their problem is a complicated one, but it is easily begun. The first government hardly had time to worry about paying the debts they so busily helped to accumulate. Fielding armies, sending representatives to the United States and other nations, defending homesteads from the constant threat of both organized military invasions and feared Indian uprisings, cost a good deal of money.

Texans regarded their vast land resources as the ultimate solution to the problem of redeeming financial pledges if they survived. But since they simply gave land away, none could be sold to raise revenue for the government's needs. Taxes were ultimately imposed by the Congresses of the Republic, but these measures could only raise a small percentage of the amount required. Some would not pay, some could not pay, and avoidance was easy.

Houston's first administration was the first to have the opportunity to face this problem, and his solution seems always to have been to keep the debt low and wait for the day when annexation to the United States would shift the problem to the more established government. But some revenue was necessary for day-to-day operations while they awaited this happy rescue, and gradually that hope faded as anti-slave and anti-expansion elements in the United States became more obstinate about admitting Texas to the Union.

The Congress required Houston in 1837 to issue $650,000 in promissory notes, payable twelve months after issuance and drawing a ten percent annual interest. These notes, often called "Star Money" because of a star which appeared on the face of the notes, circulated freely during Houston's first term and maintained their value well. Subsequent currency issued in the first Houston administration did not circulate so well and then at a depreciated value, although they did not fall below sixty-five cents on the dollar. But currency issued during Lamar's administration, often called "Redbacks" because of the color of the reverse side of the notes, dropped in value to as low as twelve cents on the dollar. Such depreciation lowered confidence in the Republic among its citizens and also internationally.

There were nearly $800,000 in notes outstanding when Lamar assumed office. His administration issued an additional $3,552,800 in notes. The Republic's treasury lacked deposits of precious metal to back the value of the paper being called money, and its land policy continued to undermine even the use of this resource of stability. Total receipts under Lamar amounted to only $1,083,661 as opposed to expenditures of $4,855,313, which meant that Lamar bequeathed a combined debt from Houston's term and his own of nearly $6 million when Houston replaced him in office.

Houston tried to stop government expenses even at the cost of government services, and his Congresses repealed all previous currency laws, a repudiation of whatever value such currency might have had. Then, they authorized the issuance in limited quantities of a still different paper money called "exchequer bills" and made these pieces of paper the only legal tender for the payment of taxes. Although the exchequer bills quickly depreciated, they were accepted at par for taxes, so they were frequently used for that purpose while other forms of moneyed value were reserved to purchase needed goods and services.

Some monies came to the Republic from customs payments and some donations arrived from private individuals, especially in the United States. But enthusiasm for the Texas cause only surfaced in times of military crisis, such as the 1842 invasions by Mexican forces. So Lamar tried to provide financial strength for the Republic through a $5 million loan. Lamar commissioned James Hamilton, formerly of South Carolina, to represent the Republic in negotiations with the Bank of the United States, then operating as a state chartered institution in Philadelphia, and with banking houses in England and France. Hamilton seemed on the brink of securing this desperately needed support several times, only to see his plans spoiled by events over which he had no control. He did secure $500,000 from the Bank of the United States, but his chances of securing the remainder from private banking houses in France with the assurance of government security failed when the responsible government official learned the fate of his relation, the Count Alphonse de Saligny, in Texas.

De Saligny had become involved in a controversy with an Austin hotel keeper, and demanded the punishment of the offending Austinite and an apology from the Texas government. When he failed to receive either, he demanded his passports and a resulting negative report kept the $5 million in France. Without it, Texas did not need the National bank Lamar had also hoped to create. This institution, he had envisioned, could work toward the fiscal stability of Texas in much the same way as Alexander Hamilton's bank had helped the infant United States of America. Like many of Lamar's dreams, the bank did not become a reality.

Anson Jones followed Houston's lead in finance, except that Jones proved more successful than Houston in turning over the Republic's problems, including many of its fiscal difficulties, to the United States. By the terms of the agreement of annexation, Texas retained control of its public lands, which also gave the new state some basis for beginning again to solve its fiscal problems under the protection of the United States.

The Republic's greatest resource lay in its public lands. It was land that had attracted Anglo-Americans to Texas, and it was the public lands, now amounting to 180 million acres, that gave many Texas leaders confidence they could surmount their problems. Since the United States government charged at least one dollar per acre, the availability of Texas land in the Spanish and Mexican periods had been able to draw thousands of Americans and Europeans to make their northern provinces productive, for Mexican authorities were granting land to stimulate immigration under the empresarial system. But the Mexicans attempted to curtail American immigration by the Law of April 6, 1830, when too many Americans were coming for their comfort. This limitation helped spark the movement which eventually became a successful revolution for the Texans.

The various Texas revolutionary governments and councils continued to use the lands of Texas as an attraction for help in the revolution itself and for the future development of the Republic. This also proved too successful as the immigrants came in increasing numbers as soon as the danger from Mexican soldiers had passed and before the generous land allotments could be stopped. Trains of immigrants increased the Texas population from an estimated 34,500 whites in 1836 to approximately 100,000 by the time the Republic ended. Total population, including Mexicans, slaves and Indians, reached nearly 150,000 by 1845. Land drew them all.

The Republic's land policy could be called liberal without exaggeration. The Republic's Constitution awarded white heads of families living in the Republic on March 2, 1836, a First Class headright of a square league and a *labor* (la-bor) of land, or 4,605 acres; single men over seventeen could receive one-third of a league, or 1,476 acres. Settlers already in possession of grants in smaller amounts were still eligible for the difference between their present holdings and the reward promised by the Constitution's writers for simply being an Anglo resident of Texas on the day of its declaration of independence. Nor were the recipients required to establish bonafide residences on their land grants.

The Texas Congress later created a Second Class headright of 1,280 acres for heads of families, and 640 acres for unmarried men, who arrived after March 2 but before October 1, 1837, and a Third Class headright of 640 acres for family men and 320 acres for single men arriving before January, 1840, and a Fourth Class headright of equal amounts for those arriving after January, 1840, but before January 1, 1842. Additional "bounty grants" of 320 acres could be claimed for each three months of military service, up to two sections. Thus, the various Congresses alienated 36,876,492 acres of Texas' public lands as a reward for those who served during the Revolution and supported the Republic by the mere fact of their residence within it.

In 1837, the Congress of the Republic satisfied still

Thomas Jefferson Rusk, Texas statesman and hero of the Battle of San Jacinto.

— Courtesy Martha Anne Turner

another requirement of the Constitution with the creation of the General Land Office. This office controlled the granting of lands as authorized by Congress, recorded land titles, and directed the surveying of vacant lands into sections. The General Land Office converted Texas to the American system of sections instead of the Spanish methods of awarding leagues of land. The Land Office also had charge of the lands awarded in large blocks when the Congresses briefly attempted to return to the empresarial system, and they had charge of the lands set aside for the support of education. Each county maintained a Board of Land Commissioners to hear claims, helped claimants survey the land, and awarded certificates of ownership. The General Land Office issued the final title, or patent, to the public lands involved, which then became private land in the name of the holder of the patent.

In 1841 the Congress restructured for a return to the empresarial system, and provided for the eventual elimination of the headright system. The Republic contracted with immigrant agents, or companies, to sponsor settlers much as Stephen F. Austin and the other empresarios had sponsored them under the Mexican government. Contracts were let to W. S. Peters and Associates, also known as the Texas Emigration and Land Company, to Charles P. Mercer, Henri Castro, and Fisher and Miller, also known as the German Emigration Company. Contractors received the land at the rate of ten sections for each one hundred families, secured compensation for surveying, and helped move the settlers to their lands.

The system produced a dispute in the Congress over a proposed Franco-Texienne Company plan to locate a colony of French people in Texas. Houston favored the bill, but a majority of the Congress did not. Instead, they granted a similar plan to the Peters group, and eventually gave the group 16,000 acres along the Red River. The Peters Company located many settlers on its lands, but eventual dissatisfaction among the land holders proved troublesome and produced a government investigation. Mercer and Castro also received their grants and began the settlement process. Castro received land along the Nueces River and the Rio Grande, and the German colony received lands that eventually attracted a significant population from Europe during the period of early statehood. Even before the Republic ended in 1845, however, considerable dissatisfaction with the contract system caused the Congress to abandon it in 1844.

Under Lamar, the Congress passed significant legislation to protect Texas landowners from credit foreclosure. The Homestead Law of 1839, partially based on a previous act of the legislature of Coahuila and Texas, provided that a citizen could hold a homestead, meaning a farm up to fifty acres or a town house and lot, and the tools of his trade, without the fear of seizure for non-payment of debt. This legislation attempted to guarantee every citizen at least the chance to make a living, and it also encouraged immigration. This protection, with some modification, has been continued by the state government and exists also in many other states of the American union. But even with their lands titled and secured, Texans of the Republic still had other problems, and one of the most unpredictable and most feared of them dealt with the Indians.

Like the problems of finance and the need to settle former military personnel and recent immigrants on land, Indian difficulties were a part of the Revolutionary legacy. There was a long standing conflict between Europeans and Indians who occupied the lands of the western hemisphere, and this conflict was especially severe among the English and their Anglo-Celtic successors. Texas Indians were no more determined in their resistance, but their territory was reached after they had had time to acquire guns and horses in their resistance.

Many Texans worried about which side the nearly 15,000 Indians in Texas might aid in the Revolution. When the military phase of the Revolution began, many of these Indians had dealt with the Spanish and then the Mexicans for years. They had treaties promising them territory and providing trading service. And some had religious connections. In 1835, the Cherokees around Nacogdoches and along the Neches River seemed to constitute the greatest threat. These Indians had come from Georgia and other southeastern parts of the United States after being chased from their homes by land-hungry Americans, so they were not expected to be friendly to the Texans. The Cherokees had made their way to eastern Texas and were promised that they could live there by the Mexicans.

Now both the Mexicans and the Texans wanted to use the Indians. The Mexicans would have liked to have had them fight the Americans, causing trouble on what would have amounted to a second front, and keeping many East Texans at home instead of being able to join the revolutionary forces. About all the Americans could hope for was the neutrality of the Indians. Sam Houston came to Nacogdoches in February, 1836, to meet with Chief Bowles. Aided by Charles Forbes and William Goyens, a free mulatto who acted as an additional interpreter, Houston met with Bowles in the parlor of Adolphus Sterne's house in Nacogdoches.

Bowles entered the house and saw Mrs. Sterne's marble top table in the center of the room; he assumed it was a seat of honor, and to Mrs. Sterne's disgust, sat cross legged on the table throughout the talks. Houston and Bowles agreed that the Cherokees would not enter the war on either side; in return, Houston pledged that the new government would give the Cherokees permanent title to their lands in eastern Texas. Houston's own residence with the Cherokees following his mysterious departure from Tennessee aided him in these negotiations, and his conduct as president of the Republic left little doubt that he had made this promise in good faith.

But the Texas Congress no longer saw a need to honor the treaty or to allow the Cherokees to continue to hold valuable land which they themselves coveted following the successful conclusion of the war. This was especially true among the citizens of Nacogdoches and throughout all of East Texas. When the Republic was established, and a kind of peace returned to East Texas, the Cherokees expected the new Texas government to honor the treaty that President Houston submitted to the Senate. They were shocked when the Senate rejected the treaty. So long as Houston remained in office, the hope of getting the treaty passed lingered, but the Cherokees grew restless when Lamar became president. Clashes resulted when whites were alarmed by the revolt of Vicente Cordova, a former alcalde of Nacogdoches, who attempted to lead East Texas Indians, Mexicans, and half-breeds against the Texas government in 1838. Cordova raised over 600 fighters for a rampage in the Angelina River country. General Thomas J. Rusk led East Texas whites in a successful effort to put down the Cordova rebellion, and the following year General Kelsey Douglass led the militia in the Battle of the Neches on July 16, 1839. Here the Cherokees were defeated, Philip Bowles was killed, and the Cherokees were pushed from Texas. President Lamar supported these efforts, as he did other expeditions to clear the Indians from the Texas lands everywhere and prepare for Anglo settlements.

An episode known as the Council House fight in San Antonio on March 19, 1840 is a good example of Lamar's Indian policy. This incident occurred when the southern Comanche chiefs requested a conference to discuss peace and to trade hostages. The Comanches arrived for the council but brought in only Matilda Lockhart, a fifteen-year-old girl, instead of the fifteen to twenty hostages they had admitted having. When asked about the remainder of the hostages, Chief Muguara claimed that the other hostages belonged to different Indian groups. They might be able to bring them in for a trade, but they insisted on conducting each ransom individually. Commissioners Hugh McLeod and William G. Cooke and militia commander William S. Fisher became outraged at what they construed as duplicity, especially when they heard the girl's story of torture and saw where flesh had been burned from her nose.

McLeod filled the meeting room with heavily armed men and demanded the release of the other hostages. Chief Maguara grew surly, and McLeod announced that the Indians would be held as prisoners until the whites were returned. A fight erupted immediately and seven soldiers and nearly all of the Indians were killed. The few who escaped carried the news back to the main Indian camp. They hastily withdrew — but they soon returned, nursing a renewed hatred for what they regarded as treachery on the part of the whites.

In August, over 600 strong, the Comanches raided Linnville and Victoria in South Texas while most of the white settlers were away on an expedition against Mexican forces. The Indians travelled all the way around San Antonio to attack these communities, convincing the Texans that Mexican agents had arranged and planned the raid. Now it was the Texans' turn to get even. Felix Huston defeated a raiding party at Plum Creek and later Colonel John H. Moore's militia attacked and destroyed several Indian villages on the upper Colorado River.

The concern felt by Texans over Indian raids, along with the periodic scares from invading Mexicans, brought back the Texas Rangers. In the colonial period, Austin had hired a few men to "range" over the countryside to intercept Indian raiding parties. Since financial troubles now prevented the government from using the regular army for this, the Rangers became the only alternative. They were organized to ride the borderlands, and despite their few numbers, were remarkably successful against hostile Indians. Their bravery and resourcefulness, and perhaps their no-holds-barred methods, earned the Texas Rangers fame and legend from that time forward. They were the first to introduce the revolver, or six-shooter, in Texas when they acquired a shipment intended for the Texas navy. The naval personnel had little use for the weapons but the Rangers did; and, now able to shoot six times before reloading, they became a formidable force on the frontier. Captain Samuel Walker even helped Samuel Colt, the weapon's inventor, to develop an improved version of the pistol which made it efficient, easy to use, and deadly.

Still, the Republic had to deal with regular military problems. Raising enough of an army to fight Santa Anna had posed a major problem even during the revolutionary period. Most Texas males were willing to serve, but their numbers were few. The various revolutionary governments had sent agents to the United States to enlist men. Adolphus Sterne, for example, actually paid the New Orleans Greys' expenses to come to Texas. Stephen F. Austin, Branch T. Archer, and William Wharton travelled to various parts of the United States promising adventure and generous land settlements at the conclusion of the war to all who would come. These efforts proved so successful that many of the "Texans" at the battle of San Jacinto were really new recruits from the United States.

That battle effectively ended the need for a large army, but more Americans came anyway. Some came as individuals, some were already organized into companies; together they numbered more than 2,000 men by the end of 1836. Since Houston had had to travel to New Orleans for medical attention to his ankle wound, suffered during the Battle of San Jacinto, Burnet had had to find another commander. Houston's leadership had been accepted grudgingly, but his successors had even more trouble with the men. Thomas J. Rusk resigned when he saw his leadership questioned; and his replacement, Mirabeau B. Lamar, also quit when the men refused to follow him, choosing instead the leadership of Felix Huston.

When Sam Houston returned and became president, he definitely did not want Huston to continue to command, so he appointed Albert Sidney Johnston to head the army. Huston challenged Johnston to a duel when he tried to assume command, and severely wounded Johnston in the leg. Under such circumstances, the army, restless for action, began to listen to various schemes for attacking Mexico. Houston knew that this would invite another invasion from Mexico, and besides, the army could not be maintained because of the expense. So he furloughed all but 600 of the men, without severance pay, although they remained eligible for the land settlements established by the Congress. This calmed the remaining personnel for the remainder of Houston's term.

President Lamar's plans called for a larger army and included several uses for one. He dreamed of extending the borders of Texas as far westward as possible. His plan included the fulfillment of the provisions of the Treaty of Velasco, which placed the boundary at the full course of the Rio Grande, and included at least half of the present state of New Mexico. Actually, Lamar's dream extended all the way to California, but in June, 1841, he attempted to secure at least the lands in New Mexico.

The resulting Santa Fe expedition is often cited as Lamar's greatest failure, but it began with high hopes. Lamar had believed that the population at Santa Fe would accept the authority of the Texas government. The town was the main trading center on a trail which led southward from St. Louis all the way to Mexico, and it would be a real prize for Lamar's administration. So he sought permission from the Congress to send an expedition to invite the New Mexicans to come under Texas authority. Both houses of Congress passed such resolutions, but since they were not in the same form, they did not legally constitute an endorsement. Lamar dispatched his commissioners and their entourage. It included General Hugh McLeod at the head of 270 persons.

Some were militiamen, some actual commissioners, some businessmen and teamsters who hoped to open a mercantile connection in Santa Fe. Most significantly, the group included George Wilkins Kendall, a New Orleans newspaperman who later wrote of the ill-fated adventure. This group anticipated a journey of 600 miles, but their misdirection and miscalculation doubled the distance they travelled. They crossed territory hostile from both the Indians and the environment, and when they reached Santa Fe, they found the stories of its willingness to join Texas proved false. A member of their own party convinced the entire group to surrender to Mexican troops, and they were marched overland to an unhappy imprisonment in Mexico. Some escaped, and the remainder were released in 1843 as a result of pressure from the United States.

Then, after an absence of six years, Mexican soldiers again entered Texas in 1842. General Rafael Vasquez led 500 men on a raid as far north as San Antonio. Arriving on March 5, his appearance caused another Runaway Scrape. Vasquez proclaimed Mexican sovereignty over San Antonio, but he withdrew after only two days. Houston used this raid as justification for his fears for the location of the new capitol at Austin, and ordered the government returned to the city of Houston. He called out the militia, and a skirmish at the Nueces River resulted before Vasquez made it safely back across the Rio Grande. Then, on September 11, 1842, Mexican troops under General Adrian Woll again occupied San Antonio. Woll also left quickly, although he took hostages with him. This time a larger militia force under General Alexander Somervell pursued the Mexicans to the Rio Grande.

Somervell refused to lead the militia across the river however, so they elected Colonel William S. Fisher as their leader and laid seige to the Mexican city of Mier. Unfortunately, the city received reinforcements while the Texans waited for a demanded tribute. When they attacked, the Mexicans overwhelmed them and captured nearly 300 men. A mass escape nearly proved successful, but most were recaptured within a few days. Finally 176 of the Mier captives were imprisoned in Castle Perote, and sentenced to death. The commander refused to execute the order, so Santa Anna commuted the sentence to the death of only every tenth man. The men drew beans— seventeen of them black — to determine who should die. These men were brutally executed and the remainder held at Castle Perote. Some escaped, and the remainder were freed on September 16, 1844, as a gesture to European diplomats who were seeking to keep Texas from joining the American union.

One other unsuccessful expedition occurred during the period of the Republic. Colonel Jacob Snively led a group in April of 1843 to intercept a wagon train en route to Santa Fe from St. Louis. Snively's 180 men encountered a force of nearly 500 Mexican troops awaiting the same wagon train, but the

Texas Navy's **Liberty** *at Galveston Harbor, 1836.*

— Courtesy of Port of Galveston

Texans defeated the larger body. Unfortunately, when the wagon train arrived, it was escorted by United States troops, who captured the Texans and confiscated all but a few of their muskets. The Snively expedition suffered dreadfully from the desert conditions on their return, and they also suffered from wounded pride. But an even worse fate was to befall the Texas navy.

During the revolutionary period, the Texans were able to control the Texas coast with four vessels. The weakness of the Mexican navy, of course, helped. By the end of 1837, the Texas navy had virtually ceased to exist. The *Liberty* had to be sold in New Orleans for debt; the *Invincible* and the *Brutus* were wrecked; and Mexican ships captured the *Independence.* The Texas Congress authorized the purchase of new vessels during Houston's first term, but all received their commissions from Lamar.

The Texas navy eventually counted seven ships in commission: one, (the *Zavala*) steam powered, the other six sail powered; the largest was the six-hundred-ton *Austin.* The remaining ships were the *San Jacinto,* the *San Antonio,* the *San Bernard,* the *Wharton,* and the *Archer.* Lamar appointed Edwin W. Moore, a former United States naval officer, to command the fleet. Moore used his ships to harass Mexican shipping in the Gulf of Mexico but later he "rented" the fleet to Yucatan rebels with Lamar's blessing. Moore defended the Yucatan coast from invasion by sea, but he occasionally used his ships in offensive action against Mexican vessels.

Houston disapproved of these activities as provocative, and when he became president again he feared that Moore's commitment to the Yucatan rebels would interfere with his own attempts to bring about a peace settlement with Mexico. He ordered Moore to refrain from sailing against Mexican vessels, but instead Moore convinced Houston's commissioner that his pressure was about to force the Mexicans into just such a concession. So Moore sailed again for the Yucatan and attacked Mexican vessels and shore positions. Houston proclaimed Moore a pirate for this insubordination and invited the world's navies to take his ships as prizes. Moore returned to Texas to demand a court-martial and vindication, but Houston ignored his demands and ordered the navy disbanded.

During the latter part of the colonial period, Texans had

complained of the Mexican government's failure to establish a system of education. Such structured educational services as existed in Texas depended on private subscription, and the most prevalent forms consisted of self-education and apprenticeship. Mothers and fathers taught their sons and daughters not only economic skills, but such "book learning" as they had acquired. Ironically, a great many Texas immigrants possessed literacy skills, at least to some degree, and they feared that their children would not learn these same skills.

When the delegates wrote the Constitution for the new Republic, not surprisingly they provided for a system of education, but no Texas Congress could find the resources to establish such a system. At least Lamar tried, earning him the designation as the Father of Texas Education. He urged the Congress to set aside portions of the public domain to establish the educational system and to provide an endowment for the schools of the future. His charge ultimately became the motto of the University of Texas when that institution finally began to function in 1883, and in a larger sense became the motto for all public education in Texas: "It is admitted by all that the cultivated mind is the guardian genius of democracy, and while guided and controlled by virtue, is the noblest attribute of man. It is the only dictator that free men acknowledge and the only security free men desire."

In 1839 Congress responded by awarding three leagues of land to each county for the support of an academy. Unfortunately, they also gave away so much land to settlers that the counties had difficulty raising funds for their schools by sale or leasing. Congress reserved an additional fifty leagues of land for the support of two universities—meaning higher education—when they were established. Since this land did not have to be located within a given county, most of it was located in western Texas, along with the lands designated for the universities. From time to time additional lands were also designated for the support of education by subsequent state governments. The discovery of oil on lands reserved for the University of Texas made that institution one of the best endowed universities in the United States.

Such victories, however, came well after the Republic ceased to exist. Education continued during its ten years much as it had prior to the Revolution. A few academies, such as Marcus

A. Montrose's San Augustine University, appeared for a time, then folded. The Congress chartered several such institutions, termed "universities," that were really elementary schools. The Nacogdoches University was the last chartered by a Texas congress. Further advancement for education in Texas had to await the solution of its many other problems.

A persistent problem, which reflected Texans' uncertain circumstances and personal conflicts between its presidential leadership, was the selection of a permanent capital. Houston began the first presidential term at Columbia, where Burnet had concluded the *ad interim* government. The community there was small, not centrally located, and was some distance from the growing population of eastern Texas. A. C. Allen and his brother J. K. Allen promoted the new community of Houston near the former capital of Harrisburg. Shrewdly, they appealed to Houston's vanity by naming their development in honor of the new president.

The government moved to Houston in 1837 and pledged to remain there at least until 1840 to help the promoters obtain resources to construct a capitol building. The capitol was incomplete, however, and even when finished did not suit many of the representatives who felt that the official seat of government should be nearer the Republic's growth line so it would remain the center of the eventual population spread. Lamar's supporters particularly felt this way, while another faction wanted to move the capital even farther to the east so it would be safe from Mexican forces. In 1838 Congress designated LaGrange as its future home, but Houston vetoed the bill, giving the pledge to remain in Houston until 1840 as his reason.

But Lamar was elected president later in that year, and he had no intention of remaining in a town named for Houston. During the first year of his term, the Congress created a commission to located the permanent capitol on a site of its own choosing, so long as it was north of the Old San Antonio Road and between the Trinity and Colorado Rivers. Allegedly, Lamar selected a hilly site on the Colorado River near the small village of Waterloo while on a buffalo hunt. He reportedly admired the view and observed that it would be wonderful headquarters for an empire. This new city of Austin matched the booster zeal of Houston and quickly readied the necessary structures for government operations. Lamar moved his administration there even before the town was ready. This placed the capital beyond the true frontier line, and left it vulnerable to Indian raids, although perhaps less so than Houston men argued.

When Houston replaced Lamar as president, he refused to make his residence in Austin. Following the Mexican military raids of 1842, he ordered the Congress to convene in Houston for reasons of safety, and demanded that all other government facilities join them immediately. The citizens of Austin learned of Houston's plan and, led by Mrs. Angelina Eberly, manager of Bullock's hotel, the Austinites resisted the removal of the government records. Houston's men made it out of town, but the pursuing defenders overtook them and forced them to surrender the archives, which then returned to Austin. Eventually, the government returned there in 1844, and has remained. The bloodless "Archives War," as this 1842 episode is termed, would be humorous but for the testimony it bears to the unsettled nature of the Republic's government.

In September, 1836, while choosing their first president and ratifying a Constitution, Texas voters also voted to seek annexation to the American union. Their relations with the United States, Mexico, and the European powers revolved around this desire for the entire ten years of the Republic's existence. Previous governments already had representatives in Washington, but Burnet designated James W. Collinsworth and Peter W. Grayson to seek annexation even before the September ballot that year. Such American leaders as Daniel Webster and John C. Calhoun favored annexation, but John Quincy Adams opposed it over the slavery issue.

President Andrew Jackson appeared neutral for a while because of United States-Mexican relations, but he sent Henry M. Morfit to Texas to investigate and report on Texas' readiness for annexation. Morfit witnessed the election fever, learned of the growing debt, and gathered the impression that Mexico was not really through with its efforts to retain Texas. But he did believe that the vast Texas lands deserved some consideration. So he recommended caution. Acting on that advice, Jackson suggested that the Congress should delay recognition and not even appear to consider annexation at that time.

Houston then sent William Wharton to press the Texas cause, and he spent most of his time working with the Con-

Old drawing shows firing of cannon down Congress Avenue in Austin during "Archives War."

gress. Wharton read between the lines of Jackson's message to the Congress that he would not act alone in the recognition. Wharton persuaded the Senate to pass a favorable resolution and the House initiated appropriations for a diplomatic mission. With these endorsements, Jackson appointed Alcee Louis La Branche of New Orleans as *charge d' affaires* to the Republic. This at least gave Texas some standing and encouraged its leaders to seek recognition from other countries while continuing to press their petition for annexation.

Houston sent James Pinckney Henderson to work for recognition from the European countries, especially England and France. A convention securing trading privileges was the best Henderson could do with Lord Palmerston in England, because Palmerston feared for his country's investments in Mexico. Henderson then moved on to the French, who were more eager to deal with him because of the Pastry War, a dispute with the Mexicans over unpaid debts to a French baking concern. The French were encouraged to move even closer to recognition when the Texans withdrew their offer to be annexed to the United States in the fall of 1838, after Houston felt the offer had stood unanswered long enough.

When Lamar succeeded Houston, he sent James Hamilton to seek loans as well as recognition. Hamilton persuaded England to recognize Texas and to offer to mediate between Texas and Mexico. The Texas Senate balked for a time at some of the provisions of the English treaty, but full relations were established in 1842. Lamar's administration also secured the recognition of the Netherlands and Belgium, but no loans.

French recognition proved a mixed blessing. Their representative, the Count Alphonse de Saligny, became embroiled in a running argument with hotel keeper John Bullock. The conflict climaxed when Bullock's pigs raided Saligny's barn to eat corn and the Frenchman's hired hands killed some of the pigs. De Saligny felt insulted by the results of the celebrated but silly "Pig War," quit the country, and ended all chances of a loan, if not actual recognition from France.

During Houston's administration, relations with Mexico remained uncertain. Mexico repudiated Santa Anna's concessions at Velasco, including the recognition of independence and especially the Rio Grande boundary line. But during Houston's first presidency, Mexico's internal problems prevented a renewal of military activity. Lamar seemed not to care when he told the Congress: "If peace can only be obtained by the sword, let the sword do its work." But Lamar did send agents to Mexico to try to deal for peace rather than fight for it. Bernard E. Bee travelled there in 1839, but he could not even gain an audience as a representative from Texas. Secret negotiations through James Treat also came to no avail. Finally in 1841, Lamar also sent James Webb, his Secretary of State, to try to work out a permanent agreement of independence. But at the same time he rented his navy to Yucatan rebels and endorsed such adventures as the Santa Fe Expedition, so there is little wonder that his peace overtures came to nothing.

Houston's return to office came when the Mexicans appeared ready to renew military activities — witness the Vasquez and Woll raids — and mistakes on the Texas side, such as the Mier Expedition, kept the two sides from meaningful talks. The renewal of annexation hopes broke the impasse. Both Great Britain and France pressured the Mexicans to work something out to keep Texas from joining the United States. The European powers hoped to weaken the United States and to maintain their influence in North America through Texas; for Mexico, this would mean less embarrassment and that they would not have to press their case against the United States. All this worked well for Texas. At the end, they were in the position of choosing between Mexican offers of independence and commercial exchange, and full annexation as a state of the American union.

Even those Texans who favored annexation kept their hopes in check since the initial rebuff by the United States. They had assumed that the United States would welcome Texas with open arms; but this attitude failed to consider the problems with Mexico that this would pose for the United States, especially at a time when relations were strained with France. They ignored the growing strength of the anti-slave lobby, which reached even to Martin Van Buren, Jackson's successor in the White House, but was especially represented in the strident opposition of John Quincy Adams. And they likewise failed to recognize the fear that many easterners felt of rapid westward expansion, especially when it involved the incorporation of resident alien cultures.

Still, the Texans had thought annexation inevitable. After

two years of disappointment, they withdrew their offer at the end of Houston's administration. Lamar did not make such an offer. Instead, he concentrated on expansion and recognition by the nations of the world. Ironically, this eventually made Texas more attractive to the United States, where many politicians feared that an independent Texas blocked expansion, and represented a potential threat, even to the United States, should Texas become a protectorate of France or Great Britain. And as Texas grew in population, particularly in a culture and an economy similar to the American nation, pressure gradually built in both nations for union.

Houston decided to renew the discussions, if a bit more cautiously, when he became president for a second time. He sent James Reilly, and later Isaac Van Zandt, to explore the attitude of President John Tyler. Since the United States was then trying to pressure Mexico to release the Texan Americans held in various prisons, many feared the prospect of war with Mexico over annexation. The abolitionists still opposed annexation, especially since the Tyler administration had significant internal problems, so the President was forced to leave the issue on the table, where it seemed to die stillborn.

Suddenly the issue was renewed by United States initiative. In October, 1843, the Americans suggested that talks be renewed on the assurance that a treaty of annexation could get through the Senate. James Pinckney Henderson joined Van Zandt to negotiate with Secretary of State John C. Calhoun. The treaty that was proposed called for Texas' annexation as a territory of the United States and for the surrender of her public lands in return for the payment of debts by the parent country. Many Texans disliked the idea of less than full admission to the union and the surrender of lands, but the treaty would probably have been approved if it had been submitted to them. Unfortunately, the United States Senate rejected the treaty on June 8, 1844 by a vote of 35 to 16 because of pressure from abolitionists.

Prospects brightened just as the issue seemed dead. Anson Jones became president, representing a new hand for Texas. Although he later billed himself as the "architect of annexation," Jones' intentions at the time seemed far less obvious. And rejection in the Senate had angered many Democrats, particularly the Southern Democrats, who made the annexation of Texas a primary issue in the presidential election of 1844. Because Martin Van Buren and Henry Clay, the two leading candidates, chose to ignore the issue, the Democrats claimed the most popular issue of the campaign for James K. Polk, who swept the election in November.

But Polk would not take office until the following March, so Tyler reintroduced the proposition as a joint resolution requiring only a simple majority of each house in Congress this time. It passed in the House of Representatives 118 to 101, and in the Senate, 27 to 25, and this time Texas got what it considered a better deal. Texas would enter the union with full statehood and retain possession of her public lands and her public debt.

France and England persuaded Jones to give them ninety days to work on Mexico, and they convinced the Mexican government to offer Texas full recognition of independence and the Rio Grande border if they would reject annexation. Jones summoned the Texas Congress and offered both proposals for their consideration. Inevitably, the Convention favored annexation. They prepared a Constitution for statehood and submitted the package to Texas voters in October. It received near unanimous approval. The United States Congress agreed to accept the Constitution, and on December 29, 1845, President Polk signed the resolution of acceptance. Texas was in the union.

The final drama came at the new state's capitol on February 19, 1846, when Anson Jones pronounced ". . . the Republic of Texas is no more." As the Lone Star flag came down, Sam Houston stepped forward and clutched the banner to his breast. Governor James Pinckney Henderson embraced the new union fully in his inaugural address: "This day, and within this very hour, has been consummated the great work of annexation."

The Republic of Texas existed officially just a few months less than ten years. But these remain important years in the development of Texas, and they were necessary to make the transition from a colony under Mexico to a state of the American union. The Republic, when the Lone Star really meant independence, danger, high potential, and grit, left all subsequent Texans something to remember.

Anson Jones, last president of the Republic of Texas.

— University of Texas Library

Lone Star State

Beginning with the Paleo-Americans – and continuing through waves of Indians, Spaniards, French, and Anglo-Celtic peoples—Texas has received its people from other places in the world. The first of these immigrants no longer mattered in 1845 when Texas became a state of the American union, for they had been gone for thousands of years. The Indians, though, still impacted, both positively and negatively, but they were few in number in comparison to the swelling Anglo population. Virtually no Spaniards or French of colonial vintage remained, having become Mexican, Creole, or American in the melting action of the New World environment, as did nearly all who invaded Texas before 1845. The Anglo-American stock dominated by that time, although it too had become something different from its British beginnings. A product of nearly three centuries of frontiering in North America, their greatest survival skill was adaptability. Irish, French, German, had all simply become American by the forces of the frontier.

In the 1830s the real invasions began. When independence from Mexico became a reality, the Texans amounted to little more than 40,000 of all colors, white, red, black, and varied shades in between. Their numbers increased to more than three times that figure by the time statehood was achieved, including more than 40,000 slaves; by 1850 there were more than 300,000 Texans, including 60,000 slaves, and at the end of Texas' first attempt at statehood, more than 600,000 Texans lived in the Lone Star state. These later invaders came for land, the same reward that had pulled the early Spanish and French groups. Such growth ordinarily would indicate peace and prosperity in any other nation on earth. Instead, the pull of the land actually came over years marked by strife against the Mexicans, the Indians, New Mexicans, their new parent government, and often amongst themselves. And, although there was some evidence of economic growth during these years, prosperity eluded Texas' colonial economy until the early part of the present century.

Establishing the government of Texas under the constitution of 1845 became the first work of statehood. The founding document benefitted from good leadership at the constitutional convention, especially from Thomas Jefferson Rusk, who served as president of the convention. The framers included J. Pinckney Henderson, a former cabinet member and minister under Houston's presidency, Isaac Van Zandt, envoy to the United Sates and member of the Texas Congress, and such notables as R. E. B. Baylor, N. H. Darnell, Abner S. Lipscomb, Hiram G. Runnels, and Jose Antonio Navarro, the only native Texan. Most came from Tennessee (18), Virginia (8), Georgia (7), Kentucky (6), and North Carolina (5), and combined such previous governmental experiences as services on the bench, in the legislature, and in Runnels' case, service as governor of a state.

They drew on the constitution of the Texas Republic for such principles as the homestead law and the prohibition of ministers of the gospel from service in the legislature. They also drew on the national constitution and on the other state constitutions, including that of Louisiana which recently had been revised. And there were some changes from the period of the Republic. Now the legislature was to meet only every other year; governors would hold two-year terms and could not serve more than four out of six years; representatives would serve for two years and Senators for four years; corporations could not be chartered except by a two-thirds vote of the legislature, and banks could not receive charters at all; the legislature could not incur debt in excess of $100,000; and married women would be protected in their property rights.

In organizing elections, Henderson won the governorship over J. B. Miller, and Albert C. Horton defeated Darnell for the lieutenant governor's job. The legislature selected Houston and Rusk as the state's first two senators, Houston drawing the short term in the alternation scheme, and these two established lines of succession still boasted of in contemporary politics. Governor Henderson appointed the bulk of the remaining officers, including the justices of the state supreme court. He appointed John Hemphill as the first Chief Justice.

The State's first test came, as the Mexicans had promised for ten years, over the act of union itself. Officially Mexico still steadfastly refused to accept the independence of Texas, but continued to regard that territory as being in a state of rebellion. In many practical matters they had come to a kind of truce with the Texans, had even promised recognition if Texas would remain independent of the United States. When Texas ignored this overture, prompted by British and French diplomatic maneuvers, many Mexicans felt they had no choice but war. For ten years they had threatened war against the United States should Texas be admitted to the Union. Now with that as a reality, Juan Almonte, Mexican minister to the United States at Washington City, withdrew his credentials and returned to Mexico. Santa Anna, president again, sounded nationalism's wounded cry. The American action confirmed Mexico's decade-long assertion that only American involvement had enable the Texans to defeat Mexican armies in 1836.

Contrary to popular belief, the war really did not involve Texas or its boundary, although both are cited as causes of the war. Texas was already a state in the American union. President Polk and the other expansionists really wanted California and New Mexico, the lands beyond Texas which stretched to the Pacific Ocean. Shortly after Polk became president, he sent John Slidell to Mexico with an offer to purchase this territory, and against that backdrop, forces in California began working toward an independence of their own. The new Mexican president, Jose Herrera, refused to receive Slidell, however, contrary to the expectations of Polk, and this rebuff convinced many Americans that war was inevitable.

What both sides used as an excuse to begin the war, and it worked well enough to allow each to claim that they had been invaded by the other, was a boundary dispute. Ever since the Treaty of Velasco in 1836, Texans had claimed the Rio Grande as their border with Mexico. When they entered the American union, the parent government had accepted this demarcation.

The Nueces River, nearly 200 miles to the north of the Rio Grande, had been the traditional boundary between the Texas colony and the established Mexican states of Tamaulipas and Coahuila, and this boundary even received statutory endorsement in the Mexican Congress during the colonial period. Mexico refused to honor the Velasco treaty and maintained that her eastern boundary remained at the Sabine River where it had been since the Adams-Onis Treaty of 1819. So the Nueces/Rio Grande River argument made only a practical, not an official difference. To hold the new territory, Polk ordered General Zachary Taylor to occupy the Nueces River line shortly after the annexation vote, and Taylor arrived at Corpus Christi in July, 1845. The Mexicans sent General Mariano Arista to the Rio Grande, thus creating a kind of no-mans-land between the two rivers.

Following the rebuff of Slidell, Polk ordered Taylor to occupy this territory, and in April, 1846 Major Jacob Brown moved to the river and set up a bivouac opposite the Mexican town of Matamoros, where Arista headquartered. Since both armies patrolled the area between the rivers, a confrontation inevitably occurred on April 24 when sixty of Taylor's dragoons stumbled into a Mexican cavalry brigade. Then Arista's men attacked Brown's camp on the river, the site of the present city of Brownsville. Taylor immediately marched to the river with over 2,300 men and full field supplies, spoiling for battle. Both sides could, and did, send communications to their political chiefs bearing the word that they had been fired upon on their own soil.

Within a few weeks Taylor won impressive battles at Palo Alto and Resaca de la Palma and readied his army for a push to Monterrey. Taylor did penetrate into northern Mexico, and later won more impressive victories at such battles as Monterrey and Buena Vista, but for the most part his war was over.

General Winfield Scott, overall commander, with Polk's approval decided on an amphibious invasion of Mexico, using Texas as a staging area, and a shorter overland march to Mexico City. Scott, of course, would lead it. Taylor chafed because he was upstaged by his rival and commander, and took revenge by finessing Scott out of the Whig nomination and the presidency in 1848. Scott assembled his invasion force at Port Isabel on the Texas coast and led the first amphibious invasion in American military history at Vera Cruz in September, 1847. He succeeded in capturing Mexico City, forcing Santa Anna's army to the north for a final battle with Taylor.

These convincing victories forced Mexico to agree — although only after tedious negotiations conducted by Nicholas Trist — to the Treaty of Guadalupe Hidalgo on February 2, 1848. It set the Rio Grande as the Mexican-United States boundary, and therefore the Texas border, and it ceded land which became the states of California, Arizona, New Mexico, Nevada, Wyoming, Utah and Colorado, for $15 million, with the U.S. assumption of the claims against Mexico.

Texans played active roles in the Mexican War. In addition to hosting the military concentrations for both Taylor's and Scott's campaigns, Texans served in volunteer units in both invasions. Four companies of Texas Rangers served with Taylor; and some of them later accompanied Scott all the way to Mexico City, making an infamous name for themselves among the Mexican population. Their lack of military discipline and regularity made the Rangers a trial for both commanders, but their ability to scout and fight earned them at least a grudging admiration. The Rangers killed Mexicans with too much enthusiasm, remembering past grievances, and Mexicans dubbed them "Los Diablos Tejanos."

Scott seemed to have better control over the Rangers than did Taylor, but he had to exert much pressure to retain it. Such leaders as Ben McCulloch, Samuel H. Walker and John S. ("Rip") Ford did not quiet easily. Even the Texas governor, James Pinckney Henderson, took a leave of absence from state affairs to lead a unit of volunteer Texans in the war. Unlike many in the United States — especially the anit-slave forces who saw the war as a scheme of slave expansionism, or the New Englanders who disliked expansionism and involvement with foreigners of Latin descent — Texans participated in the Mexican War with zest.

Even modern Texans feel somewhat defensive about the war's results. As recently as the early 1960s, the late Robert Kennedy referred to the Mexican War as a "dark episode" in American history, drawing telegrams and letters of protest from Texas governors and other officials. To most Texans it represents little more than an extension of a ten-year war which they regarded as essential to maintaining their indepen-

Drawing of Antonio Lopez de Santa Anna, Mexican general in the Texas wars and president of Mexico. Drawing by Gene Bustamante.

— Courtesy Institute of Texan Cultures

dence; to many in the north it has remained an unjustified rape of a sister American republic. The two sides viewed the activities differently; the latter looked at the result, and the addition of so much extra territory, and saw a cause of which they disapproved; the Texans viewed both cause and result with unqualified enthusiasm.

With the military threat from Mexico out of the way, Texans still faced a border crisis of another kind with the territory of New Mexico which harkened back to the same 1836 Treaty of Velasco. The Rio Grande does not stop at El Paso del Norte; it meanders northward from that ancient crossroads through central New Mexico to its forked headwaters in the San Juan Mountains of Colorado. By the treaty, all lands north and east of the river came under Texas authority, according to the Texans.

Having prevailed in that argument with old Mexico, they were not prepared to back down before their own kind. These claims included much vacant, deserted land, but it also garnered Santa Fe, the capital of New Mexico, whose culture and history had nothing to do with Texas except a common ancestry in the Spanish colonial scheme. In fact, New Mexico had a much closer economic connection to Missouri, since the Santa Fe trail ran northward to St. Louis and southward into Mexico, and caravans had moved both ways on this path long before Moses Austin and other dreamers came to Texas.

Still, the treaty, and Lamar's vision, and now more recent Texans, would have it for their own. But the New Mexicans and the United States army objected. Since General Stephen Kearney had occupied Santa Fe during the war, the military had maintained a garrison and a government in the ancient city. After the war, Governor Henderson dispatched Judge Spruce M. Baird to Santa Fe to assume control of the area and to establish Texas' authority in the region. Colonel John M. Washington commanded; and, encouraged by local people who did not want to join Texas and by national political leaders who did not want Texans to control it either, he informed Baird that he would not relinquish command unless so ordered by higher authority. President Polk, who sided with the Texans in the controversy, had already given such an order, but Washington, who knew of it, refused anyway. Baird returned to an angered Texas.

Texans had joined the union to solve its problems, but

union had brought them a new problem instead. George Thomas Wood, who succeeded Henderson as governor, summoned the state legislature and pledged to defend Texas soil against a new foe. The legislature responded by creating four counties (Worth, Buckel, Santa Fe, and El Paso) in the disputed territory. Ex-Ranger and Indian agent Robert S. Neighbors received the appointment to organize these counties, but he succeeded only in bringing El Paso under Texas authority. The three northern areas refused to organize under his leadership. At least Neighbors saved the El Paso territory, giving Texas authority over the Trans-Pecos country in that region.

When Zachary Taylor became president in 1849, he agreed with the New Mexicans, and coveted them as a separate state, along with California, as jewels in his own crown. Following Taylor's death in the summer of 1850, new President Milliard Fillmore supported the New Mexicans even more emphatically.

This impasse was resolved as a part of the Compromise of 1850, whose major parts dealt with the admission of California, a stringent fugitive slave law, the abolition of the slave trade in the District of Columbia, and the organization of New Mexico and Utah territories. The Texas border dispute was settled in the latter part. By legislation sponsored by James A. Pearce of Maryland, Texans ceded all territory north and west of the 100th meridian and the parallel of 36°30′. The boundary ran along a line to the 103rd parallel, then along that to the 32nd parallel, and then along that parallel to the Rio Grande, thence following the river to its mouth at the Gulf of Mexico.

In return, Texas received $10 million with the expectation that this would be applied to the public debt. Many Texans argued against a settlement which surrendered so much territory, but the argument that it was the best deal they were likely to get proved convincing to voters who expressed their desire in an election called for the purpose by a 2 to 1 margin. Governor Bell signed the legislation of acceptance in November, 1850.

Even the $10 million did not satisfy the Texas debt by then, for it included obligations to veterans of the various military enterprises and a much larger portion owed to security holders from the time of the Republic. Since the revenue debts were of higher priority, the Congress withheld $5 million to insure payment. The state paid the $1.25 million non-revenue debt to its veterans, but still lacked enough to settle the larger indebtedness. They proposed to fund the debt at 77 percent of par, arguing that most of the certificates were held by speculators who had purchased them for as little as ten cents on the dollar. Final settlement of these debts required more than five years, and when the state received its final $5 million payment from the Federal government, which accrued interest plus a settlement for state activities in Indian matters, they netted $7.75 million, or a total of over $12 million for the surrendered land.

Texas paid out over $10,078,703 to its creditors, netting a profit of nearly $2.75 million, most of which was dedicated to an endowment for public schools. Much of this money was later used to subsidize railroad construction and to fund the state's activities, enabling them to remand nine-tenths of their taxes for several years. The remaining tenth was required under the constitution to fund the state's schools. The state usually paid for schooling on an annual basis, often in direct payments to parents who had paid for their children's education during the year, without drawing a distinction between public and private, secular or parochial schools. At the end of the decade, Texas was again over $1 million in debt.

State politics in the first phase of statehood remained as it had been in the Republic, a matter of personalities, but the first efforts at party affiliation did develop during the 1850s. While Henderson took leave to lead Texans in the war with Mexico, Lieutenant Governor Horton filled his office until Henderson returned in November of 1846. Henderson did not run for re-election and George T. Wood, a planter from the Trinity River country, succeeded him. In 1848 Texans cast their first American presidential electoral votes for Democrat Lewis Cass instead of for the winner, Zachary Taylor. Considering Taylor's role in the Mexican War and the fact that he was a fellow slave owner, this vote is surprising except in the light of the Texan's southern background and traditional affiliation with the party of Andrew Jackson.

Wood ran for a second term in 1849, but Peter Hansborough Bell defeated him, and Bell won re-election in 1851. A veteran of San Jacinto and the Mexican War and known as an advocate of states' rights and slavery, Bell reflected the general Texas population's attitude on these subjects.

Another "old Texan," Yankee born Elisha M. Pease, won the governorship in 1853 and again in 1855. Pease had resided in Texas since 1835 and had helped build Texas from a Mexican colony to a state of the American union. His administrations were marked by boosterism, particularly in the area of river and rail transportation, in the location of additional military bases in Texas for protection against Indians, and for pushing settlement toward the west. Perhaps the most significant aspect of his administration was the passage of the school law of 1854 which employed the $2 million from the United States for education and internal improvements. Despite his long tenure in Texas, Pease remained a nationalist. During his years in the Whig Party and the Know Nothing Party, he made inroads into state politics, forcing the Democrats into more organization as well. The Know Nothings, or American Party, was a nativist, anti-foreign, anti-Roman Catholic party which operated in secret as much as possible. Such prominent Texans as R.E.B. Baylor and D.C. Dickson, who served as lieutenant governor, were said to be members of the group.

In 1857 Sam Houston suffered his only defeat at the Texas polls when he ran for the governorship against Hardin R. Runnels, who was one of the first officers nominated by a political convention in Texas. Houston had been out of the state for a decade serving in the U.S. Senate. He had lost step with the rush of new settlers, most of whom came from the Old South. They were nullifiers and states' righters, and included a few fire eaters like Louis T. Wigfall. Houston's campaign against Runnels suffered from his associations with the national government and his opposition to the secession talk precipitated by the wedges of separation then troubling the American union.

By the end of the campaign, Houston regained some of his popularity, but not enough to escape defeat. But in 1859, at the end of his Senate term and after more campaigning in Texas, the unionist Houston defeated Runnels in a time which should have been even more difficult for a union man. Ironically, this placed Houston in the uncomfortable governor's seat when the secession crisis arose in the winter and spring of 1860-61.

Part of Houston's troubles in 1857 were the hundreds of thousands of new immigrants who had arrived in Texas since his exploits in the Revolution and in the presidency of the Republic had made him the Texas hero of that earlier era. These new invaders had heard of him, of course, but theirs was a different time. While Houston led armies against Santa Anna, most of them followed John C. Calhoun's lead in nullification. Now they came to Texas, chasing the same rainbow's end as former invaders, but dragging a different cultural baggage, particularly the heavy burden of African slavery, and they did not intend to surrender their labor source just to remain in the union.

These new immigrants came from many places, but the Americans among them, almost ninety percent, mostly came from the southland, about equally distributed between the states of the upper and lower south, but all from slave country. The culture which developed in Texas increasingly reflected this argrarian, rural heritage. Texas differed from other southern states in one glaring way: it alone still had a genuine frontier settlement line with Indian hostility as a constant problem. States of the American frontier to the north shared some of this circumstance, of course, but their Indians were less hostile at this time, and their cultural source, the New England, Central State northern areas, differed as well.

The southern Americans were leap frogs; a few came to Texas from Louisiana or Arkansas, Texas' immediate neighbors, but more migrated from Tennessee and Alabama than any other place. Their Appalachian background, their intense independence, made those people Texans before they arrived in Texas. The Tennesseans and Alabamans moved directly to the frontier line to establish farms, bringing an American corn culture to border the lands where Mexicans and Indians had grown varieties of the same crop for centuries.

Next to the Alabamans and Tennesseans, Georgians and sons and daughters of Mississippi moved mostly to the pine country of eastern Texas, again as farmers, and mostly cultivated cotton, the crop which grew so well in their former homes. The few Louisianans who migrated to Texas remained along the coast growing sugar as they had done before. A few Missourians filtered in, generally moving beyond the Alabamans on to the rolling plains. These various state groups, although they did not come as sponsored ex-patriots from their native states, tended to remain together more than they intermixed. Enclaves recreated a version of their former culture in a new home.

And then there were the "foreign" immigrants. As early as the empresarial period, a few Irish and German immigrants had made their way to Texas, but these had long ago passed into the general Anglo-Celtic culture by the forces and pressures of Revolution and Republic building. Yet the Mexicans, even if born in Texas, were regarded as foreign. Of the 43,422 such "foreigners" in Texas in 1860, about 12,000 were Mexican. They were almost completely absent from East Texas, but south of San Antonio they dominated in numbers if in nothing else. Most did not speak English and did not want to learn to do so; they did not participate in the Texas experience in those years so much as they simply accepted it. Some lived on farms of their own, others worked the ranches of their own kind, and later they worked for Anglos who owned the land in large holdings but were too few to work it or to populate it. In such communities as San Antonio and El Paso, the Mexican populations were dominant, but as usual, their political power did not match their numbers since few if any voted and none served in elected office, especially after the Mexican War.

Of the remaining 30,000 or so "foreign born" Texans, nearly all were European, and these were mostly German. Some Poles, Czechs and French came, but most Anglos did not bother to distinguish them from Germans, and the French did not remain long. Their best showing was the utopian experiment known as La Reunion, founded and floundered near the site of John Neely Bryan's cabin and ferry on the Trinity River that one day would become the metropolis of Dallas. La Reunion failed, as did most such experiments, because the environment of North America would not accommodate to their idealism.

Henri Castro founded the most successful plantation of French-German speaking people at Castroville in Medina County. These immigrants were mostly recruited from the Upper Rhine country in Germany, and they shared a French-German heritage which reflected the many boundary changes of their history. Castro's 2,000 settlers thought of themselves as Alsatians, but were usually called Germans by the Texans. Some were Swabians, Wurttembergers, and Swiss. They established a bit of the Old World in south-central Texas which en-

Prince Carl Solms-Braunfels, a Prussian noble who helped colonize Texas with German immigrants.

— *Courtesy Institute of Texan Cultures*

dures still, including the oldest non-Hispanic Catholic Church in Texas.

The principal German settlements were made in the country just north and west of San Antonio. The lure for these later immigrants, or *Einwanderers*, was the same as for all Texans —land—but they were also motivated by a desire to plant their culture in the New World. The Germans did so as effectively as anywhere in the world in the Texas hill country, including the previous impact of their countrymen in Pennsylvania during the American-colonial period.

In 1842 Prussian nobles founded the Society for the Protection of German Immigrants in Texas, often called *Adelsverein*, to aid their countrymen in the work. The *Adelsverein* promised to help recreate the Fatherland in Texas by acquiring land for settlement, assisting the immigrants in making arrangements for the journey, building houses and planting crops, and providing markets for their produce.

Their idealistic agent who would fulfill these pledges was Prince Carl of Solms-Braunfels. He first purchased a defunct land grant previously awarded to the Fisher-Miller empresarial team. These lands were distant from the coast and still in danger of Indian raids. Prince Carl came ahead of the first immigrants to inspect the land, and he realized they were too distant from the coast for easy settlement. After being duped twice again by swindlers, he at last acquired lands in the country just north and west of San Antonio as an intermediate settlement area, hoping to use the first comers as a bridge to the original goal. He passed up more fertile and accessible land nearer the coast for the limestone, rocky soils of central Texas. From a base at Indianola, thousands of his countrymen journeyed into this new world to a time of despair.

Prince Carl's ways were still too much old world ways, and the first settlers fared poorly; they tried to preserve too much of their heritage that would not work in the different environment of Texas. But a more realistic leader followed. Otfried Hans, Freiherr von Meuseback, replaced Prince Carl, and symbolic of his leadership, quickly became simply John O. Meuseback, German settler. Meuseback moved the Germans from the coast to the Hill Country, as it came later to be called, to New Braunfels, and eventually on into Comanche country. He made treaties with the Indians which the settlers honored, and founded more communities, including Sisterdale, Boerne, Comfort, and eventually Fredericksburg, perhaps the best known of the German communities in a later time.

Thousands of other German immigrants followed. Most farmed, and as they adapted to the new world, prospered. A few went off to ranch and some later moved to small towns as professionals, but they retained an ethnic consciousness and spoke their own language when among their own, which was most of the time. They did not have a significant political impact on Texas because their numbers were small in comparison to the Anglo-Celts, but their cultural significance remains important because of its difference from the majority.

During the first period of statehood, the people of Texas remained mostly rural. Galveston, with fewer than 4,000 inhabitants, was the largest town, although San Antonio edged the island city out of first place with 8,000 people by 1860. Houston, New Braunfels, Marshall, and perhaps Austin, because of its political significance, could be called towns. None had anything but dirt, mud, or dust for streets, and most had only one-story buildings. San Antonio's two-story Menger Hotel, opening in 1859, was among the largest buildings in any city, outside the three-story capitol building in Austin.

These towns offered trade goods imported at high expense via New Orleans, and such professional services as medicine and the law. Indeed, the state seemed well served by physicians and lawyers, who counted hundreds in their calling in the era before medical schools and bar examinations. Their services were honestly rendered, if poorly reformed, even by contemporary standards in Europe or the United States.

There were only two factories in the entire state, a hat factory in Houston and a textile factory in Henderson county, but there were plenty of grist mills and cotton gins and sawmills. For the majority of the people who lived on farms, the life was hard. Most still lived as they had as colonists, in one-room cabins. Logs were used when available, stone when it was more convenient, as in the Hill Country. The dog run house was also common, and when planed boards were available, shacks were constructed of this material. Cracks and openings were common in the one-room dwellings; travelers often wrote of seeing the stars through holes in the roofs or between the logs.

The diet of these pioneers was monotonous at best. Few

Free Negro family on the Texas frontier. Watercolor by Bruce Marshall.

— Courtesy Institute of Texan Cultures

kept milk cows for dairy products or bothered to garden for greens. Meat, sweet potatoes and corn in various varieties, including the liquid form, was their most frequent fare. The farmers were self-sufficient by necessity; store-bought goods and tools cost money few had, so they made their own tools and utensils, as the colonists had done, because in an economic sense they were colonials too.

Most Texas farmers did not own slaves, and some resented the competition from those who did own them, but most Texans believed in slavery. They did so from a racist viewpoint; that is, they did not know what else to do with the large population of blacks, 182,000 by 1860, or nearly a third of the population. The farmer who did own slaves, and the still fewer in the planter class, knew what to do with them. They grew cotton. Slaves seemed the ideal labor force for this crop, and owners bought and bred them for this purpose. Slave investment exceeded even the value of real estate in this time. Although Texans owned less than six percent of the total slaves in America and the planter class was a slim minority of even slave owners in Texas, the planters dominated the economy, thought, politics, and culture of much of the state.

Slaves fared as well as most whites in terms of shelter, diet, and clothing, perhaps better in medical attention since no slave owner could afford the loss of property value, but less well in education and, of course, in personal freedom. This was also true for the few free blacks in Texas. Although they were not "owned," they were not truly free. In a state where most whites were freeholders of land and exercised freedom in individual movement and expression, one-third of the population did not share this blessing.

Texas reflected its frontier status in transportation. The horse was the medium of movement, either as a riding animal or to pull a wagon. Rivers offered some transportation, but none of Texas' rivers were truly navigable more than a few miles from the coast, and none by ocean vessels of deep draft. Railroads did not exist before the end of the 1850s, and then none connected the principal towns. Stagecoaches ran through Texas carrying passengers and goods to the West Coast; but few came to Texas on purpose or provided regular service. Even wagon freight remained uncertain and expensive.

Amusement in Texas can only be called limited. The people made their work a source of entertainment, with horse racing a prime example. Dancing also whiled away the hours for a few, but a Puritan ethic kept many of the Anglos from enjoying this pastime. This did not bother the Germans much, however. Barbeques, campaign speeches and church attendance might also be mentioned here, along with court day, because all offered diversion. A few touring companies performed recitations and plays. Since most Texans could read, newspapers, especially the *Telegraph* in Houston, and the *Galveston News,* reached many homes, even if they did so many days or months after publication. Temperance societies, the Masonic Lodge, and patriotic societies also provided some relief from the tedium of isolated, rural life in Texas during the 1850s.

And, as the decade closed, politics offered even more frequent diversion, as many came to question the act of union which bound them to abolitionists and other troublemakers in the North. Texas would also have its Sam Houstons, who loved the Union enough to stomach even such people as these, but by 1860 a majority in Texas had had enough of the Union after only fifteen years and were willing to try something else. After all, they had changed their government twice now, and doing so again, many thought, would not be so difficult. Without knowing it, they were preparing the way for a new wave of invaders.

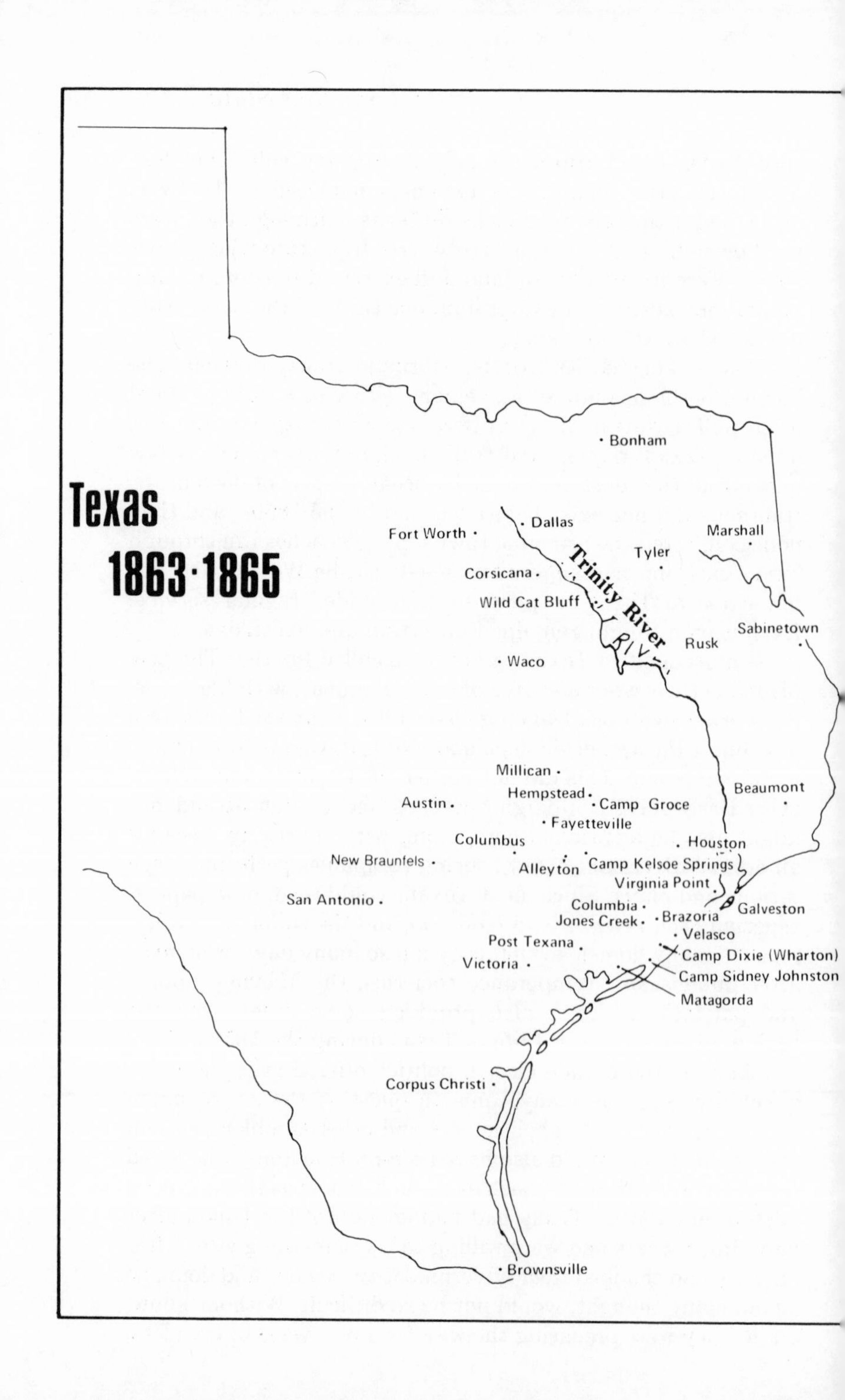
Texas
1863·1865
Bonham
Dallas
Fort Worth
Marshall
Tyler
Trinity River
Corsicana
Wild Cat Bluff
Sabinetown
Rusk
Waco
Millican
Beaumont
Hempstead
Austin
Camp Groce
Fayetteville
Columbus
Houston
New Braunfels
Camp Kelsoe Springs
Alleyton
Virginia Point
San Antonio
Columbia
Galveston
Jones Creek
Brazoria
Velasco
Post Texana
Camp Dixie (Wharton)
Victoria
Camp Sidney Johnston
Matagorda
Corpus Christi
Brownsville

7

Secession, Civil War And Reconstruction

Union with the United States lost its luster for many Texans during the decade of the 1850s. Against the backdrop of such separating wedges as enforcement of the Compromise of 1850 and with the resulting disenchantment among Texans over their loss of so much western land, continuing activities of the abolitionists, especially the violence over the settlement of Kansas, many Texans reflected their southern heritage by affirming their belief in states' rights. This is especially true as it related to slavery and race relations and their acceptance of the principle of secession as the ultimate expression of such "rights".

Hardin R. Runnels' victory in the governor's race in 1857 can be traced to these feelings in Texans, yet Houston's victory in 1859 came despite them. The legislature's selection of the ardent fire eater and secession advocate, Louis T. Wigfall, to serve in the Senate in Houston's place signifies the mood of the majority far more than does the election of Old Sam to the governorship. Houston won office with hard campaigning which invoked memories of his past leadership, but he never masked his true feelings — he was first and last a union man.

The presidential election of 1860 crystalized Texans, as it did most Southerners, into a secession posture. Texas delegates to the Democratic convention at Charleston, South Carolina, including Runnels, Francis R. Lubbock, Guy M. Bryan, R. B. Hubbard, and Tom Ochiltree, joined other Southerners in a demand for a party platform which embraced slavery and which opposed Stephen A. Douglas' majority position on popular sovereignty. Since the Dred Scott decision of 1857, southerners assumed that slavery should be forever secured; they accepted the ruling as confirmation of the right of slave owners to take their property into the territories.

But the presidential election of 1860 alarmed them. The prospect of a victory by the new and radical Republican Party seemed real. Here was a single issue group demanding an end to slavery in the territories and an end eventually to it in the states. The mainstream Democrats at a second convention in Baltimore nominated Douglas and John Cabell Breckenridge of Kentucky received the nomination of still another group of Democrats meeting at Richmond, Virginia. Most Texans supported Breckenridge and joined other southerners in the threat to leave the Union in the event of a victory by the Republican Party and its nominee Abraham Lincoln of Illinois.

Other groups emerged to head off the showdown which would result from a victory by either Lincoln or Breckenridge. The Constitutional Union Party entered the contest, hoping to block an electoral majority and force the election into the House of Representatives where a compromise candidate might be selected. Sam Houston, governor of Texas but a Unionist, tried for the nomination of this party and outdrew John Bell of Tennessee on the first ballot 68.5 to 57 votes. But when Bell was nominated, the Texan even thought of running as an independent candidate, finally deciding against such a move.

At the polls in November Texans voted for Breckenridge by a margin of three to one, emphasizing the secessionists' threat to leave the Union in the event of a Lincoln victory. Breckenridge received 47,548 votes to Bell's total of 15,463; Douglas received only 410 votes. Lincoln's name was not even on the Texas ballot.

In response to the election, on December 20 South Carolina made good its threat to secede from the American union. Georgia, Florida, Alabama, Mississippi, and Louisiana followed by the end of January, and Texas was expected to become the seventh state to secede. It did so over the political corpse of Sam Houston.

Houston attempted to ignore the popular clamor for a secession convention which began as soon as news of South Carolina's action reached the state. After secessionist leaders became convinced that Houston would not call the legislature to consider withdrawal from the Union, they usurped his powers by calling for elections within each judicial district on January 8, 1861, to select delegates for an *ad hoc* secession convention. Houston then summoned the legislature into session with a call on December 17, hoping to steal the thunder of the secessionists. The election would be held on January 8, but the state legislature would meet on January 21, a week before the convention delegates were scheduled to meet on January 28. Houston had hoped that the legislative meeting would prevent the convention from gathering. But his hopes were dashed by the delegate election itself, for many of those elected were also members of the legislature, while a majority of the remainder of the legislative members endorsed the convention.

The secession convention met at Austin on January 28 with the delegates electing Oran M. Roberts to preside. On the second day, they voted 152 to 6 to separate Texas from the United States, subject to popular approval. A committee presented a resolution that disavowed the action of the legislature in 1845, which accepted membership in the Union. By a vote on February 1, they voted to submit the resolution to the voters for final approval in an election to be held February 23.

The February 1 vote was conducted in so tense a session that when J. W. Throckmorton cast a negative vote, hisses and boos rained from the gallery and convention members. Throckmorton's courageous response "Mr. President, when the rabble hiss well may patriots tremble" gave bold testimony that Houston did not stand completely alone.

The convention added a declaration of causes to the secession vote. It included criticism of the Federal government's administration of commonly held territories to the exclusion of southerners, of the provocative activity in Kansas, of the failure to adequately protect Texans from the Indians, of northern hostility to the south and its systems (slavery), of the south's minority status within the Union, and of the election of a president who was committed to the elimination of slavery. With these considerations, the convention adjourned until March 2 to await the result of the vote.

The argument between secessionists and unionists was bitter. The *Galveston News,* and the *Texas Republican* backed the secessionists, while the *Southern Intelligencer* and the *Bastrop Advertiser* attacked them, but the outcome was inevitable: 46,129 in support of secession, with only 14,697 opposed. Ten central Texas counties, a few in North Texas along the Red River, and Angelina County in East Texas, isolated in a sea of secessionism, voted no. Every other county voted affirmative.

The convention gathered again at Austin on March 2 – Texas Independence Day – and within three days confirmed not only separation from the Union, but also Texas' affiliation with the Confederate States of America, newly organized at Montgomery, Alabama, at a convention held in February. The Texas convention had sent unofficial delegates to the Montgomery meeting, and when official word arrived from Texas of the secession vote, the Confederate group voted their acceptance even before a formal request for admission was received.

The state's convention's work continued. On March 16, they summoned all elected officials to take an oath of loyalty to the new government. Houston agonized the entire night of March 15, and the next day, although present in the capitol, he sat silently and heard his name called three times to take the oath, then he heard his office vacated by a convention vote and his lieutenant governor, Edward Clark, sworn in to complete his term. Lincoln offered Houston the use of 2,700 Federal troops in Texas under the command of General David Twiggs, but Houston refused. He had fought for Texas, he stated, and even when Texas was wrong, he would not fight against her. This romantic pledge paralleled a more substantial reason – Houston's desire to avoid bloodshed.

The presence of Twiggs' command bothered many Texans. They made an immediate demand for the Union commander to surrender his troops and all Federal property immediately. Twiggs, a native of Georgia, sympathized with the secessionists, but he tried to avoid betraying his oath to the United States by resigning. Before Twiggs was relieved, Ben McCulloch led an armed group to Army headquarters in San Antonio and demanded the surrender. Twiggs complied to avoid a fight; and his entire command, representing more than ten percent of all Union forces at the time, in effect became prisoners of war, although war did not then technically exist. Most of the men were exchanged before the war began in earnest.

The convention also prepared for elections under Confederate statehood. Party activity, present but weak in the 1850s, disappeared; secessionists controlled the state's affairs completely. Francis R. Lubbock defeated Edward Clark by only 124 votes to become Texas' first Confederate governor, with John M. Crockett, mayor of Dallas, as lieutenant governor.

Lubbock's administration supported the Confederate government enthusiastically, and he left after only one term to serve President Jefferson Davis in other capacities. His successor was Pendleton Murrah of Harrison County, who defeated T. J. Chambers by 17,501 to 12,455 votes in the 1863 election. John Henry Reagan became Texas' highest ranking Confederate civilian official when he received appointment as Postmaster General in Davis' cabinet. Since Reagan accompanied Davis on the flight from Richmond in April, 1865, he filled virtually every cabinet post just prior to their capture in Georgia. Louis T. Wigfall and W. S. Oldham represented Texas in the Confederate Senate.

Lubbock's job as the first Confederate governor of Texas was largely a work of continuing the domestic policies of the Houston-Clark administrations where war conditions permitted and grappling with new difficulties posed by the conflict. He supported the war effort and the Confederate administration without reservation, organized home guards to fight against Indians on the frontier, mustered soldiers for fighting outside the state, and motiviated the legislature to provide for the state's needs. Through a Military Board consisting of the governor, comptroller, and treasurer, Lubbock tried to establish a proper priority: win the war without undue domestic suffering. To purchase needed military supplies, the board attempted to dispose of bonds of the United States held in Texas at the beginning of the war. It suspended debtor laws because so many of the state's wage and income producing workers were serving in the military. It also raised local revenue for the support of military units in the field, and expended Confederate treasury warrants on the state's needs.

Murrah inherited a working state government, but one that suffered the same decline as did its parent government. Lubbock's administration had doubled state taxes to meet its needs. Since so many taxes had been remanded in the previous decade, this increase was a heavy blow. But still the war de-

Typical Texas recruit serving the Confederacy. Note he was armed with a double barreled shotgun and Bowie type knife.

— Courtesy Celia M. Wright

manded more revenue, and needy families of soldiers also increased their demands on the government. The state purchased cotton cards as a relief measure for homemakers to card, spin, and weave their own cotton into cloth. A portion of local tax revenues were designated for the relief of the destitute. Murrah remained a thorough Confederate until the end of the war; he presided over the steady decline of the economic productivity of his state while the public debt increased. War's end coincided with a near-collapse of the state's economy.

Texas performed much better in the fielding of men for military service. Lubbock organized his state into military districts and organized the militia for action under the state's initial commander, General Earl Van Dorn. General Paul Octave Hebert of Louisiana replaced Van Dorn as commander of the Department of Texas, but was himself replaced by General John Bankhead Magruder of Virginia, in November 1862, following a dispute over the conscription laws. Bankhead then commanded until the end of the war. Texas had no need for conscription in 1861. The state census of 1860 listed over 90,000 men between the ages of 18 and 45; of these an estimated 60,00 to 70,000 would serve in the military, over 20,000 volunteering in the first year of the war.

Usually a planter or a person of wealth organized a unit, financed its first operation, and often was elected as its initial commander. Later, conscription added increased numbers of Texans to the army. The first draft selected men between the ages of 18 and 35, but later the draft expanded to include youths of 17 and older men of 45 and 50. Texas' most prominent soldier, Albert Sidney Johnston, commanded the Western Theater of the Confederate Army until his death at the Battle of Shiloh in April, 1862. Other general officers from Texas included Felix Huston Robertson, the only native-born Texan to achieve such rank.

Most Texans served outside the state. Lubbock raised thirty-two companies in 1862, calling them the Texas Brigade. They were joined by their first commander, John Bell Hood of Kentucky, who gave them his name and leadership. Hood's Texas Brigade, later supplemented with units from Arkansas and North Carolina, fought principally in the Eastern Theater under the command of Robert E. Lee. "My Texans," as Lee called them, learned that his respect for their fighting ability often placed them at the center of most of his battles from 1862 until the end of the war. Over 4,000 men served in the unit, but fewer than 700 survived the war.

Another notable unit, Terry's Texas Rangers, under the command of General B. F. Terry, fought primarily in the Western Theater. Lawrence Sullivan Ross's Brigade, organized later in the war, fought with equal valor in the Western Theater and in the Trans-Mississippi Department. This department was created in 1863 to provide a separate military organization for the area after the Union regained control of the Mississippi River line, thus separating the far west of the Confederacy from its political capital and economic control center. General Edmund Kirby Smith of Virginia commanded the Trans-Mississippi Department, including Texas, until the end of the war.

No major battles occurred within Texas, but many significant actions were fought along its borders. As early as May, 1861, W. C. Young led volunteers from the Red River country into Oklahoma to attack Forts Arbuckle, Cobb and Washita. Then in August, John R. Baylor led a group into southern New Mexico and proclaimed the territory as far west as Tucson as the Confederate territory of Arizona with himself as governor. And General H. H. Sibley, with General Tom Green along, successfully attacked Valverde with a force of nearly 4,000 men on February 2, 1862. In March, however, he was repulsed by Union forces under Edward R. Canby at Glorietta, and New Mexico and Arizona were therefore effectively saved from all Confederate encroachment.

The Federal blockade became effective on the Texas coast in July, 1861, and the Union forces occupied Galveston in October, 1862. Magruder attacked on January 1, 1863, from a troop concentration at Virginia Point across a railroad bridge and with other men on two flat-bottomed riverboats with cotton bales lining the decks for protection. He succeeded in retaking the island, and Confederate Texans held it until 1865.

Texas' most ambitious battle occurred at Sabine Pass, a narrow inlet permitting access from the Gulf of Mexico to Sabine Lake, a saltwater empoundment of the waters of the Sabine and Neches rivers. Both rivers were navigable to rail lines. In September, 1862, Federal naval personnel forced the Confederates to abandon Sabine Pass, but it was soon reoccupied by an artillery battery commanded by Lieutenant Dick Dowling, a Houston saloon keeper. In September, 1863, General Nathaniel Banks attempted to send seventeen Union naval vessels and a force of over 1,500 soldiers through Sabine Pass to attack the interior. Dowling's guns sank or disabled two vessels in the main channel, thus blocking the way for the remainder of the ships and preventing the disembarking of the Union soldiers, who were then withdrawn to New Orleans.

The Battle of Sabine Pass was hailed by Jefferson Davis as the most significant action of the war at a time when he was grasping at straws after the defeats at Vicksburg and Gettysburg. The results even had a negative affect on Wall Street stocks and American credit in England. General Banks was more successful farther down the coast. His forces succeeded in capturing or controlling every port from the Rio Grande to just below Galveston, including Corpus Christi, Aransas Pass, and Indianola.

Banks' last attempt to invade Texas occurred in 1864. He advanced up the Red River, intending to rendezvous with forces under General Frederick Steele from Little Rock to capture North Texas. Steele was repulsed by Confederates under Van Dorn, and General Richard Taylor, son of former President Zachary Taylor, stopped Banks at Mansfield. East Texans fought as civilians, often with pikes and clubs, in this action to prevent the invasion of their state. Banks withdrew to Pleasant Hill, Louisiana where Taylor then unsuccessfully attacked the Federal positions, but Banks withdrew to the Mississippi anyway.

In a final action, John S. Ford led forces against black Union soldiers at Palmito Ranch near Brownsville in May, 1865, nearly a month after all other forces surrendered.

On the other hand, serious fighting did take place in Texas between Texans and Indians. Texans expected the Confederate army to police Indians as the American army had done before the war, but they soon learned that the high command in far off Virginia had too many Union soldiers on their hands to worry about Texas Indians. Governor Lubbock therefore organized state troops under James M. Norris for this service.

Norris attempted regular patrols in the Indian country, but these proved too easy for the Indians to evade, so his successor, J.E. McCord, substituted irregular scouting expeditions which proved more successful. As men organized for Indian service, they were repeatedly transferred to the regular army and service outside the state. Finally, J. W. Throckmorton organized a force which included many like himself who would fight Indians but not Union soldiers. The most significant Indian action was at Adobe Walls, where Union and Confederate soldiers combined to fight Comanches. The most unsuccessful action occurred at Dove Creek in January, 1864, when 370 state troops attacked 1,400 friendly Kickapoos en route to Mexico from Indian Territory. The Texans' heavy losses made them regret the attack.

Texans who remained at home did not suffer the ravages of war as did their fellow Confederates in Virginia and Tennessee, but still they had their problems. Quite a few Texans did not like the Confederate affiliation. Some, like Houston, remained relatively quiet; others such as financier S. M. Swenson, left the state, depriving Texas of needed leadership both during and after the war; and some, such as E. J. Davis, organized Union forces to fight in Texas.

Many Germans disliked the Confederacy because they favored Union nationalism and disliked slavery; often they refused to volunteer or be conscripted, and some tried to escape to Mexico. One such group was apprehended and massacred. But many Germans also served with distinction in the Confederate army. In 1862, a Peace Party, a secret society, was organized in North Texas. It aroused fear in loyal Confederates who hanged over forty Peace Party members at Gainesville and other places for disloyalty. In 1864 the North Texas area also became a gathering place for army deserters and n'er-do-wells and posed a police problem for the state.

In 1863 a conference of western state representatives at Marshall produced a plan to exchange Confederate cotton in Mexico for needed war materials. The plan called for the Confederate government to take over the trade by purchasing half of each planter's cotton and exempting the rest from impressment, to make sure the south's major economic resource would contribute to the war effort. Murrah's government devised an alternate "state plan," which called for the Texas government to transport cotton to the border, return half to the owner, and secure the remainder with state bonds. The Confederate Congress pre-empted the state's power in this area with a specific act, irritating some Texans.

The battle of Pleasant Hill, April 9, 1864 in which Confederate units from Texas took part. From sketch by C.E.H. Bonwill.

Cotton production declined steadily during the war years as more and more men entered the military services. Women, minors, draft exemptees, and some objectors continued to work and produce as best they could. But as state revenue dwindled and Confederate currency inflated, their lot was often difficult. Such necessities as salt became scarce, and people had to return to their pioneer ways to survive. They used corncob ashes as a substitute for soda, parched rye, okra or acorns for coffee, and made their own cloth. Murrah was inaugurated wearing a homespun suit partially to indicate its acceptability and partially because so many others had to wear such apparel. And paper grew scarce, forcing some newspapers to cease operations.

Texas had little industry before the war but learned to develop it from necessity. Arms works were established at Austin, Tyler, and other places; Marshall supported new factories; iron works functioned in East Texas; and the state penitentiary became the state's leading producer of cloth.

Texas became a haven for refugees from other southern states, and a shipping point for slaves whose owners were seeking to move them from conquered territory. Both migrations provided additional problems for the Texans, and many of the immigrants were not too happy with their new home. Kate Stone, of Brokenburn Plantation in eastern Louisiana, came to Tyler following the Vicksburg campaign and called her haven "the dark corner of the Confederacy." This assessment is perhaps too harsh. Texas functioned well considering its many difficulties, but its war problems were only preliminaries for the difficulties of Reconstruction.

The war ended for Texans at different times. For the survivors of Hood's Brigade and other Texans in the Army of Northern Virginia, the end came with Lee's surrender to General U.S. Grant at Appomattox on April 9, 1865. For Terry's Texas Rangers and others with the Army of Tennessee, it concluded with General J.E. Johnston's surrender to General W.T. Sherman in Bentonville, North Carolina on April 19. And General Edmund Kirby Smith surrendered the Department of the Trans-Mississippi, including Texas, on June 2.

But for most Texans, the day to remember was June 19. On that day, General Gordon Granger, representing his theater commander, General Philip Sheridan, arrived in Galveston with 1,800 Federal troops to declare the war ended and all war proclamations, including the end of African slavery, effective. White and black Texans alike would one day view this as a day of liberation, but for decades most whites seethed with resentment and most blacks did not understand fully what it meant or have an opportunity to exercise their freedom. In time it became a day of celebration for blacks, a kind of Fourth-of-July of their own.

Reconstruction means many things. Political reconstruction meant reorganizing Texas, whatever its current posture, as a constituent of the American union, and it concluded by 1870; economic reconstruction meant the resurrection and diversification of the state's economy, and this was not accomplished until after the turn of the century, if then; social reconstruction, the reorganizing of Texans into an equal society, still strives for completion.

There were five plans of reconstruction: the Lincoln "ten percent" plan, the Wade-Davis Bill, the Johnson Plan, the Fourteenth Amendment, and finally, the Reconstruction Acts of 1867. Both Lincoln's and Johnson's plans were regarded as too lenient by the Radical Republicans, and the presidents in turn regarded the Radical's three plans as much too harsh.

Lincoln announced his plan as an act of the war itself, as a way to get reconstruction started. He would have required only ten percent of those voting in 1860 to swear an oath of future loyalty to the Union; then they could begin the business of drafting a constitution, which would accept the war-time proclamation, and apply for statehood. Lincoln announced his plan in 1863, and appointed Andrew Jackson Hamilton as provisional governor to begin the operation in Texas. Hamilton, however, came no closer than New Orleans because of Banks' failure to take any part of Texas from Confederate control.

The proponents of the first radical alternative, the Wade-Davis Bill of 1864, made their plan deliberately impossible to keep the states out of the Union until the war ended so they could control the process. The bill required fifty percent of the 1860 voters to take the oath, and the "iron-clad" oath at that, requiring voters and delegates at a constitutional convention to swear they had never been disloyal to the Union or served a Confederate state in any way.

Johnson's plan, announced after his succession following

Lincoln's death in April, 1865, specified no percentage, and again required only future loyalty. Because the governments organizing under his auspices failed to demonstrate that they were sorry for the war or to admit fault in its beginning, and because Radicals disliked Johnson, those states which attempted to re-enter the Union under his plan were rejected. The Radicals countered with the Fourteenth Amendment which defined citizenship for all whites and blacks, temporarily deprived high Confederate officials of their citizenship, and attempted to secure a place in society for the freedmen through "due process" and "equal protection" clauses.

When all former Confederate states except Tennessee rejected this amendment, a condition of regaining status in the Union, the Radicals could turn to northern voters with evidence of southern defiance. The result was the final plan, the Reconstruction Acts of 1867, which defined all former states except Tennessee as conquered territory, structured them as provinces under military governors, and attempted to rebuild southern society in their own image with one exception — they insisted on complete black suffrage in the South, although no northern state had complete black suffrage.

To Texans, the road to restored statehood through these cross currents proved a torturous journey. At war's end most were weary and did not want to continue the strife. The social fabric had nearly disintegrated; paper money was worthless, land values declined precipitiously, and crops went unplanted. A mob attacked the state treasury in Austin, thinking its resources vast and rightfully theirs, but the looters found less than $5,000 in the safe. When slave owners learned of General Granger's proclamation, many deliberately did not inform their slaves, hoping to retain their labor if not their loyalty or ownership. Texans, in addition, were buffeted by changing political orders.

Granger was to be followed by other soldiers, nearly 50,000 of them within two years. Texas received far more troops than other Confederate states, partly because it was bigger and still had an Indian frontier, and partly as an arm of United States foreign policy. French interference in Mexican affairs while Americans killed each other had to be dealt with at the end of the war, and this show of force on the Texas border caused the French to withdraw. Some of these soldiers, including General

George A. Custer, who headquartered at the Deaf and Dumb Asylum in Austin, were accepted and even liked. Many were not, particularly those who lingered for four years.

Hamilton finally arrived in Austin on August 9. He appointed Unionists James Bell as secretary of state and William Alexander as attorney general, and other officers to help in the implementation of President Johnson's plan. Hamilton called for an election on January 8, 1866, to select delegates for a constitutional convention which would meet February 7. The convention was required to abolish slavery, provide for the status of freedmen, repudiate secession, and renounce both state and Confederate debt incurred for the war effort.

The Convention was composed of ex-Confederates, old-time Unionists, and many conservatives who wanted an end to trouble. They elected J. W. Throckmorton, who blended all three positions, to preside. They dodged the secession issue by presuming that the Confederate loss served as *de facto* evidence that the movement had failed, but not that it was illegal. They refused to ratify the Thirteenth Amendment, which outlawed slavery, on the grounds that the Amendment was already in effect. They did provide for the security of black persons, but limited their free access to the courts, to suffrage, and to office holding. The convention cancelled all state debt, not just the war debt, but it approved other state actions not done in connection with war. These measures and other amendments to the Constitution of 1845 were adopted and submitted to the people in an election on June 25.

In a related election for state officers, Throckmorton was elected governor over E. M. Pease, and G. W. Jones was elected lieutenant governor. These men provided Texas with what civilian government it had, along with the ever-present military government until 1869 without ever being recognized by the Congress, although President Johnson accepted them with a proclamation on August 30, 1866.

The new state legislature elected as senators David G. Burnet and Oran M. Roberts, the latter having presided at the secession convention. These officers, with three representatives, presented the new constitution to the Congress, which promptly rejected it because of discriminatory provisions concerning blacks and because of its failure to ratify either the Thirteenth or Fourteenth Amendments. The new state legislature had ignored John H. Reagan's persuasive arguments that Texas should ratify and get back in the Union as painlessly as possible. The Radicals had some cause for their rejection. Nothing in the constitution or the legislative appointments reflected the slightest change of heart by Texans beyond acceptance of military defeat. The role of blacks in the new society would hardly be different from their role in the pre-war society except in title.

The Radicals in Congress had no intention of abandoning the freedmen to the caprice of unrepentent southerners, nor of ignoring their potential votes. The Freedmen's Bureau became their agency for social reform and for policing black-white relations. The Bureau was directed in Texas by E. M. Gregory, an enthusiastic reformer. Gregory's agents assisted blacks in labor contract negotiations and enforcement, taught literacy skills in Bureau schools, and distributed direct relief when necessary.

Although the Whites resented the agents' intervening, to the Bureau's credit it performed many valuable services and its relief work benefited whites as well as blacks. One reason for white opposition lay in the political action of the Loyal Union League, an organization which existed to recruit blacks for political activities under subsequent state governments. Whites assumed that Bureau agents doubled as Loyal Union League recruiters, which was sometimes the case.

The Throckmorton government's authority was eliminated by the Reconstruction Acts of 1867, although it continued to function under military supervision. These acts removed the legal question of secession and statehood by declaring all former Confederate states legally dead. They were declared territories under the authority of Congress and the military. The former states were organized into five districts — Texas joined Louisiana and Arkansas in District 5 — and soldiers controlled their affairs. General Sheridan controlled the district through General Charles Griffin, commander of the sub-province of Texas. Later General W. S. Hancock and Edward R. Canby commanded the district, and General J. J. Reynolds commanded Texas.

One of Griffin's first acts was to replace Throckmorton with E. M. Pease following a disagreement concerning pardons for all blacks in the penitentiary at Huntsville. Griffin assumed that the blacks were in prison for being black rather than for actual

Edmund J. Davis, Republican Reconstruction Governor of Texas. From a portrait in the Texas State Capitol Rotunda.

— Courtesy the Institute of Texan Cultures

criminal acts, but Throckmorton refused to pardon them, and was fired. Pease then assisted Griffin's soldiers in registering voters for an election of delegates to a new constitutional convention. Voting registrars generally enrolled blacks regardless of literacy or other qualifications, and refused to enroll whites, whose loyalty they suspected, and who were mostly Democrats. The whites enjoyed a slight edge, 53,633 to 49,479; nevertheless, the election was held over a five-day period from February 10 through 14, and many whites stayed away, hoping to invalidate the results because the Reconstruction Acts required a majority to participate. This effort failed when some Democrats defected at the last minute.

The constitutional convention met in Austin in early June, 1868, with ninety-four members, including ten blacks. For weeks they argued over the issue of *ab initio,* or the legality of acts of the Confederate state of Texas not directly connected to the war. At stake were such issues as the validity of marriages and bond disposition, among others. The Radicals under E. J. Davis wanted to declare secession and all other subsequent acts invalid; Moderates under A. J. Hamilton favored declaring only secession and acts done to aid the war effort invalid, leaving other matters as legal functions. Between arguments the convention also chartered railroads, investigated lawlessness, discussed selling state property, and questioned the conduct of its own members.

In late summer all sides agreed to defer the convention's work until after the fall elections, each side hoping to gain from either a Republican or Democratic victory in November. This postponement also required the levying of a special tax to fund the extra session. Ulysses S. Grant's victory over the Democratic nominee Horatio Seymour strengthened the Moderate Republicans. When the convention met in January, they fell to arguing again.

E. J. Davis wanted to separate Texas into two states, east and west Texas, to disassociate the western portions from the Old South-oriented east, and to control that section himself. Hamilton successfully blocked this move. Davis also lost on *ab initio.* The convention voted to recognize as valid all state actions not connected to the war disfranchisement. He had wanted to defranchise all who had supported the Confederacy, but the Moderates insisted on allowing an oath of future loyalty except for those few ex-Confederate officials disqualified by the Fourteenth Amendment.

In a rush to finish their work, the convention adjourned on February 8, 1869, by turning all their records and resolutions over to General Reynolds, who appointed a committee to draft the constitution. Despite this unique and questionable procedure, the resulting document, although short-lived, emerged as Texas' best constitution. It centralized authority, confirmed white and black suffrage (although not female), assigned the governor a four-year term with broad appointive and administrative power, abolished many local courts, and did more for public education than any constitution or legislature both before or since by guaranteeing education at least one quarter of all state revenues.

Davis and the Radicals tried to get Grant and the Congress to reject the constitution. Failing in that, he determined to run the government of Texas under it, and this time he prevailed. In an election held on November 30 Davis defeated Hamilton by a vote of 39,910 to 39,002 in an election in which General Reynolds counted all the votes. Reynolds certified this result on January 8, 1870, and evidentally destroyed all the ballots. Hamilton, of course, complained that he had been cheated out of the election and he was probably correct, although fraud had been committed by both sides. The electorate also ratified the new constitution, 72,466 to 4,928. Pease resigned in protest over Reynolds' relationship with the Radicals, and Davis assumed an *ad interim* administration until his elected office began later in the year.

Davis convened the legislature on February 8, and that body ratified the Thirteenth and Fourteenth Amendments and elected Morgan Hamilton and J. W. Flanagan as senators. On March 30, 1870, President Grant approved Congress' act of admitting Texas into the Union. But Reconstruction lingered.

Davis dominated the Thirteenth Legislature, which met in three sessions in 1870 and 1871, because he had strong support from the Radical Republicans in Washington and from the military in Texas. His legislative program, termed the "Obnoxious Acts" by the Democrats and Moderate Republicans, made this first and only Republican governor for one hundred years anathema in the eyes of generations of Texans. Modern evaluations have found some good in his program, however. At the time, Speaker of the House Ira Evans so opposed the passage of Davis' program that the governor's supporters removed Evans from office.

The "Obnoxious Acts" included creation of a state police force and a state militia under the governor's direct authority, the authorization for the governor to patronize a state printer and to place public notices in newspapers of his choice, the enabling of the governor to appoint all vacancies in public office including those created by the adoption of the constitution — nearly 8,000 positions—and the postponement of state elections for a year to bring them into synchronization with Federal elections, thereby giving all current office holders, mostly Republicans, an extra year in office.

These acts confirmed Davis in the vast power awarded to him by Reynold's count of the vote. In actual practice Davis utilized his powers with some discretion, doubtless motivated by the knowledge that a majority of the state opposed them. Some of these provisions were needed. There was a problem of Indian defense, and the militia did perform some service in that area. There was a problem with lawlessness in Texas during the Reconstruction, and the Special Police, particularly those under the command of Captain L. H. McNelly, did yeoman law enforcement service. Davis' appointments, while always made in the light of party patronage, placed many good men in office. And Davis relented to popular demand and permitted elections in the fall of 1871.

The Republican governor was denounced by Democrats for his arbitrary declaration of martial law in Limestone, Freestone, Hill, and Walker counties. In Limestone and Freestone counties his action followed the killing of a black policeman. Davis sent over 100 militia into the area to stop an armed rebellion which failed to materialize anyway. However, in Hill and Walker counties, the militia were needed to maintain order.

Davis was also criticized for granting bonds to railroads as construction subsidies. Bonds were used because the constitution forbade land subsidies. Actually, Davis had opposed the legislative authorization of these bonds, but they were deemed necessary to help solve the state's genuine need for improved transportation, and the Democrats found it convenient to blame Davis for the expense. In this way the International Railroad Company, the Southern Pacific, and the Southern Transcontinental Railway received eight percent bonds to finance construction.

Democrats and conservative Republicans opposed Davis from the first. As early as September, 1871, delegates gathered in Austin to protest the fiscal extravagance and high taxes of the Republican regime. When elections were held in October, the Democrats won all four seats in the national House of Representatives, and the following year, Democratic presidential candidate Horace Greeley carried the state over incumbent president U.S. Grant. The Democrats again claimed all members of the House delegation and regained control of the Texas legislature.

Then they began to strip Davis of the powers obtained through the "Obnoxious Acts," repealing the police act in 1873, restricting the governor's authority to declare martial law, and reducing his appointive powers. The legislature also decentralized the public school system which Davis had begun under the Constitution of 1869, and provided for the election of state officers for the first Tuesday of December, 1873. This latter act changed the electoral process from a four-day to a one-day election.

The Democratic Party met in Austin in September and selected Richard Coke, a former Confederate army captain, as its candidate for governor and Richard Hubbard, also a former Confederate officer, as lieutenant governor. Davis received his party's nomination, and a hot election result. On election day Coke received 85,549 votes to Davis' 42,663. Both sides engaged in widespread election misconduct, but there is little doubt that an overwhelming majority of Texans preferred Coke.

Davis refused to relinquish his office. He brought suit in the state courts, which were still staffed by judges of his appointment, to declare the election invalid because it was held on a single day in violation of the constitutional requirement for a four-day election. The court agreed with the governor and declared the election void on the basis of the placing of a semicolon in the relevant constitutional clause, thereby earning itself the sobriquet, "the semi-colon court."

Davis informed Coke that he would not surrender the office and he and his supporters occupied the main floor of the capitol and requested military aid from President Grant. Austin was poised for battle, and if a fight had resulted, troops probably would have been dispatched. When none resulted, de-

"The Capitol at Austin in 1870" from an engraving in Pictorial History of Texas.
— Courtesy Institute of Texan Cultures

spite the presence of armed men who would have seized the capitol if Coke had asked them to do so, Grant refused to send the soldiers. On the evening of January 13, 1874, the Democrats gained access to the second floor of the capitol by using a ladder and, late at night, inaugurated Richard Coke as Texas' redeemer governor. Davis was forced to yield when his militia units defected.

Coke's administration continued the undoing of the work of the Repulicans begun earlier by the legislature. They replaced the "semi-colon" justices with new members, and Coke appointed Oran M. Roberts as the new chief justice. Additional judges appointed by Davis were removed and replaced with Democrats. Railroad bonds were voided, and land grants, authorized by constitutional amendment in 1873, were substituted. Also, operating expenses of the government were cut in half.

Coke called for a revision of the constitution. The legislature delayed for a time, fearing reprisal from the Grant administration, then attempted to amend the existing constitution. But only the Senate agreed to the amendments. In its next session, however, the legislature issued a call for an election of delegates for a constitutional convention to meet in August, 1875. This election endorsed the convention and selected ninety delegates, including six blacks. Democrats counted seventy-five of the delegates in their party, while the Republicans claimed the remaining fifteen delegates. Most were farmers; indeed, the strongest lobby at the convention was the forty delegates who belonged to the Patrons of Husbandry, or the Grange, and their parsimonious influence can be detected in nearly every clause of the document which resulted from their efforts. Lawyers also constituted a significant minority.

The overriding philosophy of the convention seems to have been a direct reaction to the Davis administration. The delegates determined to remove as much power as possible from the governor, leave the legislature only what it was forced to concede for the conduct of the state's business, and then to try to keep the legislature from meeting except when absolutely necessary. The delegates began their work by reducing their per diem to $5.00, or $3.00 less than the legislature received. They likewise reduced the pay of the governor and every other elected official, and permitted the legislature to meet only

Confederate General Robert E. Lee received part of his military training on the Texas frontier in the 1850s.

every other year except by special call. The governor's appointive powers were greatly reduced; the comptroller, treasurer, land commissioner, and attorney general were to be elected officers. The governor's authority to declare martial law was limited. He could veto laws and exercise the item veto on specific parts of legislation. And while he was instructed to "faithfully execute" all laws of the legislature, his powers to do so were greatly limited by the constitution itself.

The convention specified that all court judges from Justice of the Peace to the Supreme Court would be elected, and that the number of courts be reduced. It also established a dual system for civil and criminal proceedings at the appellate level.

The constitution permitted land grants to subsidize railroads, and reauthorized a homestead program for the settlement of western lands. The delegates debated the use of a poll tax as a requirement for voting, then rejected the idea, and also defeated a move to extend the suffrage to women. By omitting many offices created by the previous constitution, the delegates sought to limit state activities and to save money. This is especially evident in the school system, where the delegates undid the best work of the previous constitution by abolishing the office of state school superintendent, by eliminating compulsory attendance, by establishing segregated schools, and by making no provision for local funding. State funding was also reduced. The farmers proved a bit more generous with higher education by continuing the land endowment for a future University of Texas and increasing lands reserved for this use.

Despite its rejection by both the Democratic and Republican conventions, the Constitution of 1876, still in use in Texas, received public endorsement by a margin of 136,606 to 56,652 on February 15. Its restrictive nature was perhaps appropriate for the times, but it has limited the state in the modern period.

The fact that many measures handled by the legislature must eventually be approved as constitutional amendments by the people has provided a plebiscite on significant issues, but at the same time it has prevented the legislature from handling routine matters itself. For example, the authorization of hospital districts in communities is hardly a matter of statewide concern, but such matters may be handled only as amendments. By 1983, nearly 400 amendments had been proposed, and nearly 250 of them have been approved. And the constitution endured. Efforts in 1919 and 1975 to replaced it were rebuffed, mostly because the revisions were judged even worse than the Constitution of 1876.

The era of secession, Civil War, and political Reconstruction closed with the adoption of the restructured constitution. Once more control of Texas affairs lay in the hands of conservative, now mostly native, people. But these last invaders, the soldiers and Radicals, had changed much. The place of blacks in society could never be the same, although their role would change still more in the decades ahead. Farmers reigned, but industrial development was not far behind, and by the end of the century would prove a strong competitor for control. Women emerged from the period in a somewhat strengthened, if still secondary, position. For the moment, perhaps, Texans thought their house was back in order; they could not have imagined the changes that would soon come from many directions.

Indians attacking a Butterfield Overland coach on the Texas plains. Sketch by Theodore R. Davis from Harper's Weekly.

— Courtesy Institute of Texan Cultures

The Western Frontier

The westerning impulse rivals nationalism and reform as the primary motivational force in America. Even in times of national stress or actual combat with foreign enemies, the nation spread westward in continuation of its frontier experience. Texas was populated in the four decades preceding the American Civil War by such forces; and even during that conflict and the Reconstruction period which followed, Texans continued to advance the frontier line. Until the end of the nineteenth century, Texans and other Americans rushed to complete the occupation, settlement, and exploitation of their frontier.

Indians headed the list of impediments to such expansion; or perhaps better stated, conquest and removal of the Indians constitutes a fundamental part of the frontier process itself. By treaty or weapons, the Texan-American conquest of the land and its Indian population was necessary to render any territory suitable for civilian settlement, for ranching, farming, or other economic enterprise. During the war, Confederate Texans had expected their central government to fight the Indians for them and had learned that they must do so themselves; at war's end, they expected the Federal government to send its soldiers to Texas for that purpose, but again they learned that they must help themselves, for a while at least. Most Federal soldiers in Texas stayed busy with such tasks as voter registration and maintaining order in the eastern communities, or they were posted on the Rio Grande for anticipated action against the French in Mexico. Perhaps also the memory of

David Twiggs' forced surrender in 1861 rankled some commanders and made them reluctant to fight Indians to protect the Texans.

Time, and the Indians themselves, removed these obstacles. Two actions freed the soldiers for other duties: the French quit Mexico rather than fight the Americans; and the Reconstruction process finally produced a civilian government. Most importantly, though, renewed and continued Indian raids, especially by Comanches and Kiowas, forced the United States army into action beside the Texans' Special Force, and later the Rangers, to eliminate the Indians from Texas almost completely. In 1865, seventy-eight people were killed by raiding Indians, and another 162 were killed in 1866 and during the first half of 1867. The war, plus the Indian activity, had effectively stopped the advance of the settlement line; in the period immediately after the war, the line actually receded in some areas. Wise and Denton counties both suffered significantly during this period, and Waco and Gainesville also became outposts as a result of the resettlement.

Despite the political differences of the regime, state forces under Throckmorton, Pease, and Davis did their best to defend the frontier against the common enemy. In 1867 the Federal government as well as the state government again addressed the problem. Federal agents negotiated the Treaty of Medicine Lodge Creek with leaders of the Comanche and Kiowa tribes. It created a 3 million acre reservation for these peoples in the Indian Territory. These agents also agreed to support the Indians by annuities and to restrain unauthorized whites from coming on reservation lands.

Renegade bands continued to raid in Texas. Some did so from habit and others continued the raids because their leaders had not participated in the negotiations. Also the activities of the Comancheros caused an increase of such activity. The Comancheros were traders from New Mexico who received stolen cattle, horses, and other goods from the Indians in exchange for weapons, ammunition, and whiskey. In 1872 a desperate Texas rancher named John Hittson raided their stronghold to regain stolen cattle.

As a result of continued Indian resistance, the United States Army re-established a line of frontier forts in 1868. Soldiers reoccupied older posts abandoned at the beginning of the Civil War and established new posts, including Forts Concho and Griffin. Mostly they staffed these posts with "Buffalo Soldiers," or black troops under the command of white officers, but the small number of troops and the wide separation of the posts kept them from top efficiency.

President U.S. Grant tried a new tack in 1869. He accepted the "Quaker Peace Policy," or the employment of Quaker Indian agents, on the assumption that the Quakers could establish the same kind of relationship with Texas Indians as they had effected in Pennsylvania two centuries earlier. Time and technology, however, made this impossible. The Texas Comanches and Kiowas had the use of horses and firearms — two powerful forces of resistance — and they were less advanced than the forest Indians of Pennsylvania. More important, they had a two-century history of clashes with frontier Europeans as a cultural inheritance.

Texas agent Lawrie Tatum did his best, but he had to admit that policing Texas Indians was a military job. So a more aggressive military policy was adopted, along with greater state activity, particularly by the Rangers after their resurrection in 1874. This policy of force, and the extermination of the buffalo by hide hunters, finally controlled the Texas Indians. The dangers of facing the Federal troops or the Rangers, plus the need to depend on the reservation for food supplies, restricted most Indians after the decade of the 1870s.

In 1871 the Salt Creek Massacre signalled an end to the Quaker Peace Policy and the beginning of the final push against the Indians. Generals William T. Sherman and Randolph B. Marcy visited Texas in April of that year on an inspection tour. They themselves narrowly escaped death when an Indian raid led by a chieftain named Satanta struck a military wagon train following the generals to Fort Richardson. All but five of the soldiers were killed. Realizing that their own train had narrowly escaped the same fate, Sherman and Marcy committed the military to a more active policy. Sherman personally went to the Fort Sill reservation to arrest Satanta and returned him to Texas to stand trial for murder. Satanta was convicted and sentenced to life imprisonment at Huntsville, but Governor E.J. Davis paroled him in 1873. Sherman was outraged. He wrote Davis that he hoped that the governor would be Satanta's first victim when he started raiding again.

Davis escaped that fate, but Satanta soon took the warpath again. Colonel R. S. Mackenzie, commander of the Fourth Cavalry, drew the assignment to end the Indian problem in Texas with force. Mackenzie had served under Grant during the Civil War and was regarded as one of the brightest young officers in the army. He came to Texas in 1868, as head of the Fourth Cavalry, and continued to rise in the estimation of his commanders as an aggressive leader. Mackenzie first led punitive expeditions against the plains Indians in 1871 and 1872, sometimes fighting but always chasing the Comanches from the area, reducing the number of raids and the loss of life and property significantly. In 1873 he moved to the Rio Grande border in the Eagle Pass area to push Kickapoo and Lipan Apache Indians into Mexico, and his tactics all but eliminated Indian problems in that area.

Mackenzie became the chief American officer in a great roundup of Indians in 1874, the last major Indian campaign in Texas. Colonel Nelson A. Miles led a column of soldiers southward from Kansas to rendezvous with other columns led by Colonels William Price from New Mexico, and John Davidson from Fort Sill, and Colonel George Buel's command from Fort Griffin. Mackenzie's column moved directly to the High Plains. Over 3,000 men took the field under these various commands to round up the Indians and herd them to the reservation in present Oklahoma. Mackenzie captured the greatest number of Comanches, who had taken refuge in the Palo Duro Canyon. His troopers scaled down the canyon's walls and captured over 1,400 horses, which Mackenzie ordered shot to prevent the Indians from escaping. The Indians were then marched to their home on the reservation. What kept most of them there afterwards was the absence of the buffalo as a food supply on the Great Plains.

The buffalo hunters came to Texas in the 1870s after successful hunts in Kansas. Buffalo ranged over most of the continent before the coming of the Europeans, although their numbers were greatest in the plains country where abundant grasses supported massive herds. Coronado had reported sighting these animals, which he called cattle, in 1540, and suggested that some day the plains might be good for ranching. The buffalo takes its name from the French explorers who

Texas traveler makes stop at Fredericksburg.

— Courtesy Institute of Texan Cultures

first saw the animals in the Great Lakes country and called them *bouefs*, or beef.

By the mid-nineteenth century, Anglo-Americans had already harvested or chased the buffalo from the eastern part of the continent. Some of them were harvested as a part of the fur trade, for the heavy hides and thick hair could be made into warm winter clothing by whites as well as Indians. The Indians, however, used the whole buffalo: they ate most of what was not hide or bone, then found such uses for even these remains as shelter, clothing, tools, weapons, and decorations. The whites wanted only the hides, although the meat could be eaten, and the tongue could even be considered a delicacy.

When the railroad construction crews of the 1860s required meat to eat, hunters such as William F. "Buffalo Bill" Cody hired out to the construction companies to provide buffalo meat for the camp cooks to prepare. Cody alone reportedly killed over 4,000 buffalo for this use. A boom in this extravagant industry developed in the 1870s and 1880s when tanners learned that the heavy leather could be worked as well as cow hides. As the hunters exhausted the supply of buffalo in Kansas, they moved north and south, pursuing the great migrating herds. Hunters would work their way up wind of a herd and pick off the leaders to establish a stand, then shoot animal after animal with .50 caliber Sharps rifles until sometimes their weapons would overheat.

Skinners then took over. They removed the hides, stretched the skins by tying them to stakes, and scraped off the excess meat after it rotted. The hides would then be stacked for a wagon ride to market. The meat and bones of the animals would generally be left to rot on the plains, although a rich trade later flourished briefly in gathering the bleached buffalo bones for grinding into a calcium fertilizer.

Among the earliest hunters in Texas were Bob and Jim Cator, who arrived in the Panhandle country in 1872. J. Wright and John Mooar, George Causey, Joe S. McCombs, and even Bat Masterson and Billy Dixon from Dodge City soon followed. Dodge City hunters headquartered at Adobe Walls, and even established a crude town with A. C. Myers and James Hanrahan promising stores and saloons to service the hunters.

The Indians naturally resisted this threat to their food

supply, and a raid on the Adobe Walls encampment became one of the precipitants of the Mackenzie raid. On June 27, 1874 a band of over 700 Comanches and Kiowas attacked the hunters at Adobe Walls. The most widely recounted incident connected with this unsuccessful attempt to chase the hunters from the region was a shot by Billy Dixon which felled an Indian on horseback at a distance of one mile. The Indians withdrew when they could not flush the hunters out of the Adobe Walls and knew that more whites were on the way.

By the end of the decade the buffalo were mostly gone from the Texas plains, and with them the Indians as well. This removal of Indian and buffalo made way for ranching and farming in the same region.

Although it grew from Spanish beginnings, the Cattle Kingdom is uniquely a Texas story. It was nurtured by the Mexican *charro* and eventually spread over most of the western United States and into central Canadian provinces. The reign of the cattle barons was also brief, from the 1860s until the 1890s, but Spanish priests and ranchers and settlers had prepared the way as early as the sixteenth century. And, beef production remains an important industry in Texas today.

What primarily distinguishes the Cattle Kingdom from the cattle industry was its method of working the animals, especially the great herds that trailed northward in the post-Civil War period to supply the markets of the east. The romanticized cowboy, always on horseback, characterized this kingdom. There were as many cattle actually raised for farm use and for the market east of the Mississippi River as west of that continental divide, but they were worked only on foot, in small numbers, and behind enclosures. Their total numbers were great, but the perspective remained small. In Texas and in the west, cattle were worked from the horse and herds might number into the thousands. Fences came later.

The first Texas cattle came with the *entrata* of Coronado and Onate, and with the soldiers and priests who claimed the land for Spain. Mission Indians learned ranching skills as a part of their reduction to help prepare the country for Spanish settlers who would arrive later. The bovine descendants of the first stock unloaded by Cortez at Vera Cruz walked and grazed across Mexico and into Texas, took hold, changed with time into longhorn, and seemed to multiply geometrically. It was often said that they did best when left alone.

The result was a great natural resource by the time the later Europeans arrived in Texas. The riparian ranches of Jose Escandon, located along the Rio Grande as early as the 1740s, centered the Mexican industry in that border country. And the missions still herded cattle, as many as 15,000 head at Espiritu Santo and 10,000 head at Rosario.

When the Anglos arrived in Texas they found the cattle roaming freely, although some presumably belonged to Mexican ranchers. The Americans took as many as they wanted to eat and used the hides and horns for such things as chair bottoms and as a way to keep their powder dry. Few colonists regarded themselves as ranchers, since the cattle were free and mostly roamed on public land. War and Yankee appetites changed this situation.

The diamond-shaped area between the Nueces River, the Rio Grande, and the Gulf of Mexico is often called the cradle of Texas cattle industry. The warm climate and scrub growth of this region seemed ideal for the cattle whose numbers increased dramatically to several million head by the time of the Texas Revolution. In 1860 cattle were estimated to outnumber people in Texas by a six to one margin.

The Spanish made a few cattle drives to New Orleans, but such exportation was inhibited by their government's policy of political and trade isolation from the United States. The American colonists in Texas had also made a few drives. James Taylor White, who some regarded as Texas' first Cattle Baron, made drives from his ranch in present Liberty County to Louisiana, and Edward Piper made a drive to Ohio in 1846. Other trail drives moved across Louisiana or Arkansas for sale in Missouri or on the Mississippi River if a boat captain could be persuaded to load the live animals.

These drives mostly stopped after 1858 when irate farmers from eastern Texas all the way to Missouri protested the cattle tramping on their fields and pastures, and especially the persistence of a trail-borne bovine disease they called "Texas Fever" which never seemed to bother the herd but killed the farmer's domestic stock with devastating swiftness. Sometimes the drovers also faced unscrupulous raiders, particularly in Arkansas, who stampeded the herds to pick up strays or robbed the drovers as they returned home. So prior to the Civil War, the cattle industry became mostly a hide and tallow business. Vast

Ranch hands at the Matador Ranch in northwest Texas. Photo from the Southwest Collection, Texas Tech University.

— Courtesy Institute of Texan Cultures

numbers were slaughtered, usually on the coast for convenient shipping, and the hides would be harvested. The meat would then be boiled for tallow, and some of the remaining sinew would be shipped to New Orleans or dumped into the sea.

The Civil War brought the cattle industry in Texas to a standstill. A few herds were trailed to the Mississippi River and crossed to the eastern part of the Confederacy, but this became impossible after 1863 when Union gunboats controlled the river. With so much natural production and such little harvest of the herds, returning veterans found that cattle had increased in numbers but not in value. While few in Texas wanted to buy cattle anyway, there was a great demand for beef in the northern cities, where economic stimulus from the war and increasing European immigration created a hungry market.

As early as the fall of 1865 a few cattlemen rounded up stock without paying much attention to actual ownership and trailed them to Sedalia, Missouri, where they brought as much as $30 or $40 a head. Other drives went as far as Iowa. Resentment against the drovers and the "Texas Fever" returned with the drives. If the herds moved to the west to cross Oklahoma to get around the settlements, as many did up the Texas Trail to Fort Smith, they had to face hostile Indians most of the way.

A entrepreneur named Joseph G. McCoy solved the problem in 1867. McCoy moved onto the plains of western Kansas and founded the town of Abilene. Its streets were wide so cattle could be driven right through town to holding pens beside the tracks, which he also had convinced the railroad company to build. His town sported boarding houses, saloons, brothels, and other trail's end delights for the drovers he hoped to attract by riders whom he dispatched down a trail blazed by Indian trader Jesse Chisholm in 1865. The first herds came up the Chisholm Trail to Abilene in 1865 on faith, and found it to be all that had been promised. That first year over 35,000 head of Texas longhorns walked into Abilene; the next year the number more than doubled; and in 1869 it reached over 350,000 head.

As the population in Texas shifted westward, the trails also moved west to avoid conflict with settlers and to enjoy an unfettered right of way to the railheads in Kansas and Nebraska. The Western, or Dodge City Trail, ran north from San Antonio through Kerrville, Albany, and Vernon, near the Red

River at Doan's Crossing, then due north to Dodge City where the Santa Fe Railroad waited to take the cattle east, or on to Ogallala, Nebraska, where the Union Pacific Railroad carried the beef to market. The drovers mostly watered at the Long Branch Saloon or some similar establishment.

In 1866 Charles Goodnight and Oliver Loving drove a herd from the Middle Concho River northward to Fort Sumner, New Mexico. Later the Goodnight-Loving Trail ran on through Raton Pass into eastern Colorado. In 1884 the National Cattlemen's Association, in a rare abandonment of states' rights, tried to get the national government to take over a trail that would skirt state and local quarantines. The measure was considered in the Congress but never came to fruition.

The natural process of trailing herds to these northern markets began with a roundup. In the early post-war period, these activities might not be conducted with too much concern for ownership; after the development of large ranches, called spreads by the cattlemen, they were conducted with scrupulous attention to brands and property rights were honored. In the beginning the rancher conducted the drive himself, but later he could use the services of regular commission agents such as John T. Lytle, Charles Schreiner, or John Henry Stephens, who would take the stock north at the rate of $1 per head.

The trail herds were not as large as fiction writers often suggest. Anywhere from 1,500 to 2,000 head would constitute a good-sized herd. A trail boss headed the outfit, but since he had to sleep, keep books, and represent the outfit at quarantine inspections and the like, the trail boss usually had the assistance of a ramrod, or foreman. A camp cook moved ahead of the herd and prepared a meal, usually of staples and the ever present beef. The cook was often aided by a swamper, or less skilled cook, who performed various chores around the camp. The cook pointed his wagon tongue to the North Star each night to provide a sure direction for the next day's drive.

The drovers rose before daylight, breakfasted, and caught their first of perhaps three mounts of each day from their "string" of horses in the remuda and began the day's ten-mile ride. A trail herd could be visualized as a human body, prone, and pointed to the north. A scout would ride ahead of the herd to report on trail conditions — water and grazing mostly — but also Indian or settler hostility. Point men rode on either side of the head of the herd to keep it bunched and moving in the right direction. The most experienced and skilled cowboys rode there to control the herd and to mill it in case of stampede. Along the body of the herd flankers rode to chase strays back, and inexperienced cowboys or discipline cases rode drag, eating the dust of the herd as it slowly moved along. In this fashion a dozen or so men could move 2,000 cattle over 1,000 miles to market. Boredom and monotony were their greatest burdens, although bad weather and stampedes always loomed as dangers to life and safety.

Some trail hostility ceased after it was learned that a parasitic tick was the actual carrier of the "Texas Fever." The drovers then dipped the cattle before starting the drive to rid them of the parasite and remove the danger to domestic cattle farther north. Fences still closed the trails, though, and the trail rides themselves were never easy. In addition, herds arriving late in the market year did not draw the high prices that earlier arrivals obtained, so cattlemen sometimes wintered their herds in Kansas and Nebraska for sale the following year. They learned that the cattle could survive the northern winters and even prosper on the richer grasses of the upper plains despite the shorter growing season.

So the Cattle Kingdom spread through the plains of the United States. The cycle of the longhorn then, was to start out on spreads in Texas, be trailed as yearlings to northern ranges to fatten on the meadow grasses, and then be sold to commission agents and packing companies. Soon the demand for better grades of beef, severe winters, market glut, fences, economic changes, and the arrival of the Hereford cattle put the trail drives and the longhorns out of business.

In Texas, though, great ranches were born from the Cattle Kingdom. As early as the 1840s, H. L. Kinney established a trading post and ranch in the Rio Grande country. And in 1852 Richard King and Mifflin Kenedy, riverboat operators who came to the Rio Grande, acquired the Santa Gertrudis grant and built it into a major ranch. King and Kenedy divided their property in 1868, and King developed his holdings into the famous King Ranch with the assistance of his son-in-law, Richard Kleberg. Kenedy obtained other lands for ranching in what is now Kenedy County.

In the Panhandle, buffalo hunters such as the Mooar

brothers and Jim Cator established large spreads, as did the famous Abel H. "Shanghai" Pierce. Charles Goodnight located an Irish partner named John Adair in Colorado and returned to Texas to found the JA Ranch in the Palo Duro Canyon with Adair's money and his own know-how. Goodnight used the canyon walls for fences and controlled access to his spread with only a few line riders at the lower end of the canyon.

The largest ranch operation in North America, The Matador, grew from a buffalo hunter's dugout when A. M. Britton and H. H. Campbell bought range rights from Joe Browning in 1878 in Motley County and founded the Matador Cattle Company. Scottish investors purchased the ranch in 1882 and operated the vast holdings from Texas to Canada until 1952.

The XIT Ranch in the Panhandle is Texas' most famous spread besides the King Ranch. This vast 3 million-acre ranch resulted from a land settlement to the Capitol Syndicate for constructing a new state capitol building in Austin. Texas, lacking cash but rich in land, transferred title to the area at a rate of approximately $1 per acre while it was selling the state's other lands for as little as fifty cents per acre.

Unable to sell its land, the Syndicate went into the ranching business until land values rose. It built six thousand miles of fence to enclose its land and ordered supplies in box car lots. The Syndicate gradually sold off much of its holdings at a profit. The XIT allegedly earned its name because it spread across ten counties, thus the "X" or Roman numeral standing for the "ten in Texas."

The day of the great open ranches and the cattle drives passed with the coming of enclosed ranches and farms to occupy the western regions of the state. This change resulted from several forces. For one thing, the state desired to develop its public lands. Too, the construction of railroads, and such technological developments as barbed wire and the windmill made enclosure and rowcrop agriculture possible.

The Constitution of 1876 enabled Texas to return to the use of its land to subsidize railroad construction. And the railroads wanted to settle the lands along their tracks to improve their market. This was the normal pattern in the remainder of the United States, but it had to follow a slightly altered path in Texas. The Texas legislature controlled the public domain within the state just as the Congress did in the western territories, and also adopted the national policy of awarding sixteen sections of land for each mile of track laid by the railroads.

The railroad companies in Texas were usually forced to take the land in the undeveloped western part of the state, not necessarily where their tracks were laid, and they had to accept it in a checkerboard fashion since the state retained alternate sections. Companies had to survey the land at an average cost of fifty cents per acre, which was also the cost of the state-owned land, so the companies could not sell for a profit although another law required them to sell it to someone within eight years of the original grant. Despite these provisions, over 30,000,000 acres of public domain were alientated to the railroads.

Some companies unloaded the land to settlers at a loss, but others merely transferred this land to a subsidiary company which satisfied Texas law but kept the land in their control for later sale at higher prices. In 1883 the legislature stopped the railroad grants.

The state also sold their alternate sections and, in 1894, the Four Section Settler Act enabled a bonafide settler to purchase as much as four sections for fifty cents per acre. The state government leased grazing rights on the public lands, including the school lands, at rates which were beneficial to cattlemen. At first the cattlemen, who were accustomed to using the public lands freely, balked at this change, but later they turned the policy to their advantage. They usually managed to purchase their headquarters and other essential developments and leased the rest of their spreads. Sometimes employees would front for the cattlemen in these arrangements, so they could consolidate holdings through purchase or lease into vast acreages.

Cattlemen also used barbed wire to fence out settlers from such land, or fence them in on their own land to deny access to water supplies or to market. But the farmers came anyway. At first they bought land from the large cattle and land development companies, such as the XIT, and from the railroads and from the state government. The dryness of the country slowed their westward march, but as they learned to plow deeper for moisture and to conserve even the dew with heavy mulches, farming became possible. The invention of the windmill to

Charles Goodnight, one of the pioneer Texas cattlemen.

— *Courtesy Panhandle-Plains Historical Museum, Canyon*

pump what had been termed "underground rain" transformed the fertile Caprock country of the Panhandle into the new center of rowcrop agriculture in Texas.

And farmers used barbed wire also. In a treeless land with no available fencing material, their crops were at the mercy of the cattle, which would as soon graze on farm crops as prairie grass. Smooth wire had been available but ineffective. In the late 1870s barbed wire arrived on the market, patented by J. F. Glidden, produced by Isaac L. Ellwood, and marketed in Texas by H. B. Sanborn and John W. "Bet-A-Million" Gates. Barbed wire proved an ideal solution for both the farmer and the cattleman.

Problems arose when either group fenced out the other from

water or markets, and bitter struggles sometimes erupted in all parts of the state. At first cattlemen mostly built drift fences, then enclosed their entire spreads. They fenced out others from water holes and streams, but resented the farmers' fences which kept them from trailing herds to rail lines. So much fence cutting was done by both sides that an estimated $20 million loss resulted. Gates were required at three-mile intervals, and fencing off access to private property was prohibited. These new laws and the Texas Rangers eased the crisis.

Other conflicts occurred between cattlemen and sheep herders. Sheep were herded in Texas as early as were cattle, but the business did not flourish until the end of the nineteenth century. G. W. Kendall had established a large sheep ranch in 1857 in what is now Kendall County, and many early cattlemen also raised sheep for meat or wool. By 1870 an estimated 1,223,000 head grazed in Texas. Their numbers increased to over six million by 1880, declined until about 1930, then increased to over eleven million by the 1950s. Angora goats were also brought to Texas in 1849, and over four million goats in Texas now produce ninety-seven percent of the nation's mohair.

The rivalry between cattlemen and farmers and sheep herders has been distorted by fiction and imagination. The conflict was real, but it mostly concerned disputes over the use of the land, not deep-seated prejudice. Usually ranchers valued farmers as a source of vegetables, eggs, and extra labor, and as a source of civilization and increased land prices. And they did not so much resent the sheep as they wanted to use the land the sheep occupied for cattle. The belief that cattle and sheep will not graze on the same land or drink from the same stream can be easily disproven by penning cattle and sheep together and watching the natural process of grazing and drinking take place. Range animals do not know the difference, but the cattleman looks at the short cropped grass that the sheep have eaten and measures the loss in pounds of beef.

By the end of the nineteenth century the Cattle Kingdom had declined, but the cattle industry, along with farmers and sheep and goat herders, continued. Texas was settled by 1890; its counties were organized and towns were founded from the Sabine to the Pecos and from the Red River to the Gulf. Texas appeared on the road to economic recovery from the Civil War. But greater industrial development and population increase awaited in the new century.

Growth and The Reform Impulse

The rise of the Cattle Kingdom and the advance of the line of farmers on the frontier sustained one part of Texas' recovery from the losses of the Civil War, but major industrial and social forces changed all of the state by the beginning of the twentieth century. These changes appear most obviously in the railroad construction boom, the development of industrial strength in lumber and milling, a cash crop orientation in agriculture with resulting tenancy, and in the rising protests of blacks, labor, and farmers for a greater share of the rewards of Texas' expanding economy. Above all, the leadership of James Stephen Hogg as a man of the people focused the thrust of the late nineteenth century reform.

Railroad construction, in a way, laid the track for Texas' movement toward industrialization. The need for cross ties and lumber for boxcars and depots stimulated the sawmilling industry; then the rail lines hauled more lumber than any other product to eastern and even foreign markets. The railroads provided Texas with a transportation network desperately needed for economic expansion, and the great post-Civil War building boom elevated the state to national leadership in miles of track with nearly 10,000 miles by 1904. The railroad was introduced to America in the 1830s and its advantages over wagon transportation for freight or horseback or stage rides for passenger service over great distances quickly gained recognition.

Late nineteenth century locomotive at Brownsville, a part of the St. Louis, Brownsville, and Mexico Railroad.

— Courtesy Texas Southmost College Library, Brownsville

One of the leading political arguments within Texas in the 1850s had centered around the decision of whether to subsidize rails or river transportation. There were fewer than 500 miles of track in the state in 1860—mostly in the vicinity of Houston — indicating that the river supporters got the best of the argument. But this is not necessarily true. Beginning in 1852 Texas offered eight sections of land, increased to sixteen sections two years later, for each mile of track. Some construction companies organized, including the Henderson and Burkville Railroad, the first to receive a subsidy, but construction work was glacial and political tensions over secession doubtless slowed the process of capital accumulation even more. Then the war stopped railroad construction completely.

The various reconstruction governments favored renewal of railroad construction. Because the Constitution of 1869 proscribed the land grant method of state subsidy, the state legislature granted bonds to railroad companies for four years, then amended the constitution in 1873 to enable the state government to return to land grants, and continued that process under the Constitution of 1876. In all, the state granted over 30 million acres to various railroad construction projects, although the railroads realized little cash from this largely because they usually had to accept the land at great distances from the tracks, alternating their grants with sections of school lands, and they had to buy their own rights of way, pay for the surveying of the land, and then sell the land within eight years of acquiring it.

The railroads did receive other subsidies from counties and cities along the tracts, and sometimes deliberately routed the lines to include or exclude communities depending on their generosity and cooperativeness. Community leaders who realized the value of the rail lines to future growth donated depots, rights of way, roundhouses, tax exemptions, and sometimes cash bonuses for directing the tracks their way. Small communities such as Dallas greatly benefited from their rail connections. Dallas had no alternate transportation and only dreamed of some day making the Trinity River navigable to the Gulf. But the railroads made Dallas a transportation and trade center and one of the five largest cities in the state by 1900.

Jefferson in East Texas, on the other hand, failed to realize the railroad's potential. Jefferson, a city of perhaps 5,000 people on the eve of the Civil War, profited from its bayou connection to the Red and Mississippi rivers and rose to a rank second only to Galveston as a port of entry. In the 1870s the Jeffersonians saw no reason to grant subsidies to the Yankee millionaire Jay Gould for construction of the Texas and Pacific Line through their town. Miffed, Gould routed his line through Marshall, sixteen miles to the south of Jefferson, and by the end of the century, Marshall had become a bustling community and Jefferson had nearly ceased to exist except as a quaint memory of antebellum glory.

Abilene, Sweetwater, and other communities along the Texas and Pacific were born of the railroad itself. The principal lines in Texas included the Texas and Pacific, the Missouri, Kansas and Texas (KATY), the Fort Worth and Denver, the International and Great Northern, the Missouri Pacific, the Santa Fe, and, of course, the Southern Pacific. Construction began on the Texas and Pacific in 1870 with Grenville Dodge, fresh from completing the Union Pacific lines to Utah in 1867, in charge of the line. Dodge contemplated a line from East Texas to San Diego, California and began construction in 1873, but he stalled after reaching Fort Worth in 1875. Gould acquired control of the line shortly afterward and began laying track again in 1880. He hurried to meet Collis P. Huntington's Southern Pacific racing eastward toward El Paso from California. The lines met at Sierra Blanca, about eighty miles east of El Paso in 1882, and by agreement, both companies used the lines into the city. Later, Huntington built an alternate route to San Antonio via Laredo, and acquired over thirty rail companies through consolidation to complete his Southern Pacific trunk line all the way to New Orleans.

The major construction period extended from 1876 with the return of a predictable governmental policy of support, and ended in 1882 when the state ceased granting land to railroads. About one-half of Texas' 10,000 miles of track were laid during this period. More miles of track were laid in Texas in 1877 than in any other state, and the following year Texas rail construction equalled the entire nation's total.

The availability of rail service helped revolutionize other aspects of Texas industry. Most Texas industry, primarily lumber and the processing of agricultural products, had remained extractive and domestic since colonial times. And what was not done on the farm or ranch for the owner's use was migratory, that is, saw and grist mills moved from place to place to be near the source of materials. With the coming of the rails, the material could be hauled to centralized factories and then the product could be carried to markets on the same tracks.

The total value of all Texas manufactured products in 1870 was under $12 million, or only about 25 percent of the agricultural product's total. Fewer than 2,500 shops employed about 8,000 workers, which was about one percent of the total population. Galveston remained the manufacturing center of the state with a gross production value of $1.2 million. Grist mills, 533 of them in 1870, were the dominant producers in the state. By 1900 the number of mills declined to 289 yet the value of the product doubled, and by 1890 the number of shops engaged in manufacturing in Texas increased to 5,200 and employed over 36,000 workers. The total value of their products reached $70 million. By 1890 lumber had displaced flour milling as the state's leading industry, and by the turn of the century cotton seed oil pushed milling into third place.

The lumber industry is a good example of an extractive industry which became a big business. Saw mills operated in Texas from the earliest times. One operated at San Augustine as early as 1816 and another was established in Nacogdoches in the 1820s. East Texas contained a prime unharvested stand of virgin pine, and mighty stands of hardwoods along its many streams. At first the mills operated only for the benefit of local communities because of the transportation difficulties; but, with the demand for wood products by the railroads — which then hauled the lumber once their tracks were in place — the forest industry became the state's industrial leader until the age of petroleum.

The lumber industry headquartered in the area from the Sabine River on the east nearly as far west as the Trinity River, but was centered in the thickets north of Beaumont and Orange, a 68,000 square mile region with perhaps as many as 300 billion board feet of lumber still growing. Capitalists such as H. J. Lutcher, G. B. Moore, and especially John Henry Kirby, moved into this country for a massive exploitation which continued until the 1920s when the virgin timber country had been cut over, and which continues under planned harvesting as the region's second largest industry.

The early timber barons harvested the timber and moved on to the next stand until they had denuded the region of most of its marketable timber. Over 600 mills participated in this exploitation and development, ranging from jackleg operations to the mighty Kirby Lumber Company with major mills at Kirbyville, Silsbee, and Beaumont. In some ways the timber barons operated like the cattle barons, acquiring vast acreages, maintaining employees in company towns, paying wages in script money redeemable only at the company stores, and holding labor sources by any means that worked. In their defense, they provided work to thousands of persons who might otherwise have had none. The Kirby Lumber Company is often credited with being Texas' first million dollar corporation.

The cotton seed oil and cake business emerged as a consequence of the state's farmers turning to this secondary cash crop until over half the planted acreage in Texas grew cotton. The tenacious seeds were removed by the gin and were discarded to rot for decades. When it was learned that a rich light oil could be squeezed from the seeds, over one hundred mills turned this process into a $14 million business by 1900. And the cotton cake, or what was left after the oil was extracted, was found to be an excellent nitrogen fertilizer and useful as livestock feed.

The Texas agricultural picture changed considerably during the period after the Civil War. The center of farming shifted to the black lands of Central Texas, then moved out on the high plains after the discovery of sources of irrigation and the acquiring of dry farming techniques. Cotton became the dominant crop even in the antebellum period, but in the postwar era it became the cash crop specialization. In 1870 the total value of the crop was $10 million; by 1900 it increased to over $100 million, with bale production increasing from 35,000 in 1870 to over 2.5 million in 1900. But the price also dropped from 35 cents per pound in 1865 to as low as 5 cents per pound by 1900, and farm income from cotton dropped from $88 million to $68 million per year, meaning that a farmer must increase his production annually to stay even. This spiral contributed to a significant increase in the sharecrop, sharetenant, and crop lien systems in Texas.

A Central Texas farm family around the turn of the century in Falls County.

Before the Civil War, inexpensive or free land was available to all, and most farmers tilled their own soil. The financial reverses of the war and recovery periods, the exhaustion of the public domain, and economic uncertainty forced many to sell their property or forfeit it for taxes or other debts, then come back to farm it on shares for the new owner. Under the sharecrop system, a farmer became a laborer who was paid a share of the crop. The land owner contributed the land, shelter, equipment, seeds, and credit for the crop and usually received three-quarters of the produce. Since he had provided credit, he often also ended up with the sharecropper's quarter, and the vicious cycle started over every year with the cropper falling further into debt all the time.

Under the share-tenant system, the farmer rented the land for a share of the crop but provided the other things for himself; thus he earned a larger share. Under the crop lien system, the farmer borrowed against an anticipated crop. If the crop made it, he paid off his debt with money to spare; but if the crop failed, he frequently had to borrow that much more at high interest rates for the following year.

Most farmers fell constantly into debt no matter how hard they worked or how much they produced. They blamed the system — banks, insurance companies, railroads, and many other culprits — and in their frustration joined the Greenback party in the 1870s and later supported free silver in the hope that more inflated money would lighten their burden. Farmer Alliances, the Populist Party, and eventually the Farm Bureau also attracted a large following among agrarians.

Laborers also joined the protest. Big business means concentrated labor, and eventually leads to collective action among laborers to achieve better working conditions and higher wages. Labor unions as such did not exist in Texas before the Civil War, although benevolent associations did operate in some trades. In 1866 a group of longshoremen formed a benevolent association in Galveston, and in 1870 Norris Wright Cuney formed a similar organization for blacks. The International Typographical Union was organized in Houston, Galveston, and Austin in the 1870s and many laborers also joined the Knights of Labor, a national organization with individualized membership. The Knights claimed they preferred legislation over strikes to achieve their goals, although they did stage several dock strikes in Texas.

The United Mine Workers organized in Texas in 1884 in the coal mines in Erath and Palo Pinto counties. Spectacular strikes against the Gould rail lines occurred in this decade, and stonemasons struck against the company which was building the new state capitol. Longshoremen, draymen, and others, including the bizarre cowboys' strike in 1883 — in an isolated, spontaneous and non-union effort of over 300 cowboys to obtain higher wages — idled over 8,000 workers and their industries for over 700 working days in the 1880s.

The most celebrated protest of the period involved liquor. Texans had always enjoyed easy accessibility to liquor, but even before the Civil War temperance societies had sought to change this. Now, the United Friends of Temperance, the Bands of Hope, a juvenile group, and especially the ladies of the Women's Christian Temperance Union tried to vote Texas dry with a constitutional amendment in 1886.

The issue became the most divisive and bitterly contested issue in the state for the remainder of the century. The *Texas Christian Advocate* and the *Texas Baptist Herald*, along with such popular figures as John H. Reagan, Senator Samuel Bell Maxey, and David Culberson, led the "pros" in the fight, while the "antis" counted James S. Hogg, George Clark, and Roger Mills in their camp. The amendment failed. There were only 120,000 votes for it as opposed to 220,000 to keep liquor available. Nevertheless, the issue remained a heated one for decades, and occasional "wet-dry" elections under the state's current local option laws still provoke the greatest local interest and election participation.

Politics in the post-war era featured reform. The redeemers "reformed" Texas as best they could, and later reformers tried to restructure the imperfect society of the redeemers. Richard Coke began the process with a determined effort to reduce the expenditures of the Davis administration. Even before the adoption of the parsimonious Constitution of 1876, Coke trimmed the state's spending in every way possible. His action was made necessary, Coke claimed, because he had assumed control of a treasury with no more than $40,000 and expenses of $1.2 million against an anticipated annual tax revenue of only $500,000. Obviously, something had to change.

Coke attempted, with some success, to re-negotiate state bonds, fund some of the outstanding debt with new bonds, raise some taxes, and increase land grants to settle the state's debts. Under his administration some business taxes were levied, but a reform in the method of collection actually resulted in a loss of revenue from railroads and telegraph companies. Occupational taxes were passed; some, such as that on fortune tellers, were intended to be regulatory. And a $1 poll tax on every adult male was passed, but it proved difficult to collect.

After being elected to a second term in 1876, Coke resigned to accept the U.S. senate seat being vacated by Morgan Hamilton. He joined Samuel Bell Maxey, who had replaced James Flanagan the preceding year. Lt. Gov. Richard B. Hubbard succeeded Coke in office and continued the administration along the same lines as his predecessor. He ran for a second term in 1878 but deadlocked in the nomination process with J. W. Throckmorton and William Lang. Justice Oran M. Roberts received the Democratic nomination to break the impasse.

Roberts, who won the election and received a second term in 1880, was the most significant governor between E. M. Pease and James S. Hogg. Even more fiscally strict than Coke, he forced the reissuance of state bonds at reduced rates, reduced veteran's pensions, demanded a reduction in school funds — he vetoed the school appropriations twice until the legislature complied with his wish to provide no more than one-sixth of the state's money for education — reformed the methods of tax collection to realize a higher yield, and introduced new taxes such as the Bell Punch Tax on liquor by the drink and the Drummer Tax on travelling salesmen doing business in Texas. The latter tax may have been counter-productive.

Roberts also urged an acceleration of the public domain grants to settlers as a method of bringing the land into production and as a source of tax revenues. The resulting Four Section Settler Act and the Fifty Cent Law made land available to settlers at moderate rates; but they virtually exhausted the state's holdings, except for school lands, by the end of the decade. This program also was subject to rampant speculation, which Land Commissioner W. C. Walsh tried desperately to combat.

In 1882 John Ireland secured the Democratic gubernatorial nomination and ran successfully against a coalition of the Greenback and Republican parties which nominated George W. Jones. Ireland opposed the wholesale disposition of the public domain and convinced the legislature to modify the land laws to incorporate the idea of graduation, or graded land values, coupled with the auction method of sale, both of which were calculated to increase revenue from land sales. Otherwise, Ireland continued Roberts' penny-pinching methods of administration and secured election to a second term in 1884 with a large majority. Ireland's administrations urged reform in such areas as the state's prison system and supported higher education. They also witnessed the bulk of the labor disputes and the fence cutting wars.

In 1886 prohibition dominated the reform thrust in Texas. The Democratic party nominated the old civil warrior L. S. Ross for governor, and the young, energetic James Stephen Hogg for attorney general. Ross won this race and was returned for a second term in 1888, but the real power in his administration fell to Hogg.

It was a time of reform in the state as well as in the nation. In congress, John H. Reagan introduced legislation to create the Interstate Commerce Commission, and co-sponsored legislation which became the Sherman Anti-Trust Act. In Texas, the legislature enacted the second state anti-trust law in the nation, prohibiting price fixing and other trade restraints by monopolies and trusts.

Hogg began his reform activities against insurance companies, which operated in violation of state regulations. In February 1887, he issued a circular letter to local prosecutors which promised state aid on any cases filed in district courts. A flood of prosecutions followed, and dozens of poorly financed insurance companies went out of business. State Insurance Commissioner L. L. Foster estimated that Hogg's initiative saved Texas premium payers in excess of $1 million.

Hogg lost some cases. For example, he failed in his defense of the Drummer Tax before the United States Supreme Court, which declared the tax unconstitutional. And he lost some prestige in his feud with Judge Frank Willis, who presided with what Hogg considered biased tactics in a celebrated case dealing with grass leases in cow country. Hogg's accusations precipitated a legislative investigation of Willis which proved inconclusive, but the action alienated cattlemen from Hogg. He did not seem to mind, for he was more a champion of the common people.

Hogg and Ross were re-elected to a second term, and Hogg shifted his reform efforts to the railroads, forcing them to provide full service to Texas users on the grounds that the public domain and local subsidies had largely financed the railroads and they owed good service to the public. He forced some of them to resume abandoned lines, to extend other services, to keep grades and rolling stock in good repair on the basis of existing state regulations, and he worked hard for a constitutional amendment to create a Railroad Commission to regulate all aspects of the railroad business in Texas.

The rail lines retaliated through a marketing agency called the Texas Traffic Association, which they also used as a cover to fix rates. Hogg brought action under the state anti-trust law which forced the Association out of the state. It later reorganized across state lines as the International Traffic Association to escape state jurisdiction. Hogg also argued with Jay Gould over the issue of receiverships for lines going bankrupt in Texas, a convenient device to evade debt obligation. Hogg insisted that state-appointed receivers should administer such affairs to insure that state interests would be served; Gould preferred federally appointed receivers because the national administrations were more disposed to the railroad companies.

Hogg ran for the governorship in 1890 on a platform of reform and made the election a referendum for the Railroad Commission amendment. He received the support of the Farmer's Alliances and other protest groups, but the railroads, cattlemen, and other business interests opposed him. He won the Democratic nomination at a convention in San Antonio and went on to victory in November for both his candidacy and for the amendment to create the Railroad Commission. Hogg's opponents still tried to block the Commission in the legislature, but that body created the Texas Railroad Commission on April 3, 1891, and it ultimately became the most powerful and effective such agency in the nation.

Hogg appointed John H. Reagan as chairman of the Commission, and L. L. Foster and William P. McLean filled remaining positions. Reagan proved an ideal appointment. An old-time Texan, he had served in the Confederate cabinet and afterwards in the U.S. Congress. Honest, efficient, and generally respected, Reagan helped the Railroad Commission get established, weather the storm of court actions brought unsuc-

Governor James S. Hogg
— Courtesy University of Texas Press,
Painting from Barker Texas History Center

cessfully against it by the railroads, and upon his retirement in 1903, left a functioning agency as a legacy of his leadership.

Hogg was re-elected to a second term in 1892 but the election proved a harder fight than had his first election. The Populist Party nominated Thomas L. Nugent, robbing Hogg of some of his reform and agrarian support, and conservative Democrats even opposed his nomination. At a state convention in Houston, the group known as the Car Barn Democrats met in the trolly car barn and nominated Hogg; another group of Democrats met in Turner Hall to nominate George Clark. The Republicans sensed their best chance for a victory since 1870, but they also split over the leadership of the party by racial faction under Norris Wright Cuney, a black, and a group known as the Lily Whites. And the Prohibitionists nominated Albert C. Prendergast.

Hogg won re-election, although the large field left him a plurality governor. In his second term Hogg continued his efforts to regulate business and to advance the people's cause. The Hogg Laws, as his program became known, featured the Alien Land Act, the Perpetuities and Corporation Land Law, and the Stock and Bond Law. The Alien Land Law required foreign owners of Texas lands to dispose of such property within six years; the Corporation Land Law required businesses to divest themselves of real estate holdings within fifteen years; and the Stock and Bond Law gave the Railroad Commission supervisory authority over stock and bond issues by rail lines to put an end to watered stock evils.

At the end of Hogg's second term, he promised his full support to Reagan, but a new force in Texas politics, E.M. House of Galveston and Austin, intervened. House was a retired cotton merchant and a behind-the-scenes manipulator who dominated Texas and even national politics for the next three decades. He decreed, for example, that Attorney General Charles M. Culberson should succeed to the governorship. House seized control of the party, then helped Culberson defeat the Populist candidate Jerome C. Kearby as well as the Prohibitionists and the Republicans. Culberson also won a second term in 1895 in an election in which Texans supported Democrat William Jennings Bryan over the Republican candidate William McKinley for the presidency.

Culberson continued Hogg's reform thrust, especially in

the courts. His attorney general, M. M. Crane, won a case under the anti-trust legislation against the Waters-Pierce Oil Company, a subsidiary of Standard Oil. Waters-Pierce later returned to the state under the control of Standard Oil. On the other hand, Culberson and Crane lost the Greer County case before the Supreme Court. This was a boundary dispute over which fork of the Red River constituted the true boundary between Texas and Oklahoma, which resulted in the forfeiture of Greer County to Oklahoma.

Texas experienced a dramatic increase in population during the last quarter of the century, especially during the decade of the 1870s. The state began the period with a population of 818,579 and increased to 3,048,710 by 1900, making Texas the sixth largest state in the nation, up from nineteenth in 1870. This increase was equally distributed between new births and immigrants coming mostly from the Southern states. Texas remained predominantly rural, but the urban population increased from 6.7 percent to 17.1 percent by 1900. The Negro population increased during these three decades, but their percentage of the total population dropped due to the more significant increase in the numbers of whites.

Foreign-born residents of Texas remained in the same ratio to American-born Texans. Persons born in Mexico still constituted the largest number of non-United States citizens in Texas, but their numbers were less than the combined European-born residents. The Mexican population percentage remained steady until after the turn of the century when revolutions swept across Mexico in successive waves. Many of these movements began in the border country along the Rio Grande, causing significant migrations of Mexicans to Texas to escape the dangers of war. Later, economic opportunity in Texas increased the flow of Mexicans to jobs north of the border.

The rural complexion of Texas can be easily seen in the population of its counties. In 1870 the five counties with the greatest population were Washington, Harris, Rusk, Fayette, and Caldwell, and the five largest towns were Galveston, San Antonio, Houston, Brownsville, and Jefferson; by 1900 the five largest counties were Dallas, Bexar, Harris, Travis and Tarrant, and the largest cities were San Antonio, Houston, Dallas, Galveston, and Fort Worth. The latter list matches counties to cities much closer, indicating the beginning of a trend to the cities which continued throughout the twentieth century.

Texas made significant strides in higher education during the closing decades of the century. Building on Federal largesse in the form of the Morrill Land Grant Act, Texas A&M College began in 1876 with six faculty members and forty students. A&M's ROTC program trained more officers than did West Point for service during World War II. Because the A&M College was for white male students of the agricultural and mechanical arts, a black counterpart was created at Prairie View in 1885, but was quickly converted into a "normal," or teacher preparation school.

Sam Houston Normal School, now University, began operating in Huntsville in 1870, and became a model for several additional teacher preparation colleges created by the legislature in 1917. The University of Texas, the old dream of Mirabeau Lamar, finally became a reality in 1883. Austin was selected as the site for the main academic campus and the medical branch was located at Galveston. The University began with thirteen faculty members and 221 students, and has grown to an institution of over 40,000 students in Austin, a system of campuses located in Dallas, Tyler, Arlington, and in the Permian Basin, and four medical colleges.

Texas Christian University began in 1873 in Thorpe Spring as Add-Ran College, named for benefactors Addison and Randolph Clark. The Disciples of Christ endorsed the University, moved it to Waco for a while, then relocated it as Texas Christian University at Fort Worth in 1910. Baylor University, at Independence, affiliated with Texas Baptists since 1846, moved to Waco in 1886. Other Baptist schools founded during this period include Howard Payne University at Brownwood in 1889, and Hardin, now Hardin-Simmons University, at Abilene in 1891. The Catholic Church supported St. Mary's in San Antonio for men and Incarnate Word and Our Lady of the Lake for girls. Methodists established Southwestern University at Georgetown in 1873 and Texas Wesleyan University at Fort Worth in 1891. The Presbyterian Church established Trinity University, now in San Antonio, at Tehuacana, and Austin University at Sherman, originally located in Huntsville.

In other artistic matters, Texas was dominated by a woman at the close of the century. Elisabet Ney, wife of the scientist Dr. Edmund Montgomery, brought her international reputation from Europe in 1870 to reside at Liendo Plantation, the property of the early Texas settler Jared Groce. Ms. Ney was a most unconventional woman for the time and place who delighted in shocking her provincial neighbors. She swore, rode horseback astride, and smoked in public. In her studio she sculpted works of art. Her statues of Austin, Houston, and Albert Sydney Johnston are best known to Texans, especially those which may be seen in the state capitol building. Her statue of "Lady Macbeth" is in the National Gallery in Washington, and her "Sursum" is in the Chicago Art Institute.

Important Texas painters of the period included H. A. McArdle, whose "Battle of San Jacinto" and "Dawn of the Alamo" hang in the Senate chamber at the capitol, and William H. Huddle, whose "Surrender of Santa Anna" also hangs in the capitol building. The most important writer of the period was William Sidney Porter, better known as O. Henry, who came to Texas from North Carolina in 1882. Porter worked at several jobs and professions, served time in the prison at Huntsville, and wrote of many of his Texas experiences in short stories of lasting quality. Mrs. Percy Pennybaker wrote a state history text in the 1870s which educated generations of Texans about their state, while John C. Duval and John Henry Brown penned more substantive historical works.

The capstone of art and politics for this period of reform was the construction of the state capitol still in use in Austin. The writers of the Constitution of 1876 had authorized three million acres of public domain to construct the new state capitol. No work was begun until after the other capitol building burned in 1881. Subsequently, the legislature created a capitol board to dispose of the land subsidy, and added an additional 50,000 acres to cover architectural costs. Mattheas Schell of Illinois secured the bid as contractor for the building, agreeing to accept the land itself as his fee. Schell soon involved other Illinois businessmen, including Charles B. and John V. Farwell, A. C. Babcock, and Abner Taylor. Ultimately Taylor saw the building through to completion. The work was frustrated at many points. Taylor wanted to use limestone to construct the building because of its availability; but the board declined to accept limestone because of its propensity toward discoloration; Taylor agreed to use granite. So, because granite required more skilled masons, he imported stonecutters from Scotland, only to have the rest of his union force strike because of the use of alien labor, a problem which was solved by hiring scab laborers. Taylor also tried to change the specifications to substitute slate for the copper roof called for by the architectural plans on the grounds that slate better suited the climate, but Attorney General Hogg forced him to stick by the original contract lest Texas taxpayers be cheated.

The building's dedication fell on May 16, 1888, a day of heavy rain in Austin, and the copper roof contracted from the temperature change and leaked on the proceedings. Taylor was then forced to reroof the building with slate at his own expense. The builders, who had organized as the Capitol Syndicate, were forced to seek a loan from financial concerns in London, who then received the 3-million acre payment as security. Since the building had cost the contractor about that much money, in effect the builders paid an average of one dollar per acre while adjacent lands still sold for fifty cents. Unable to sell their land at a profit, they formed the XIT ranch and entered the cattle business until land prices rose.

The capitol remains a magnificent building, only slightly smaller than the United States capitol building in Washington. Constructed of native pink granite, its interior woods and stones house the governor's office, both chambers of the legislature, and the business offices of the legislators. The State Capitol building is a tourist attraction, a seat of government, and a symbol of the age in which it was built. Barons of Texas cattle, lumber, and oil industries, as well as teachers, lobbyists of every conceivable cause, media representatives, and every other kind of Texan imaginable, visit it and use it daily as a tangible monument to Texas' past and as a path to its future.

10

Progressivism: Some Good, Some Bad

The twentieth century variety of American reform often goes by the designation of "progressivism," meaning a belief that humanity, both individually and collectively, can be improved by legislation. Often this belief works its way into positive legislation such as child labor regulation, laws to preserve and promote public health, or laws to improve the lot of scholastics or prison inmates; and sometimes negative progressivism rears its head in presumptuous dictations of public morals, nativism, and religious intolerance. Most of the time progressivism is positive and applaudable. But always it presumes that some know what is best for all, and its leaders are willing to use the law and even extra-legal methods to enforce orthodoxy. Progressivism is always well-meaning; its motives are noble and righteous.

Texas' pre-eminent progressive leader after James Stephen Hogg was E. M. House. House engineered the election of Charles Culberson to succeed Hogg as governor, and then in succession decreed that the next governors of the state should be Joseph D. Sayers (1899-1903), S. W. T. Lanham (1903-1907), and Thomas Mitchell Campbell (1907-1911), perhaps the most progressive of all. Oscar Branch Colquitt, although less progressive than his predecessors, continued their trend in his two terms; but by the time of his elections, House had lost interest in Texas politics and transferred his attention to helping Woodrow Wilson win the presidency in 1912. Each of these

Senator Joseph W. Bailey
— Courtesy Austin-Travis County Collection

governors preferred the label of "conservative" despite the progressiveness of their administrations.

The Texan who most epitomized the opposition to progressivism in Texas politics was Joseph Weldon Bailey, the so-called "Last Democrat" and prototype for "Baileyism." Bailey was a successful lawyer for the Waters-Pierce Oil Company, the Kirby interests, and other large corporations. He served in both the U.S. House of Representatives and the Senate in a political career which began in 1891 and spanned three decades. Bailey served as counsel to Henry Clay Pierce, president of the Waters-Pierce Oil Company, during the anti-trust litigation, and advised the company to reorganize in a fashion which would disguise its continued affiliation with Standard Oil. In a second case in 1906, the Waters-Pierce Oil Company was again found to be in violation of the anti-trust law and fined $1.8 million.

In a public hearing it was learned that Senator Bailey had served as a silent counselor and received fees in excess of $100,000. Bailey admitted taking the money, but claimed that it was payment for legal services, and that he earned his living by practicing law. He was exonerated by legislative investigating committees and re-elected to the Senate. In 1908 he headed the state's delegation to the National Democratic Convention. For a decade, pro-Bailey or anti-Bailey positions polarized nearly every politically active Texan, but prohibition remained the most divisive issue during the first three decades of the century.

The prohibitionists refused to accept as conclusive the defeat of the constitutional amendment for prohibition in 1878, and they steadily worked to submit another amendment while pushing with equal diligence at the local level for wet-dry elections. By 1919 Texas had 167 dry counties, 61 partially dry counties and only 21 completely wet counties; but the majority of Texans lived in the wet counties, which hosted the major urban centers. From 1900 until 1911, the prohibitionists advocated another amendment through such organizations as the Texas Local Option Association, organized in Dallas in 1903, and the Anti-Saloon League, organized in 1907.

The Texas Brewers' Association and the Retail Liquor Dealers Association labored with equal diligence for the survival of their businesses, but the prohibitionists rode the crest of the progressive wave to reform society through legislation. In 1902 they helped establish a poll tax as a requirement for voting, hoping to eliminate pro-wet votes. They demanded another prohibition amendment with a plebiscite in the election of 1910, and the Democratic Party supported their call while nominating Colquitt, a wet. The election was held on July 22, 1911, and state-wide prohibition failed again by a vote of 231,096 to 237,393, a margin of only 6,000 votes. The outcome encouraged the prohibitionists to work even harder. In 1915 they learned that the brewers' association had violated state election laws with certain contributions, but they could do little because the new governor, James E. Ferguson, threatened to veto any liquor legislation.

The coming of war helped the prohibitionists' cause. More Americans and Texans were willing to listen to the voices of prohibition at this time in order to save grain for the soldiers and for the relief of starving Europeans. In Texas the legislature forbade the sale of liquor within ten miles of military bases. Texas Senator Morris Sheppard introduced the bill that became the Eighteenth Amendment to the national Constitution, prohibiting the sale or distribution of alcoholic beverages. The state quickly ratified the amendment by a vote of 188,982 to 130,907, and anticipated its effect with state-wide prohibition. Within a year the Volstead Act implemented prohibition for the entire nation. Over 2,500 saloons closed in Texas, but illegal stills and bootlegging soon replaced the legal sale of liquor, leading to widespread violation of the law.

In the 1920s Governor Pat Neff used the Rangers to combat what he called the worst crime wave in the state's history and called on the legislature for even tougher liquor laws. They responded in 1923 by making the possession of one quart of liquor as *prima facie* evidence of guilt. His men raided stills, arrested violators, and tried to combat speakeasies, but many Texans continued to use alcohol anyway.

Texas also became active in national progressive politics. House visited with William Jennings Bryan and learned of a New Jersey governor named Woodrow Wilson who sounded like his kind of man. He moved to New York, became a supporter of Wilson, and helped pull progressive Texas into line with this Yankee Progressive rendered more palatable by Virginia birth. Texans supported Wilson at the Democratic Convention and earned the name "the immortal forty" because they remained loyal to Wilson through vote after vote in his contest with Missouri congressman Champ Clark. Texans also supported Wilson in the campaign against the Republican president William Howard Taft and former president Theodore Roosevelt.

At House's insistence, Ranger Captain Bill McDonald served as Wilson's bodyguard during the campaign. Wilson repaid the Texans with generous appointments to his cabinet. Albert Sidney Burleson became postmaster general, and former Texan David Franklin Houston served as secretary of agriculture. House moved to Washington and became Wilson's closest advisor, his alter ego, and his guest-resident in the White House for a time after Wilson's first wife died.

Women played a significant role in the prohibition movement through such organizations as the Women's Christian Temperance Union. But they were limited to persuading males to vote for prohibition, for they were denied suffrage in Texas. Petitions calling for women's suffrage had failed at the constitutional conventions of 1869 and 1876, and in several legislative sessions. The Texas Equal Rights Association, a group of suffragettes, organized in 1893, but its effectiveness was lessened by internal quarrels over a national affilitation. Beginning in 1913, an annual convention of the Texas Women's Suffrage Association called for the vote for women. The movement eventually included hundreds of local societies, including several male organizations. And there was a group headed by Mrs. James Wells of Brownsville that opposed extending full citizenship to women because of the "evils" which would result.

In 1915 and 1917, petitions for a constitutional amendment to permit the female vote failed in the legislature, but in 1918 the special session which ratified the prohibition amendment also passed measures to permit women to vote in the primaries. The following year William Hobby requested an amendment allowing women to vote in the general election as well. The amendment passed, but even before it could become effective, the Nineteenth Amendment to the United States Constitution was ratified by the legislature in June and became effective in time for the national election in 1920. Texas became the first state in the South and the ninth in the nation to ratify this amendment. Women still did not serve on Texas juries until 1954, however, and equal property rights remained clouded for decades.

One progressive measure for Texas and the nation grew out of a natural disaster. On the first weekend of September in 1900, a tropical hurricane struck Galveston. The waves drove bathers from the beaches on the afternoon of September 7, and by early the next morning 120-mile-an-hour winds struck the island. The tide swept over the entire island, the highest wave achieving an estimated height of fourteen feet. The city of 38,000 lay submerged under at least five feet of water for hours; every building suffered some damage, many were swept away entirely. Over 6,000 people lost their lives. The storm raged across Texas, and in testimony to its intensity, farmers 300 miles inland claimed it made the sky so black that chickens roosted at four in the afternoon.

In the face of such destruction, Galveston simply ceased to operate for a time. Then the Galvestonians pulled themselves together, organized relief, and attempted to dispose of the dead by dumping them at sea as a health precaution. When most of the bodies floated back to shore, they were burned in huge pyres. The city organized a commission form of government on an *ad hoc* basis with each commissioner responsible for one primary city function to handle problems of police and fire protection, sanitation, and supervision of cleanup. The method worked so admirably that the legislature chartered the city commision for Galveston in 1901, and the form of government soon found adoption in scores of other cities throughout Texas and the nation. Houston, for example, adopted the city commission system in 1905.

In 1913 Amarillo refined the system with a council-manager method which placed day-to-day city functions in the hands of a professional administrator. This form of government also found acceptance. In 1912 the legislature adopted a progressive measure which added a more democratic method to civic organization. Cities of 5,000 or more were thereafter empowered to incorporate by drawing up their own charters without legislative sanction.

Other progressive measures included a reform of the system of political nomination, regulations for labor and business, and reforms in taxing and prisons. Since the rise of parties in Texas, the nomination of candidates remained ostensibly a work of delegates at party conventions, but often the conventions were controlled by a small clique. In 1903 a preliminary election code revision passed the legislature, and a further modification in 1905 by the Terrell Election Law created the basic system still in use in Texas. This law called for a party primary in which anyone can file for office, with winners receiving delegate support at the convention on an instructed basis. A further modification in 1918 provided for a second primary, or runoff election, when a candidate failed to receive a majority in the first primary.

Less positively, in 1923 the legislature allowed the political parties, principally the Democratic party, to exclude blacks from the primary elections on the grounds that such elections were private, not public, exercises. White primaries continued until 1944 when the Supreme Court ruled in Smith v. Allwright, a Texas case, that the primaries were an integral part of the election process and that systematic exclusion of any group constituted illegal disfranchisement.

Thirteen years before the U.S. Congress passed the Keating-Owens Act to prohibit child labor abuse, the Texas legislature prohibited the employment of children under twelve years of age in industrial plants and under sixteen years of age in mines, distilleries, and breweries in 1903. These age limits were raised to fifteen and seventeen in 1911. Other progressive labor measures limited the number of consecutive hours that trainmen could work without rest, set requirements for protection against the weather for streetcar motormen, and prohibited a company or corporation from forcing its employees to patronize the company's products or make purchases from company stores. And later businesses were prohibited from paying employees' salaries in script or tokens in lieu of legal tender. The legislature also limited the working day for telegraphers to eight hours.

The Robertson Insurance Law, passed in 1907, required all insurance companies operating in Texas to invest at least seventy-five percent of their reserves from premiums paid by Texans in real estate or securities within the state, and required that their securities be deposited in Texas banks. The legislature sought to prevent the flow of capital from the state and also to make sure that the insurance companies were sufficiently solvent to pay claims filed by Texans. The companies argued that Texans investments were uncertain and twenty-one companies decided to cease operations in the state, which probably indicated that they were undercapitalized and uncertain themselves.

The progressive legislature also created a Department of Agriculture and a Department of Insurance and Banking to monitor and report on activities in the state within their respective areas. In 1909 the state required a guaranty system for banks similar to the Federal Deposit Insurance Corporation, but later repealed the system because cautious bankers claimed they were forced to pay for the mistakes of their more reckless colleagues.

Several tax revisions were attempted with uneven success. In 1905, legislation attempted to enforce a more accurate rendition of property; and in 1907, the legislature attempted to bring personal property and corporations under the tax system, but they realized little success.

There were also efforts to bring some reforms to the state prison system. The Texas system consisted of the main unit at Huntsville, several farms, iron smelting plants at Huntsville and Rusk, and two juvenile installations. Convicts were also leased to counties for road maintenance and to others for a variety of purposes. Fees from the leasing system and profits from the farms kept the system solvent, but an investigating committee reported that prisoners were often mistreated by the lessors and often received severe corporal punishment. These disclosures resulted in the Prison Reform Act of 1910. It abolished the leasing of convicts, required the classification and segregation of prisoners, ended the requirement that prisoners wear striped suits, and provided a small wage for labor done by prisoners.

The loss of revenue from the leasing system quickly eliminated the profit the prisons formerly reported and made the penal system dependent on the state legislature. Most legislators talk tough about prisons and the necessity for punishment, but the Texas legislature has usually provided adequate financial support and provided for recreational and educational opportunities for most prisoners in later years. But personal abuse by individual guards and deliberate affronts to authority by some prisoners kept prison life in some turmoil.

Major progressive legislation followed in the administra-

Governor and Mrs. Jim Ferguson with supporters.

— Austin-Travis County Collection

tion of Gov. James E. "Farmer Jim" Ferguson. Ferguson announced his candidacy in 1914. His background was rich in personal experience but poor in political preparation. Ferguson came from Bell County, worked as an itinerant laborer, read for the law, and finally became an established banker and businessman at Temple. He announced for the highest office in Texas without ever having run for or served in any political position before. Ferguson was known as an anti-prohibitionist, but he sensed that the electorate had grown tired of that issue and simply dismissed it by promising to veto any liquor legislation regardless of which side it might favor. This created the perception of neutrality but was actually a strong position in opposition to prohibition.

Ferguson made his principal pitch for votes to farmers. Tenancy had continued to increase in Texas, and had reached the point that two-thirds of the state's farmers tilled someone else's land for a share of the crop. Ferguson sympathized with their plight and with their resentment of the unstable share-system in which shares of the crop fluctuated from year to year. He campaigned hard in rural areas, only ten of his 155 campaign appearances being made in a town or city. He defeated Thomas H. Ball, the candidate of the prohibitionists in the primary, and faced only token opposition in the November election. Ferguson made good on his pledge for a Farmer Tenant Law to fix the share rates at one-quarter for cotton and one-third for other crops; but the law was declared unconstitutional.

Ferguson's efforts proved more successful on other fronts. His administration saw the passage of the Rural High School Law, providing for the consolidation of rural schools and making possible a pooling of resources for improved educational facilities. Compulsory attendance and the movement for free textbooks were also advanced. In 1917, the work of decades by the Texas Good Roads Association and others resulted in the creation of the Texas Highway Department, which eventually provided Texas with one of the best highway systems in the nation.

Ferguson's first administration ended in 1916 amid rumors that he had used state funds for such expenses as his own groceries and other personal expenses, but he managed to gain re-election. Then shortly after he began his second term, Ferguson became involved in an argument that became a vendetta against Robert E. Vinson, the new president of the University of Texas. Ferguson resented criticism from university faculty members and wanted some of them fired. Vinson resisted the governor's attempt at interference with the administration of the school, and Ferguson retaliated by vetoing the legislative appropriation for the university. The board of regents offered to underwrite the entire university budget, and powerful alumni demanded the governor's impeachment. The Travis County grand jury indicted Ferguson on July 21, 1917, for nine separate counts of misuse of state funds, and the speaker of the House of Representatives called the legislature into session to consider impeachment even though he lacked the power to do so.

Ferguson, perhaps hoping to avoid the criminal courts, authorized the session. The trial resulted in exposure of many of Ferguson's tactics, including a $156,000 unpaid loan from liquor interests, bank loans which he used to cover other loans at different banks, state deposits in banks under his control, and improper influence of state officials. Ferguson's conviction on ten of twenty-one charges made him the first, and so far only Texas governor to be impeached and convicted of malfeasance in office. Ferguson resigned one day before the announcement of the verdict, which barred him from seeking elective state office in the future. Lt. Gov. William P. Hobby succeeded Ferguson.

International affairs intruded on the domestic progress in Texas, but even they remained partly of a progressive nature. Texas' first concern after the beginning of the world war in 1914 was for its boundary with Mexico. The Rio Grande border had remained troubled since Texas had joined the American union; then from 1906 until after the American entrance into World War I, the border teemed with successive waves of Mexican revolutionaries, who first overthrew longtime Mexican dictator Porfirio Diaz, then warred among themselves for leadership.

Flores Magon, Gilberto Guerrero, Francisco I. Madero, Bernardo Reyes, Victoriana Huerta, and Venustiano Carranza, each in turn, organized a revolutionary movement to overthrow the previous victor. Usually these movements began from exile in Texas, where plans were laid and arms were obtained to fight in Mexican border towns and ultimately place the new leader in office. Fighting in Juarez naturally concerned

El Pasoans, and the story was repeated in border towns all the way to Brownsville. American military personnel reinforced installations from Fort Brown to Fort Bliss to keep the peace north of the border.

The most unsettling part of the border trouble came with the disclosure of the Zimmerman note, a proposal of the German foreign secretary that should Mexico declare war on the United States, the Germans would see that Texas and other lands that were lost in the Mexican War would be returned to them. This outraged most Texans and made them more anxious for war with Germany.

Raids north of the border by revolutionary leader Poncho Villa, in a blatant attempt to lure American soldiers into Mexico to topple the government for him, brought the U.S. troops. Gen. John J. Pershing mounted an expeditionary force to invade Mexico to capture Villa. Carranza, the Mexican president, welcomed Pershing at first because his regime would be aided by the capture of the rebel; but when the Mexican people showed resentment at this latest American invasion, Carranza threatened war.

Belligerency with Mexico was averted by a declaration of war against Germany by the United States on April 6, 1917, for continued violations of America's neutral rights by the German navy, and the Wilson administration's fear that the British and French were near collapse in Europe. This intelligence came from a variety of sources; but one of the most important of them was E. M. House, who became Wilson's liaison with the leaders of the major powers. House travelled to Europe several times in hopes of mediating the differences, but gradually came to side with the British-French alliance.

Other Texans of prominence during the war included John Nance Garner, chairman of the Ways and Means Committee in the House of Representatives, who paid Wilson weekly visits to help coordinate executive-legislative efforts; Tom Connally, a young Texas congressman for whom Garner wrangled a slot on the Foreign Affairs Committee; and Sam Rayburn, then in his third term in Congress and the sponsor of the War Risk Insurance Act, which provided $10,000 insurance for servicemen.

Texans at home prepared for the war in various ways. The Zimmerman note and Mexican border trouble had already meant a reinforcement of all military installations along the

Texan Lester Miller with airplanes he had flown before World War I. Born on a farm between Greenville and Commerce, he was typical of the state's first pilots.

boundary. Training camps were now located throughout the state, including Camp MacArthur at Waco, Camp Logan at Houston, Camp Bowie at Fort Worth, and Camp Travis at San Antonio. Fort Sam Houston became headquarters for all Texas operations, and Fort Crockett on Galveston Island prepared for coastal defense. On Registration Day, June 5, 1917, more than 400,000 Texans signed up for the draft and eventually 989,751 registered. Nearly 200,000 Texans served in some branch of the service, and 5,147 of them lost their lives, although fully half of the casualties fell victim to disease, especially influenza. Still, 1,200 were killed in action in Europe and nearly 1,500 more died from wounds.

The state government responded to the demands of the war. The State Council of Defense coordinated state efforts, which included the enlargement of the National Guard and the Rangers. It protected the property of servicemen against forced sale for debt, it remitted poll taxes for servicemen, and it promoted patriotism in public schools. Texans bought bonds and savings stamps, cultivated victory gardens, and "Hooverized," that is, went without meat or wheat products or pork on certain days so these products could be used for servicemen or hungry Allies. And, of course, they did without liquor. Sometimes, however, their efforts were negative, as when Germany-Americans were persecuted, sauerkraut was shunned, or Governor Hobby vetoed the appropriation for the German department of the University of Texas.

Perhaps the most colorful aspect of the war in Texas was the work of the Aeronautical Division of the Signal Corps. Benjamin D. Foulois, arriving in San Antonio in 1910 as the first pilot of the division, had — despite a series of mishaps — learned to fly the corps' only airplane. In 1911 he flew the first military mission from Laredo to Eagle Pass, setting a world's record for distance. New airplanes and pilot trainees arrived in 1911. The division then briefly moved to Georgia but returned to Texas in 1913 to establish the San Antonio Aviation Center. Foulois led the First Aero Squadron to assist Pershing in Mexico, then shipped over to Europe with his commander to fly against German pilots.

In 1917 the Aviation Section consisted of only thirty-five officers and few aircraft, but the war increased the numbers of both. Kelly Field — named for George E. M. Kelly, who had died in a training crash in 1911 — was established at San Antonio to train pilots. Later Randolph Field, "The West Point of the Air," opened in 1928 and all American military pilots were trained there until the outbreak of World War II.

E. M. House was still with Wilson at the end of the war. The Fourteen Points, which Wilson presented to the conference at Versailles, bore House's mark, and many believe that the idea for a League of Nations originated with him. House remained in Europe after the signing of the treaty. And after Wilson's remarriage, the two men grew apart.

The war, as wars are wont to do, stimulated Texas industry. The value of manufactured products doubled, and significant increases were noted in cottonseed oil and meal, in manufacturing, and in building materials. The shipbuilding industry also received a boost. The post-war era, though, was a season of strikes, as labor demanded a greater share of the rewards of this industrial development. In 1920 the Galveston longshoremen struck for higher wages and for the privilege of a closed shop. Violence and disorder pushed the legislature to pass the Open Port Law, which made it a violation to interfere with anyone working in the transportation industry. Eventually the law included the rails as well as shipping.

The post-war era likewise witnessed political changes. Hobby filled out Ferguson's second term, then won a term in his own right in 1918. In 1920 Texans elected Pat Morris Neff, a Waco attorney, over Joseph Bailey and three other candidates. Neff, who later served as president of Baylor University, was the first Texas governor to hold a college degree.

The progressive thrust continued in Texas despite the interruption of the war. In education, the value of school property increased dramatically from $9 million in 1900 to over $72 million by 1920. The number of scholastics rose from 708,125 to 1,233,860, and the number of teachers increased from 15,019 to 31,880 in the same period. While state funding increased from $4.50 to $14.50 per pupil, however, Texas remained thirty-ninth in the nation in per capita expenditure.

Elementary education fared better than secondary education. Many people felt that elementary education was sufficient for the publically supported institutions, or else they required the labor of sons and daughters to make a living. The University of Texas led the fight to make high school attendance mandatory and served as a kind of accrediting agency with its admissions policies. The University also founded the Interscholastic League in 1911 for athletic and academic competition to popularize high schools. The rural consolidation law made fewer but better schools available, and free texts made books available to all.

Higher education also received attention. In 1917 the legislature authorized additional teacher preparation schools; and, although the war briefly interrupted the process, by the mid-1920s East Texas, Southwest Texas, North Texas, West Texas, Sul Ross, and Stephen F. Austin colleges, all now universities, began operations. Texas Woman's University, Texas College of Mines (now the University of Texas at El Paso), Texas A&I University, and Texas Tech University were founded to provide schools for women, for West Texas, and for occupational education. In the private sector, the William Marsh Rice Institute, now University, began in Houston in 1912, and the Southern Methodist University was founded in Dallas.

In national politics, the Seventeenth Amendment provided for the direct election of senators, and Senator Morris Sheppard introduced the legislation which became the Eighteenth, or prohibition amendment.

In the 1920s, the Ku Klux Klan became a powerful force in Texas politics. Founded in Georgia in the aftermath of the world war, this secret organization borrowed its name and tactics from the political enforcement organization from the Reconstruction Period. The Klan held anti-Negro racist beliefs, but these were not in the forefront because segregation had come to the nation and to Texas. Blacks caused little social trouble and did not participate in politics heavily in the 1920s. The Klan was also anti-Jewish and anti-Catholic, and anti-foreign in a Know-Nothing way.

Imperial Wizard W. J. Simmons brought the movement to Houston in 1920 to further "one hundred percent Americanism" and to guard the conduct of all citizens. The Klan used secrecy, threats, and actual violence to enforce codes of conduct on all citizens, especially where questions of morality were concerned, often with the assistance of law enforcement officers and other public officials. Sometimes these officials were also members of the Klan. Texas Senator Earle B. Mayfield greatly profited from Klan support, and he is thought by many to have been a Klansman.

Many Texas nights were illuminated by the burning of crosses and made melodic by the singing of "Onward Christian Soldiers" and "The Old Rugged Cross" by these hooded knights who tarred and feathered, whipped, threatened castration, cut hair, and performed other chastisements against those they deemed moral offenders.

At first Governor Neff seemed to tolerate these activities in his anguish over the crime wave in the 1920s, which was mostly brought on by the prohibition violators; yet it was a time of violent criminal activity, with Bonnie Parker, Clyde Barrow, and Raymond Hamilton to name but three of Texas' best-known fugitives, who were robbing banks and performing other acts of violence. This was the age of the automobile, the motel on wheels, which revolutionized morality, especially among the young, as well as aided the escapes of the outlaws. Petting parties, flappers, speakeasies, and the open discussion of sex marked a social revolution which many were not prepared to accept. The Klan seemed a way to restore, or at least preserve, a different way of life. A Texan, the Dallas dentist Hiram W. Evans, eventually became Imperial Wizard of the national Klan organization, which aided the local Klan efforts to control Texas politics.

Mayfield's election in 1922 with Klan assistance produced a reaction. In 1924 Democratic presidential candidates Oscar Underwood and William Gibbs MacAdoo kicked off their campaigns in Texas to oppose the Klan, and seemingly from out of nowhere Mrs. Miriam A. Ferguson, quickly termed "Ma" by combining her initials, announced her candidacy for the governorship as an opponent of the Klan. Jim Ferguson had run for the presidency and for the U.S. Senate in 1920 and 1922, but could not run for state office. So Ma, his wife, ran in his place, boldly claiming that she was a stand-in for him with the oft-repeated line, "A vote for me is a vote for Pa," and pledging that Texans would get two governors for the price of one. She ran second in the first primary, then defeated Felix D. Robertson, the candidate backed by the Klan, in the second primary. The Republicans ran George C. Butte, a University of Texas professor. Butte received nearly 300,000 anti-Ferguson votes in the general election, but Mrs. Ferguson easily defeated him with 400,000 votes.

And Texas got two governors in their bargain. Jim Ferguson established an office in the capitol and made most of the decisions of state, including over 2,000 pardons. The former governor also dispensed contracts for textbooks and road construction as if he were the chief executive. The Fergusons defended their generous pardon policy, significantly increased from fewer than one hundred pardons by Neff, on the grounds of economy, but there is little doubt that cash bought some of the pardons. L. W. Kemp, a Texas Contractor's Association executive, pointed out the relationship between Ferguson and the road contracts. He published his findings in *The Goat Bleats,* a publication so-called because Ferguson had threatened that Kemp would become the goat of the scandal if he revealed it. The Fergusons responded to it with their own publication, *The Ferguson Forum,* which always contained large ads from those wishing a state contact.

The scandals caused Mrs. Ferguson's defeat in 1926 by Attorney General Dan Moody, a true progressive, who persuaded the legislature to undertake a revision of state government. The Highway Department was revised to provide more public participation in contracting methods, and a State Board of Education was created to coordinate state efforts in that field. Moody won re-election in 1928 over a Ferguson-backed candidate, Louis J. Wardlaw. In 1928 the Democrats held their national nominating convention in Houston. Franklin Delano Roosevelt nominated Alfred E. Smith of New York, a Yankee, a wet, and a Catholic. For the first time since Reconstruction, Texans gave their electoral votes to a Republican, Herbert C. Hoover.

The greatest single development in the early twentieth century for the Texas economy — and ultimately for all of the state's activities — came from growth in the oil industry. As early as 1866 Lynn T. Barret had drilled in the first oil well in Texas at Oil Springs, just south of Nacogdoches. Without a market for oil, and having shallow wells with only a ten-barrel per day production, the discovery amounted to little. Others, in Brown County, in 1878 and Bexar County in 1886, had similar fates. But in 1894 at Corsicana, a well drilled for water produced oil in significant volume, and attracted J. S. Cullinan, who founded the first refinery in Texas there to handle the nearly 900,000 barrels a year flowing from nearby fields. Cullinan built a market for his product, demonstrating the use of

Spindletop, the largest single producer in Texas, was brought in January 10, 1901 to inaugurate the Texas oil industry.

Artist's conception of the oil boomtown days of Burkburnett, near Wichita Falls in north central Texas.

oil as a fuel for the railroads and as a dust settler and surface protector for Texas roads.

Then on January 10, 1901, Anton Lucas brought in the Spindletop gusher on a salt dome just south of Beaumont at a site designated and named Gladys City by Patillo Higgins, the prophet of the Texas discoveries. Higgins had predicted that oil would be found there for years and had exhausted all his own funds in an effort to do so. Even Lucas had bargained away most of his interest in the well when it finally blew in as the greatest single producer in Texas history. The well shot oil over 100 feet into the air until it was capped nine days later. By then a lake of oil surrounded the derrick.

Beaumont changed from a city of a few thousand to a bustling, booming town overnight. Rooms rented by the hour to oil men, food prices doubled, then doubled again; excursion trains ran from Houston and New Orleans for tourists to see the sight; and drilling rights ran up to $100,000 per acre for proven areas. Wooden derricks were almost as thick as corn stalks in the Spindletop area, and enterprising boys found empty whiskey bottles to fill from the ditches for sale to tourists for $1 while oil prices dropped to a few cents per barrel at the well head. Within ten years the Spindletop field produced nearly 50 million barrels, then deeper drilling brought out another 20 million barrels in the 1920s, and the field is still in production.

The Guffey Oil Company of Pennsylvania, soon changed to the Gulf Oil Company and established a refinery at nearby Port Arthur to ship the oil; the Texas Fuel Company, now known as Texaco, was founded by Cullinan, James S. Hogg, and J. W. Gates, among others; it also established a refinery. The Magnolia Oil Company, now Mobil, was also established at Beaumont. Other discoveries followed at Sour Lake in 1902, at Batson in 1903, at the Humble field in 1905, and at Goose Creek in 1908. The discoveries spread to the west at Petrolia in 1906, Electra in 1911, Powell in 1906, Burkburnett in 1903, Mexia in 1912, and on and on. Perhaps the best-known oil boom, largely because of a movie named "Boom Town" was the Ranger boom in the early 1920s. Filled with bogus promotions and other wildcat activities, the Ranger boom epitomized all the good and the bad of unrestrained exploitation.

The oil boom spawned related industries. Howard Hughes Sr. bought the rights to a drilling bit invented in Beaumont by a bicycle repairman and made millions selling oil field equipment. The Kirby Lumber Company profited from selling timber to build drilling derricks and plank roads to drilling sites. And a pipeline industry was born to carry the oil from wells to refineries to holding tanks to ships to consumers. All this created a major tax resource for Texans, but they were reluctant to use it for generations. Texas is still one of the few states without a true natural resources extraction tax. But in the property values of refineries and production fields, Texas schools and other public entities have benefited greatly from *ad valorum* taxes.

Perhaps the greatest contribution of oil, other than the obvious benefit of vast new riches, lay in the reaction of Texans to the new-found wealth. Texas became an industrial leader in the nation, and Texans became aware of the new role this created on the national political and economic scene. The "get rich or go broke" syndrome has affected the state's psychology in various ways, but one of the most notable is in its pride, called arrogance by some. With the richest and biggest oil fields joining the nation's cradle of the Cattle Kingdom, Texans looked forward from the 1920s with eagerness, unsuspecting that bust follows boom. But the depression of the 1930s and the renewed international conflict awaited Texans as they did other Americans.

A sewing room in a Texas city, a feature of the Depression days.

— Courtesy Austin-Travis County Collection

11

Depression, War and Readjustment

President Herbert Hoover assumed office in March, 1929, on the crest of the post-war prosperity that pushed up profits and other economic growth indicators in a seemingly endless spiral. But the spiral ended abruptly in October with the crash of the stock market on October 24, Black Thursday, and for the next dozen years America endured its worst economic depression. Many Texas farmers and laborers later claimed that they were unaware that 1929 differed from any other year; agriculture still accounted for nearly seventy percent of the state's investment and employment, and agriculture had been depressed since the end of the war. Yet things got worse for the farmers and laborers in the 1930s.

Probably no single explanation can account for the cause or depth of the depression, but many can be advanced. For too long credit—especially by the purchase of stocks on margin—had been abused by nearly everyone; industry had overexpanded from the war stimulus, and inventory accumulations exceeded the peace-time consumption capacity; low return for farmers and low wages for laborers kept Americans from purchasing consumer items; and technology contributed to increasing unemployment among the unskilled. And, most importantly, an international financial crisis contributed to the fall of America's financial structure.

The obvious signal of the beginning of the depression came with the failure of hundreds of stocks to hold their value in the

October crash. Then hundreds of businesses closed, especially among financial institutions, and later in manufacturing. Farmers could no longer sell their produce to processors and many lost their lands which were mostly mortgaged; and tenants, constituting seventy percent of the Texas agricultural work force, were laid off along with the factory workers. By 1930 the economic wheels of the nation ground to near-stillness, and Texas, because it was not yet heavily industrialized, followed the nation but fared a little better for the first year of the depression.

Soon, 5.4 percent of Texas whites and 8.8 percent of the blacks were on relief; many thousands more were aided by relatives or friends. Armies of Texans joined other Americans in a kind of drifting, hobo odyssey; looking for any kind of work and knocking on the back doors of residences to ask for food became an accepted practice. Cities spouted shanty towns of the unemployed, where the disillusioned and unemployed parodied Hoover's pledge that prosperity lay just around the corner by naming their shanties "Hoovervilles"; newspapers became "Hoover blankets" when used for cover against the night's cold; and jackrabbits and armadillos, depending on the section of the state, became "Hoover hogs."

Hoover was not personally at fault for the depression which came so early in his administration. But he received blame nonetheless, as did Texas Governor Ross Sterling, who had defeated Miriam Ferguson in 1930 by a vote of 473,371 to 384,402 in a runoff after they had survived from a field of eleven candidates in the first primary. Sterling, a successful contractor and co-founder of the Humble Oil Company, agreed with Hoover that direct relief was unwise and that the best way to correct the problems of the state and nation would be to help business. He approached state administration in this fashion, and called for a state bond issue to improve highways without asking the legislature to address the problems of the unemployed.

The most significant program of Sterling's Administration grew from an Austin conference attended by leaders of cotton-producing states that called for state action to limit cotton acreage in hopes of raising prices. Cotton was selling for only 6 cents per pound in 1931; and, although Texas produced over 5 million bales that year, most farmers lost money. The

Texas Legislature responded with the Cotton Acreage Control Law, which limited cotton acreage to thirty percent of any individual's holdings. Other cotton-producing states followed suit, but postponed implementation until at least seventy-five percent of all cotton states had passed similar legislation. Thus, only Texas enforced acreage control prior to the passage of the Agricultural Adjustment Act of the New Deal.

Some Texans favored the law as at least one hope to raise prices, but others pointed out that the law forced them to lay off more tenants. The Texas Court of Civil Appeals declared the law unconstitutional in March of 1932. More tenants left the land for the cities, however, and more farms were lost to debt foreclosure. Conditions for Texas farmers were made even worse by the Dust Bowl conditions, which prevailed during the 1930s as tons of precious Texas topsoil blew away in the winds from drought and decades of ignoring conservation methods.

For East Texans the depression became somewhat more bearable after the discovery of the giant East Texas oil field on October 30, 1930, by Columbus M. "Dad" Joiner, a wildcatter who brought in the Daisy Bradford No. 3 well on a site near Kilgore. Within two months Joiner completed several more wells, confirming a field over forty miles long and from four to eight miles wide. Kilgore's population increased by 5,000 people literally overnight as the unemployed hurried there to find work. Over 1,000 wells were drilled within six months; and in the field's first year, production reached over 100 million barrels and climbed to 200 million barrels by 1933, an amount exceeding the total production of the remainder of the state.

The East Texas field enriched the wildcatters and independent producers, who developed the field in the absence of the major oil companies. The so-called "majors" had stayed away from the field, even after the first discovery wells proved successful, because they had not believed the field would become a significant producer. By the time the truth was learned, the field was tied up by the independents with exclusive leases. While this foresight produced wealth for the hundreds of independent producers, it also denied the more orderly development which the major companies would have brought to the field.

Over-production soon dropped prices from a dollar to ten cents per barrel and jeopardized the stability of other oil investments in the state. Governor Sterling responded to the pleas of a group of oil men for help by requesting that all operators in the East Texas fields voluntarily shut down operations. Some independents swore to keep their wells flowing and to back up their right to do so with weapons if necessary. Sterling proclaimed martial law and maintained order by sending the National Guard under the command of Jacob F. Walters. Considering Sterling's affiliation with Humble Oil and remembering Walter's civilian occupation as an attorney for the Texas Company, East Texans accused both men of shutting down the East Texas fields to protect their own investments elsewhere.

The field re-opened in September with a "daily allowable" of 225 barrels per well, which later was dropped to only 100 barrels per day. Prices rose, but many independents could not resist the temptation to allow their wells to produce "hot oil," or production in excess of the daily allowable, which they marketed at the higher prices. Hot oil production probably surpassed legal production, but it produced little satisfaction for land owners who could never be certain that oil companies were paying a true royalty. Even the producers found that their own men often pumped extra barrels for surreptitious sales of their own. Violence erupted from resentment caused by the distrust, so when the Supreme Court held that Sterling's use of the National Guard had been unconstitutional, the Railroad Commission Chairman, Ernest Thompson, requested the use of Texas Rangers to restore order.

The hot oil also produced many new independent refineries. Nearly ninety skimming units and cracking units were established in East Texas to produce what was called "cheap gas" that was marketed by independent retailers. The major companies responded to the competition by exercising their economic muscle; they began the systematic purchase of independent wells, refineries, and retail outlets, and eventually achieved control of over eighty percent of the East Texas oil business from well to station pump.

If oil helped some Texans get through the Great Depression, others looked to political leaders for relief. Within the state, voters turned Sterling out of office in 1932 in favor of the return of Mrs. Ferguson, and, for the presidency, gave their hearts and votes to Franklin Delano Roosevelt over Herbert Hoover. The national Democrats ran well in Texas because one of their own, Speaker of the House John Nance Garner of Uvalde, accepted Roosevelt's invitation to become his vice president. Garner enjoyed great popularity and power at home, in the Congress, and in the council of the Democratic Party. Many Texans felt that a vigorous campaign might have made him the Democratic nominee instead of Roosevelt, but in 1932 Garner seemed content with his assignment.

Once in office, Garner helped Roosevelt push the New Deal program of relief and recovery through the Congress, including the Emergency Banking Act, the Agricultural Adjustment Act, and the National Recovery Act; much of the New Deal legislation was declared unconstitutional by 1935 by a conservative Supreme Court. Garner was upset when Roosevelt then attempted to "pack the Court," that is, increase the number of justices from nine to fifteen and allow him to appoint a favorable majority. He and other Texans were even more upset in 1940 when Roosevelt announced for a third term. Garner left Washington in disgust in 1941, never to return.

Jesse Jones of Houston also became a powerful force in Roosevelt's New Deal by heading several agencies. He had first joined the Reconstruction Finance Corporation, created during the Hoover administration to extend government loans to businesses to keep them in operation. Roosevelt promoted Jones to the chairmanship of the RFC, later made him Federal Loan Administrator in charge of all Federal loaning agencies, and in 1941 also made him Secretary of Commerce. By holding several offices, Jones became second only to Roosevelt in wielding the New Deal's financial power to effect recovery.

When Roosevelt failed in his bid to restructure the Court, he decided to restructure the New Deal. Already the Emergency Banking Act and the crisis in the nation's financial institutions had produced Federal regulation and assistance for banking institutions through the Federal Deposit Insurance Corporation. It guaranteed deposits in member banks, and permitted only member banks to do business with the Federal Reserve System. Federal examiners closed weak banks and certified strong banks to reopen after a 1933 banking "holiday." Later Roosevelt revamped the Federal Reserve System to give it more regulatory control over the nation's financial security.

Scores of separate laws duplicated the omnibus AAA and NRA in more constitutional ways, and direct relief to unem-

Governor Miriam Amanda J. Ferguson, Texas's only woman governor.

ployed Americans and Texans came in the alphabet soup of the New Deal, the CCC, or Civilian Conservation Corps, which employed and trained young men in conservation projects, the NYA, or National Youth Administration, which kept young people in schools and off the job market, and the P.W.A., or Public Works Administration, the W.P.A., or Works Projects Administration, to construct such public facilities as schools. A Social Security Act, beginning as old age assistance and eventually encompassing survivor's and disability benefits, affected all Texans.

Businessmen often resented such large-scale Federal involvement, at least after their businesses returned to prosperity, but wage earners mostly stuck with Roosevelt until his death in April, 1945. His "fireside chats" on radio held their attention as if he were a savior, and the personal concern he seemed to have for the welfare of ordinary people made many of them lifelong Democrats.

Within the state, Mrs. Ferguson's second administration proved less controversial than her previous term. The liberal pardoning policy returned as an economy measure; it made some sense, for the state operated at a deficit because of lost revenues from the depression. The governor, with her even more influential husband behind her, requested a state sales tax to offset the deficit. But the legislature refused her request, and also denied the recommendation of the Sterling-appointed Woodruff-Graves Committee to reorganize all state commissions, agencies and departments from 129 agencies down to twenty, begging cost as the reason. The legislature did provide for a special $20 million bond issue for relief funds; and it redistricted congressional jurisdiction, it legalized prize fighting and 3.2 percent beer, and it followed the national lead in repealing the Eighteenth Amendment by ratifying the Twenty-first Amendment and repealing statewide prohibition. They decided to return to a system of local option for liquor sales, more or less returning Texas to its pre-prohibition posture, with some counties wet, some dry, and some divided on precinct lines on the issue with seven different options.

In 1934 James V. Allred won election as governor over six other candidates, including his strongest competitor, Tom Hunter. Allred's administration proved one of the most progressive in the state's history. He campaigned for a public utility regulatory commission, a pardons board, and a modern police system. His service as attorney general convinced him that all of these were needed. Allred failed to obtain an increased tax on crude oil because of opposition from producers who had the support of workers who feared that any tampering with oil would ultimately prove harmful to them as well. He did succeed in combining the Rangers — who had fallen into disrepute during Mrs. Ferguson's administration by indiscriminant appointments — with the Highway Patrol into a new Department of Public Safety. The DPS became an efficient, modern police force. He also won an old age assistance package by a constitutional amendment coupled with pertinent legislation.

These measures helped Allred secure a second term in the election of 1936. But in 1938, deficit spending, brought on by the continuing necessity for relief—nearly 200,000 Texans were on direct relief and another 100,000 worked for Federal relief agencies—caused many Texas voters to look for a change. They turned to a radio singer and flour salesman named W. Lee O'Daniel.

O'Daniel arrived in Texas in 1925 from Ohio to work as sales manager for a Fort Worth firm which marketed Hillbilly Flour. He appeared on a radio show each day at noon that attracted a statewide following with hillbilly and "sacred" music performed by O'Daniel and three musicians known as the Light Crust Doughboys. O'Daniel's show became a kind of electronic Poor Richard's Almanac with advice, homilies, and flour commercials. He was known as "Pappy" because the show started each day with "Pass the biscuits, Pappy" as O'Daniel's introduction.

O'Daniel and the Light Crust Doughboys toured the state by bus giving musical shows, which incidentally and perhaps accidentally made him one of the best-known personalities in the state. An admirer mailed O'Daniel a card suggesting he run for governor in 1938. When the performer asked listeners for advice, he received nearly 55,000 requests that he run. He did so, claiming that his platform was the Ten Commandments and the Golden Rule. He continued to tour with the band, giving free shows and passing flour barrels for campaign contributions. O'Daniel's opponents ridiculed his methods without realizing that every nickel in the flour barrel constituted a pledge of a vote. O'Daniel's original objective was doubtless just to sell more flour; it surprised even him, as well as the established politicians, when he won nomination without a runoff and received 95 percent of the vote in the November election.

O'Daniel's tenure as governor was not particularly productive for the state. Characterized by confrontation with the legislature, it ended shortly after the start of his second term when he won a special election to succeed Senator Morris Sheppard. As governor, he advocated a "transaction tax," which was a mask for a simple sales tax. But the legislature opted instead for increased taxes on proven revenue sources, especially on tobacco and natural resources, and a new tax on gasoline and selected business receipts in insurance, telephone, and other utility companies.

O'Daniel was succeeded as governor by Lieutenant Governor Coke R. Stevenson, who served the remainder of the term, then twice won re-election in his own right. Stevenson presided with quiet and conservative tactics over a return of prosperity brought on by World War II; he bragged in future elections that he had directed Texas' finances back into the black. The winds of war, as novelist Herman Wouk termed the Asian and European events of the 1930s, should have warned Americans and Texans of the coming of the war well in advance of the Japanese attack on Pearl Harbor on December 7, 1941, and the German declaration of war a few days later.

Like other Americans, Texans had observed the work of the German and Japanese forces in their respective theaters. They had seen the Roosevelt administration move to help the European allies and the Chinese—often with disapproval. And they had registered for the draft with other Americans after the passage of the Burke-Wadworth Act in 1940. But the Japanese attack caught most people by surprise on a lazy Sunday late in the fall of 1941. Because of his important position on the Senate Foreign Relations Committee, Texas Senator Tom Connally was among the first of those summoned by President Roosevelt to the White House to receive official confirmation of the attack. It was Connally who introduced the resolution for a declaration of war against the Japanese on December 8.

Texas soon became a training center for all branches of the military. The Third Army, which trained from Arizona to Florida, headquartered at San Antonio; later the Fourth Army, which readied men for European action, also headquartered there; and thirteen other Army training bases operated within the state. Texas became the center for all aviation training for the Air Corps with Brooks, Kelly, Randolph and Lackland Fields at San Antonio and at thirty-six other installations located at such cities as Lubbock, Wichita Falls, San Angelo, San Marcos, and Midland. The National headquarters of the Air Force Training Command was even located at Carswell Field near Fort Worth. In addition, the Navy maintained air training facilities at Corpus Christi and Grand Prairie. Two hundred thousand men received flight training in Texas, including 45,000 pilots, along with thousands of bombadiers and navigators. At least a million and a quarter personnel were trained in the state in various services.

Many of these trainees were native Texans. As usual, a greater percentage of Texans than of citizens of any other state served in the military forces. Perhaps as many as three-quarters of a million Texans, including over 12,000 women, served in the Army, Navy, Marines, Air Corps, or Coast Guard. Nearly 8,000 women served in the Women's Army Corps (WACs), and 4,200 served in the Women Accepted for Volunteer Service (WAVES), or the women's division of the Coast Guard or Marines. Texans likewise paid the price of war with high figures among the killed and wounded: 15,764 died in Army service, mostly in combat; 7,258 died while serving in the Navy, Coast Guard or Marines; and the numbers of wounded greatly exceeded these figures. In addition to the thirty-six Congressional Medals of Honor earned by Texans, ten more earned the Navy's Medal of Honor. The most decorated soldier in the United States Army during the war, Audie Murphy, hailed from Farmersville, and the Navy's most decorated serviceman, Samuel D. Dealey, who was killed in action, came from Dallas. One hundred thirty-five Texans achieved the rank of general in the Army, including Dwight D. Eisenhower (born in Denison), who became Supreme Allied Commander in Europe; and twelve Texans advanced to the rank of admiral of the Navy, including the Pacific Fleet Commander, Chester Nimitz of Fredericksburg. Oveta Culp Hobby, second wife of former governor William Hobby, became head of the Women's Army Corps with the rank of colonel.

While Texans fought in all theaters of the war, there were some units that were linked directly to the state. The Thirty-Sixth Division, composed largely of Texans, landed at Salerno,

Italy. The first American troops on the Continent, they fought for 400 days through Italy, France, Germany, and Austria, carrying the Lone Star flag beside Old Glory all the way, and often being called the Texas Army. The Ninetieth Division, the One hundred and Thirtieth Division, the First Cavalry Division and the One Hundred and Twelfth Cavalry Division also contained an inordinate number of Texans.

On the home front, Texans went back to work with the prosperity brought to business by the demands of the war. Aircraft factories at Fort Worth, Garland, and Grand Prairie, and shipyards at Orange, Beaumont, Port Arthur, and Houston, attracted laborers from the farms and smaller towns because of the higher pay they could offer. Some workers were forced to stay in positions designated as crucial to the nation's defense, and they received deferments from military service. Prices, wages, and rents were frozen in Texas, as they were for the remainder of the nation. Texans drew ration stamps for gasoline, sugar, coffee, shoes, and other items, and spent "red points" or tokens to purchase allotments of meat; cigarettes rationed themselves by being in short supply.

Synthetic rubber plants were opened on the coast to provide a usable substitute for rubber from the by-products of the petroleum industry, since the Japanese had cut off the natural rubber supply from plantations in Asia. Munitions plants, such as IDECO in Beaumont, built bomb casings, and the Lone Star installation near Texarkana readied other armaments; a steel mill opened at Daingerfield, and a tin smelter operated at Texas City. Established industries such as petroleum, natural gas, and the East Texas paper and pulp business boomed; they provided employment and contributed to the war effort. Individuals bought savings bonds and stamps, which helped check inflation and made money available for the war effort.

In the absence of silk stockings, ladies painted their legs with a liquid which resembled stockings when it was dry, and little boys more often played "soldier," emulating fathers and older brothers who had gone away to war. The labor shortage put women to work in jobs men would have found difficult to find only two years earlier. They worked in defense plants as riveters, welders, electricians, and mechanics. They also collected scrap metal, paper, and the "tin foil" from cigarette packages for reuse long before recycling became an environmental passion.

Victory gardens sprouted in back yards and vacant lots, and little flags with stars on them appeared in windows to indicate that a man or woman from that household was away in service. Too many of these households received a black bordered telegram from the Army or Navy telling the survivor that their service person would not return.

The increasing urban population with a new mixture of countryfolk of all races in new economic and social relationships sparked different reactions. Some Mexican-Texans benefited from the opportunity to demonstrate their patriotism by military service, and perhaps some blacks enjoyed that opportunity as well. One of the genuine heroes of the Day of Infamy, December 7, was a Waco black named Doris Miller, a ship's steward who manned an anti-aircraft gun and shot down an enemy airplane despite his lack of training with the weapon. For years Miller was denied full recognition for his achievement largely because of race. Racial mixing in several cities with defense plants produced recurrent tension and one spectacular riot in Beaumont in 1943.

Governor Stevenson presided over Texas at war with a dignity which increased his popularity, but others' political affairs proved contentious. O'Daniel weathered a strong race for a full senatorial term against former Governors Allred and Moody, the "Gold Dust Twins" as he called them. When Roosevelt announced for a fourth term in 1944, a group called the Texas Regulars became his strongest opponents. They also formed the nexus of the conservative Democrats who bolted their party in national elections to support Republican candidates Eisenhower and Richard Nixon in later campaigns.

The years of depression and war changed Texas and Texans in almost every way. Dramatic population growth during the century brought Texas to a total of 7,711,194 by the 1950 census, making it the fifth largest population among the then forty-eight states, up from 3,048,710 in 1900. Growth progressed steadily at a rate of approximately twenty percent each decade, but internal fluctuations by category distort this apparent picture of even growth. For instance, while whites and blacks both show an increase in total figures, the whites increased at a greater rate, and their rate of increase greatly

Governor Lee O'Daniel and the some 60,000 Texans who witnessed his inauguration on January 17, 1939.

outdistanced that of such other non-white groups as Chinese, Japanese, and Native Americans. Blacks remained more rural during the war, although many left the state for higher wages and more social acceptance elsewhere.

The foreign-born population also grew, but with unevenness. Mexicans constituted approximately 70 percent of this group, with Germans, Czechs, Anglos, Russians, Austrians, Poles, and a scattering of other nationalities, dividing the remaining 30 percent. Thousands of Mexicans had left their homeland to escape the revolutionary strife during the first two decades of the century and then returned to Mexico during the 1930s when they suffered the loss of economic opportunity, exclusion from Federal relief programs, and an increase in anti-Mexican feeling among Anglo-Texans. The census of 1930, for the first and only time, listed Mexicans as non-whites. The message was clear to most Mexicans. Yet many returned during the war, and additional migrants crossed the border to fill jobs created by war demands. The feelings of difference persisted in many communities, however, and many businesses refused to hire Mexicans so long as others, whites or blacks, could be found to fill the jobs. This has caused many contemporary Texans to assume that such attitudes are long-standing and date from the Alamo and San Jacinto; in fact, significant anti-Mexican prejudice is of relatively recent origin.

More and more Texans moved to towns and cities. In 1900 only 17 percent of the population could be classed as urban; by 1950, 60 percent of the state's citizens lived in towns. In 1900 the largest cities in order were San Antonio, Houston, Dallas, Galveston, Fort Worth, Austin, Waco, El Paso, Laredo, and Denison. By 1950 Houston and Dallas both had passed San Antonio, which ranked third, followed by Fort Worth, Austin, El Paso, Corpus Christi, Beaumont, Waco, and Amarillo. The shift to towns also showed a tendency to the west and to coastal industrial centers.

Industrial growth stimulated by the war also changed earlier economic patterns within the state. In 1930 petroleum refining, lumber, and food processing led Texas businesses. Livestock processing had long been an established business, and the location of meat packing plants at Fort Worth by Armour and Swift, but two of nearly seventy packing plants in the state, marked this industry's growth. Pecan shelling, processing and shipping citrus and truck crops from the valley, and the manufacturing of other food products continued or increased in importance through the post-war years. The end of prohibition restored a thriving brewing industry, especially in San Antonio and Galveston.

But the real industrial story lay in the rise of new industries brought on by the war and the demands of the post-war world. Pulp production in East Texas greatly accelerated with the arrival of Time, Inc., as a major purchaser of processed pine trees. Natural gas, flowing through pipe lines such as the "Big Inch," heated homes and fueled industries as far away as the Atlantic Coast. Machinery, a true legacy of war production, expanded as IDECO converted from bomb shells to oil derricks, and such plants as the Le Tourneau Company at Longview manufactured earth moving equipment instead of war machines. The aircraft industry suffered a loss when the war ended, dropping in employment from 80,000 persons to 5,000, and shipbuilding declined in the same proportion. But the basic plants remained, and, particularly in shipping, awaited the next boom.

The petro-chemical industry, the combining of the organic elements of petroleum with other chemicals, was born of the war and continued to thrive in the post-war era. Texas plants produced nylon, orlon, dacron, tetraethyls, and plastics, such as styrene and polyethylene. The Texas Gulf Coast petro-chemical complex produced as much as 80 percent of the nation's supply of such products by 1950. Texans also worked at the production of aluminum, antimony, and tin, and continued to produce steel at the plant near Daingerfield.

The war accomplished what the New Deal had not — a return of prosperity. The New Deal helped Texans weather the depression with relief employment, but the war brought them jobs and a renewed sense of self-worth; it thrust Texas forward as a major force in both the nation and the world in the post-war era. In the 1930s no Texan could have anticipated the vast changes to be wrought by depression and war, and none could have anticipated in 1946 the very different new world that awaited.

Coke R. Stevenson served as Governor of Texas for five and a half years in the 1940s, leaving office January 1947.

12

Texas in the Post-War World

The news of Franklin Roosevelt's death from a cerebral hemorrhage in April of 1945 numbed Texans as it did other Americans. The man who had attempted to lead the nation out of depression, and had led it during its most severe war since the 1860s, would not be there at the finish, which then seemed so near. Harry S Truman assumed the presidential duties and continued the war to a successful conclusion in Europe in May and in Asia in September, with the assistance of men like Sam Rayburn of Bonham who had become speaker of the House of Representatives. Truman made the decision to use the first atomic bomb against the Japanese cities of Nagasaki and Hiroshima in August, which hastened the end of the war by months, perhaps years, but in so doing changed the world forever. The awful mushroom cloud still threatens annihilation of all humanity.

Texans returned from military service and defense jobs to remake their world. The land had changed, for now oil derricks and manufacturing plants and chemical plants appeared in all sections. But plenty of farm land and trees and coastal sands remained to remind them of the Texas of old. And the political wars were as colorful as ever.

The governor's race in 1946 pitted a preacher-turned-college professor, Homer Price Rainey, against a field of thirteen candidates, including a quiet man named Beauford Jester. Rainey, recently fired from the presidency of the University of

Texas, had gotten into trouble at the University shortly after he became president in 1939 by quarrelling with the board of regents over what he termed interference in such administrative matters as faculty hiring and firing, library holdings, and administration of research funds. The board dismissed Rainey in 1944 and he immediately became a celebrity; he began a radio program which attracted large audiences because of his controversial nature, and in 1946 he sought the governorship as vindication for his stand.

All of his opponents except Jester, a former University of Texas regent, attempted to smear Rainey for his defense of "immorality" at the University. One of them even held campaign rallys "For Men Only" to read lurid passages from books in the University library. By the end of the campaign, Rainey and his opponents had so fouled each other that Jester won easily, billed as the only candidate who could assume the governor's position without "slime and filth" on his hands. He won re-election in 1948, but his race was eclipsed by an even more dramatic U.S. Senate race.

Congressman Lyndon Baines Johnson had challenged W. Lee O'Daniel in 1941 in a special election in the Senate. Johnson campaigned on his closeness to Roosevelt ("He was just like a daddy to me"), and lost by only 1,100 votes. Johnson challenged O'Daniel again in 1948, but this time the race also included Coke Stevenson, the popular figure who had succeeded O'Daniel as governor and performed well for the state during the war. Facing two such formidable figures, O'Daniel abandoned the race.

The contrast between Johnson's and Stevenson's campaigns proved great. Johnson barnstormed in a helicopter, the "Johnson City Windmill," in the first use of such devices in campaigning; he would swoop down on unsuspecting farmers, land in football stadiums and parking lots, and move rapidly from town to town in a rush of energy. Stevenson, on the other hand, moved quietly about the state in his Plymouth station wagon, buying only five gallons of gasoline at a time to allow more stops; he reminded voters that he had "made money" for the state by administering state finance into the black during his term of office. On election eve Johnson's wife Claudia, better known as Lady Bird, mounted a telephone campaign which helped turn the tide for her husband in the closest race in the state's history.

After some confusing initial reports, the final unofficial figures stood at 494,330 for Stevenson and 493,968 for Johnson. But as official returns filtered into the Democratic Execucutive Committee over the next two weeks for the official canvass, Johnson eroded Stevenson's slim lead to take a 494,191 to 494,104 victory, a margin of 87 votes which earned Johnson the name of "Landslide Lyndon" and changed the political history of the nation. Stevenson attempted to block Johnson in the courts, but Supreme Court Justice Hugo Black turned down his appeal on the grounds that a state election in a party primary lay outside the court's jurisdiction.

Johnson assumed office in 1949 and within six years had become the Democratic leader of the Senate. Paired with Rayburn in the House, these two Texans dominated national politics for a decade. In 1948 Harry Truman surprised many by carrying Texas as well as the nation, to win a presidential term of his own. But Truman and the national Democratic leadership had moved away from most conservative Democrats, and the arrival of Allan Shivers as governor clearly established that difference.

Shivers became governor on July 11, 1949, when Beauford Jester suffered a fatal heart attack. Shivers served nearly all of Jester's term, then won election to three more terms on his own right. He presided over a harmonious session of the legislature during his first term, but thereafter confrontation with the national Democratic leadership marked Shiver's career as governor. Ben Ramsay of San Augustine won election as Shiver's lieutenant governor, and he served all three terms with Shivers in that capacity. Together they represented the decidedly conservative nature of state party leadership which remained intact for three decades.

Shivers led the remnants of Texas Regulars in opposition to Truman; they opposed the national administration when scandals over influence peddling in Washington seemed to testify to low morals, they disliked Truman's civil rights policies and his opposition to Senator Joseph McCarthy's anti-Communist campaign, and they especially disliked his veto of legislation which would have confirmed state control of oil exploration and profits in the tidelands. In the early 1950s most Texans, even some who would later have their feet of clay revealed in state scandals, stood for morality in government and resented the "five percenters" in Washington and the gifts of fur coats and deep freezers to government officials. Conservative Texans supported McCarthy's campaign to root out Communists in government, especially in the State Department, although his tactics were ruthless and unfair to those unjustly accused.

Texas Congressman Martin Dies of Lufkin, McCarthy's counterpart in the House of Representatives, chaired the House Un-American Activities Committee to seek out Communists in labor unions, the entertainment industry, and in other fields. The Dies Committee held spectacular hearings where persons suspected of membership in the Communist Party often pleaded the Fifth Amendment against self-incrimination, which alone convinced most Texans of the guilt of such witnesses; to Texans, any real American would be willing to stand up and proclaim his loyalty. So the Texas state legislature required a loyalty oath and a disclaimer of membership in "un-American" organizations of all students in public colleges and state employees had to sign such oaths before receiving paychecks each month. Suspected Communists in labor unions, especially in the oil, chemical, and shipping industries, were denounced.

But the tidelands controversy excited Texans in oil, and eventually those whose only interest was the traditional states' rights issue, more than any other. The issue had been raised in the 1930s when Secretary of Interior Harold Ickes had claimed that the Federal government, not the states, should control mineral exploitation along the nation's shores. Since there was not much drilling activity on the shores then, and because of the interruption of the war, the issue went unresolved until 1947 when the Supreme Court confirmed the Federal position in a case against California.

Shivers and Attorney General Price Daniel of Liberty argued that Texas should be exempt from this ruling because of its unique background as a Republic. The Republic had negotiated itself into the union, unlike California which had been a territory, and had reserved self-determination rights for a distance of three leagues out to sea, or a distance of ten and one-half miles, not the customary three miles. The court did not agree, so the Texans worked to get quit-claim legislation through the Congress.

When Truman vetoed the legislation, Shivers and Daniel declared political war. Shivers, who controlled a major portion of the delegates to the national Democratic Convention in Chicago in 1952, determined to nominate a conservative who would be sympathetic to Texas on the tidelands issue. Liberal Democrats, led by Maury Maverick of San Antonio, attempted to unseat the "Shivercrats," but succeeded only in pledging them to support the nominee, whoever it might be.

Curiously, the Texas Republicans also sent conflicting delegations pledged to Ohio Senator Robert Taft and to General Dwight D. Eisenhower, a native of Denison but a citizen of the world. At that convention, the Eisenhower, or more liberal delegates, won. When the Democrats nominated Illinois Governor Adlai Stevenson, a liberal, the "Shivercrats" followed their leaders and broke the convention pledge. Instead, they bolted the national party to support Eisenhower while voting a straight ticket on state offices. The Republicans responded by not running candidates for governor, attorney general, and several other offices held by Democrats supporting Eisenhower.

So Shivers' main fight for governor came in the primary, where he faced and defeated a liberal named Ralph Yarborough. John Ben Sheppard won the attorney-generalship, while Price Daniel, who had given up on waiting for Shivers to quit being governor, won a seat in the U.S. Senate. In the fall elections, all three ran as the nominee of both parties, and Eisenhower won Texas' electoral votes and the presidency, the first Republican to win either since 1928. Eisenhower repaid the Texans by signing the tidelands quit-claim legislation, which had been pushed through the Congress by Rayburn, Johnson, Daniel, and other Texans. Shivers faced Yarborough again in 1954, and for the first time in his three races he had to go into a runoff, which he won by nearly 100,000 votes.

In local matters, the Jester-Shivers years showed major achievements for Texans, then dissolved in scandal. The Fifty-first legislature, the last to sit during Jester's term, met longer than any previous legislature and passed measures that were significant for years to come. This legislature gave emphasis to sustained growth by passing the state's first $1 billion budget. State hospitals received attention with the creation of a State Board for Texas State Hospitals and Special Schools to oversee the work of regular care, mental treatment, and handi-

Governor Allen Shivers rolls his own at a Stamford rodeo.

— State Archives Photo

capped assistance. Minimal science requirements for medical professionals and the licensing of chiropractors received authorization.

The state prison system also drew significant attention. Despite efforts of administration since the last significant prison reform made during the progressive period, conditions in prisons had become inadequate for the modern period, partially due to overcrowding. This legislature appropriated funds to modernize the prisons, and subsequent legislatures carried the program forward.

Perhaps the legislature's most significant efforts lay in the field of education, and this work carried over into the Shivers administration. A study completed in 1947 revealed a serious need to revamp the state's education system; the study resulted in legislation sponsored by Representative Claude Gilmer and Senator A. M. Aikin. The Gilmer-Aikin Law provided minimum foundation support for teachers' salaries in an effort to increase and equalize pay throughout the state, but it also required that teachers must qualify for salaries and increments based on merit and preparation through a state certification program and the frequent return to colleges for updated training. A state board of education, with one member elected from each congressional district, was created with authority to employ a commissioner to administer the Texas Education Agency, the general supervisory body for all public elementary and secondary education in the state.

Governor Shivers called the legislature into special session in 1950 to find funds to complete the biennium, then called on the next legislature to address the government's need for additional revenue. The legislature responded with additional taxes on natural gas, and increased all other taxes included in the Omnibus Tax of 1941 by ten percent. The first redistricting bill in thirty years was passed by this session of the legislature, giving urban centers more, if still inadequate, representation. During Shivers' third administration, the legislature again raised the tax on gasoline, now dedicated to the highway fund, and increased the "sin" tax on cigarettes and alcohol. It also created a Commission on Higher Education to help mesh the efforts of the state's universities and colleges, and passed extensive regulatory legislation dealing with insurance companies, the first such legislation since the Robertson Insurance Law of the Progressive Era.

The insurance business in Texas operated under loose regulations by the 1950s. The stock and securities legislation which had seemed adequate fifty years earlier had not anticipated the remarkable growth of the state's population or wealth, and subsequent legislatures failed to keep consumer protection legislation adequate to deal with the modern problems. For instance, a company could be capitalized with as little as $25,000 and could issue unlimited stock; so stock sales became the principal income instead of premiums for hundreds of fly-by-night operations. When such companies went out of business, gullible purchasers of their polices or of their valueless stock lost millions of dollars. Over 1,300 companies were chartered in Texas in the early 1950s; and an additional 700 chartered in other states did business here because of the weak regulations and lax enforcement by the state government.

Lieutenant Governor Ben Ramsey called the legislature's attention to the failure each year of scores of these inadequately capitalized and regulated insurance companies. The legislature responded with twenty-two regulatory laws to put the insurance companies back on a sound basis. They created a Board of Insurance Commissioners to regulate companies doing business in the state under the new regulations. They included a minimum requirement of $250,000 for capitalization, the rating of policy premiums, and state checks on the activities, as well as the registration, of agents. The board members began with zeal; they forced some companies into receivership and refused licenses for others; and they inspected all companies so they would be prepared to force others out of business should they fail to follow the laws. Still the bankruptcies continued, and with the failure of the U.S. Trust and Guaranty, and especially the I.C.T. Corporation, a holding company ruled by Ben Jack Cage that controlled seventy-two insurance and finance companies, the state reaped the consequences of long delay in insurance regulation.

When U.S. Trust and Guaranty folded, it was disclosed that the company owed five times as much in claims as it held in reserves, but had been continuing in business anyway, partially through payments to state legislators. The largest scandal came about when Ben Jack Cage absconded to Brazil with most of his company's assets as it went into receivership, costing stockholders and policy owners millions of dollars.

Later it was learned that Insurance Commissioner Garland Smith had accepted expensive vacation trips from insurance companies.

These scandals led the next legislature on a quest to investigate gifts and other illegal activities of state officials, which quickly turned into the state's major scandal of the decade. They discovered a scheme involving the $100 million fund established in 1950 to purchase land for resale at modest rates to veterans, with a five percent down payment and a three percent interest rate with up to forty years to pay. The program was intended as a state supplement to the Federal G.I Bill of Rights benefits. Land Commissioner Bascom Giles administered the fund, with Governor Allen Shivers and Attorney General John Ben Sheppard as the other two members of the Veteran's Land Board. When working properly, the program benefitted thousands of Texas' servicemen who returned from the war.

But crooked promoters found a way to cheat the system by purchasing large tracts of land for resale to the state for the veterans' program. All lands purchased by the state for resale to veterans were to be first examined by the veterans. Then the state was to hire an appraiser to certify the land's value. By requiring all tract sales to come directly to his office, then using selected appraisers, Giles circumvented the checks built into the system and authorized vast sums for the purchase of land of much less market value. Promoters ghosted the veterans' purchases by paying the down payments for them, and the unsuspecting veterans occupied land without realizing that the state had paid too much for it or that their notes would eventually be higher than they realized.

The fraud was first investigated by DeWitt County Attorney Wiley L. Cheatham, who enlisted the Department of Public Safety, State Auditor C. H. Cavness, and eventually Attorney General Sheppard in the investigation. Giles' culpability was substantiated by these investigations and by his unwitted admission in an interview with Kenneth Towery, editor of the *Cuero Record.* Towery won a Pulitzer Prize for his reporting, Giles received concurrent sentences of six years each on ten counts of fraud, John V. Bell, a Congressman and former state Senator, was convicted of receiving illegal fees from the operation, and many others, particularly real estate agents, were either indicted or ruined.

Shivers and Sheppard were soiled by their association with Giles, although their major indiscretion seems to have been their failure to more carefully discharge their responsibility as land board members. Sheppard's cooperation as attorney general had proven essential to the successful completion of the investigation. Neither, however, sought re-election, although both remained active and influential in state affairs.

When Shivers decided not to run for governor in 1956, Price Daniel knew his time had come. But Reuben Senterfitt, Ralph Yarborough, W. Lee O'Daniel, J. Evetts Haley, and J. J. Holmes thought the moment belonged to them. O'Daniel withdrew before the primary, but the others made the campaign interesting. Haley's arch-conservatism, his activities against liberals, and his opposition to racial integration formed one end of the spectrum, and Yarborough's populist liberalism formed the other. Daniel was somewhere in the middle with the most votes, and he won the runoff against Yarborough and the general election against a Republican candidate named William R. Bryant. Few men have assumed the governorship with such thorough preparation.

Daniel revealed at his inauguration that he had taken an official oath of service three times as a member of the legislature, once as Speaker of the House, and once as a serviceman, three times as attorney general of Texas, and once as a member of the U.S. Senate. Daniel had risen to prominence as attorney general by fighting the tidelands battle for the state; then as Senator he had introduced the legislation which Eisenhower eventually signed to quit-claim the tidelands of Texas. Daniel continued in the Shivers tradition by winning re-election in 1958 and 1960, but ultimately made the mistake of seeking an unprecendented fourth term in 1962.

Conservative oilman and rancher William A. Blakly of Dallas temporarily replaced Daniel in the Senate, but Blakly lost a special election the following April to Ralph Yarborough, whom Daniel had defeated for the governorship. Yarborough filled out Daniel's term, then won two of his own, providing an unusually liberal voice for Texas in Washington and securing such significant legislation as the Cold War G.I Bill, the Padre Island National Seashore, and the Big Thicket Biological Preserve.

Governor and Mrs. Price Daniel enter the Governor's mansion, 1957. Daniel later served as U.S. Senator from Texas.

— Courtesy Dallas Morning News

Daniel's administration ferreted out more scandal from previous years. Investigations revealed further malfeasance among lobbyists who were accustomed to giving expensive gifts, meals, and free transportation to members of the legislature. The most infamous case involved Representative James E. Cox, who accepted a $5,000 bribe from Dr. Howard Harmon, president of the Texas Naturophatic Physicians, to kill a bill that would have prevented the practice of naturopathy in Texas. Cox denied accepting the bribe, but Harmon had taped the transaction; Cox then weakly retorted that he had himself been trying to trap the lobbyist.

Daniel weathered a primary challenge in 1958 from W. Lee O'Daniel and San Antonian Henry B. Gonzalez, then faced down the formidable conservative challenger Jack Cox in 1960. Daniel won only after a bitter contest in which each tried to be more conservative than the other; he then easily defeated Republican William M. Steger. But Daniel was not the star of the 1960 race in Texas. Senate Majority leader Lyndon B. Johnson, despite a heart attack suffered in the mid-1950s, decided to enter the race for the presidency, although his position in the Senate was also up that year and a loss for the higher office would force him to leave Washington for the first time since 1938. Johnson solved the problem by getting the legislature to pass a measure enabling him to run for both offices at the same time.

Johnson proved the last principal contender to the candidacy of Massachusetts Senator John F. Kennedy at the Democratic Convention although both were alarmed by a last-ditch effort of supporters of two-time loser Adlai Stevenson. Johnson tried to claim that he was a "westerner" instead of a "southerner" to shed a tarnished civil rights image, but westerners had claimed no president since Herbert Hoover because of the sparce electoral votes in the section.

Kennedy won the nomination on the first ballot, then surprised the world the next day with an invitation that Johnson join the ticket as the vice-presidential nominee. Kennedy's liberal team did not want Johnson, nor did Johnson's Texans want him to join Kennedy. Rayburn and Daniel both opposed the move, and former Vice President John N. Garner reportedly told Johnson over the telephone, "Lyndon, the vice-presidency ain't worth a pitcher of warm spit."

Kennedy wanted Johnson because he judged him to be the

best qualified in the case of unanticipated succession, and because Johnson would add to the ticket's appeal in the south; Johnson wanted the higher office, even at the expense of his greater power as Senate Majority Leader. So "All the Way with LBJ" came to mean the second slot on a ticket which defeated Republicans Richard M. Nixon and Henry Cabot Lodge. Johnson also won the Senate race he had simultaneously run against Republican challenger John G. Tower, a political science instructor at Midwestern University. Governor Daniel appointed Blakly as interim Senator again, and in a special election in 1961 which saw over seventy candidates file in the no-runoff, winner-take-all election, Tower won. He was reelected in 1966, 1972, and 1978, partially because the Democrats ran me-too conservatives who simply could not be more conservative than Tower, and partially because of his novelty as the first Republican senator since Reconstruction, but mostly because he campaigns hard, keeps good contacts in the state, and has risen high in national Republican councils.

When Daniel tried for a fourth term in 1962, he was defeated in the primary by the Johnson protegé John Bowden Connally, a wealthy Floresville and Austin attorney for oil man Sid Richardson who had served as Secretary of the Navy in the Kennedy administration until resigning to run for governor of Texas. Connally also defeated right-wing former General Edward A. Walker, Marshall Formby from West Texas, and the crusading former Attorney General Will Wilson. Connally then defeated Jack Cox, who had turned Republican, in the November election, and like Shivers and Daniel, served three terms before deciding not to run again in 1968.

The most significant legislation to come from the last Daniel administration was the sales tax, which Connally continued and increased. First suggested in modern times by Mrs. Ferguson and advocated by O'Daniel, this regressive tax is often touted as the only "fair" tax since all pay it to the degree that they make purchases within the state. But since it is not structured on ability to pay, and ignores the amount of money left to the purchaser after the tax is paid, liberals regard it as an anathema. Even Daniel, a conservative, disliked the tax and disliked even more being the governor who had to pass on it, so he allowed it to become law without his signature. The state sales tax began modestly as a two percent levy with generous exclusions for food and medicines, but under Connally it was increased to four percent and cities were given the option of adding an additional one percent for local revenue. Liberals and conservatives agree that the sales tax has provided the state with sufficient revenue for expanded state activities, preventing the state government from engaging in deficit spending, which is prohibited by the Constitution. For these reasons, the sales tax is counted as a benefit.

Texan Lyndon B. Johnson flew to Washington on the evening of November 22, 1963, as president of the United States. He had begun the day as vice president on a tour of the state with President Kennedy, who had come to Texas with an eye on the 1964 election in a pre-campaign trip, hoping to heal a breach between Johnson and Yarborough Democratic forces. Both men were on the tour, although they did not ride together in parades at San Antonio, Houston, or Fort Worth. At each stop Mrs. Kennedy had been presented with a bouquet of red roses as a gesture of friendship.

On November 22 the President was to speak at the World Trade Mart in Dallas just after noon, and he had proceeded there from the airport in a motorcade that moved down Elm Street past the Texas School Book Depository Building, then approached a railroad underpass before moving along a freeway to the Trade Mart. Many had feared an untoward incident in conservative Dallas, where the Vice President and Mrs. Johnson had received rough treatment earlier and U.N. Ambassador Adlai Stevenson had been struck with a sign by a demonstrator. None could have anticipated the tragedy that awaited at the triple underpass by the School Book Depository, or the undeserved national blame that would be focused on Dallas and all of Texas after the events of that afternoon.

The day had gone well, however, and the city's streets were lined with well-wishers. At half past noon as the President's motorcade approached the underpass, shots were fired. Some thought they came from the underpass or from a "grassy knoll," the slope of the underpass. Later, the Warren Commission, the government's blue-ribbon investigating commission, said that all came from the Depository and had all been fired by Lee Harvey Oswald, a former Marine and a Communist defector to Russia. Oswald had returned, worked for the Free Cuba Committee, and was then living in Irving with his Russian-born wife. Oswald was captured in the Texas Theatre soon after shooting police officer J. D. Tippit and held in the Dallas Police Headquarters.

The bullet which struck Kennedy passed through his body and gravely wounded Governor Connally, who was riding in the jump seat ahead of the President. Both men slumped into the arms of their wives as the limousine sped to Parkland Hospital. Johnson's car followed immediately and he was protected by Secret Service men in a nearby trauma room while doctors worked on the slain President. When the "bag man," the agent with defense secrets who always remains with the president, moved from Trauma Room One to Johnson's room, the awesome power of the American presidency walked with him.

Johnson hurried to Air Force One where he took another oath of office, and returned to Washington with the former President's body for a weekend of anguish which gripped the entire nation.

While being taken to the Dallas County Courthouse on Sunday morning following the shooting, Oswald was slain while national television cameras focused on the back of Jack Ruby as he shot the accussed assassin in the stomach. Oswald died, still denying that he had harmed anyone. Ruby, in turn, died of cancer before his sentence of execution could be fulfilled. The nation was denied a trial and perhaps the truth about the tragedy, and left to speculation and suspicion. Because it had happened in Texas, the new president's home state, and in Dallas, a conservative city not noted for its past support of Kennedy, both received unjustified criticism.

Johnson quickly became a powerful president. In Kennedy's memory, Johnson secured passage of important civil rights legislation and economic measures which Kennedy had been denied by a seemingly blocked Congress, and went on to defeat Republican Barry Goldwater in 1964 for his own term in a way that made "Landslide Lyndon" only a stale joke. Johnson's War on Poverty brought the VISTA program and the JOB Corps to Texas, along with countless other liberal programs not appreciated by Texas conservatives. But problems with the continuing war in Viet Nam caused him to decide not to run for re-election in 1968. In that year, Democrat Hubert H. Humphrey narrowly won Texas but lost the presidency to Republican Richard M. Nixon, who returned to carry the state in 1972.

Lyndon B. Johnson is sworn in as President in 1963 aboard Air Force One at Dallas by U.S. District Judge Sarah T. Hughes as Mrs. Johnson and Mrs. John F. Kennedy look on.

In domestic affairs, Connally put together a program which caused moderate and conservative forces alike to call him the greatest governor in the state's history. He pushed through a major legislative program with new coordinating agencies for state and local governments, revised the welfare program and higher education, created the Coordinating Board to oversee the universities to avoid duplication and to found more institutions, and generally gave the state a good, businessman's administration. The Supreme Court declared the state poll tax unconstitutional during Connally's administration, and under his direction the legislature created a new system of annual voter registration. He appointed more blacks to state offices than any previous governor.

When Connally decided not to seek re-election in 1968, his lieutenant governor, Preston Smith, a movie theatre operator from Lubbock (Smith was essentially colorless and inarticulate, but at the same time he could be an endearing man), demonstrated that political astuteness could emerge in unsuspected places. For years he had patiently cultivated voters throughout the state, so now he moved easily into the governor's office; young Ben Barnes became lieutenant governor, and many predicted that he would soon be governor. Gus Mutscher ruled in the House of Representatives. Together these three ran the state until scandal brought them down.

Smith secured an impressive package from the legislature, including increased aid for vocational education, two new medical schools—including one for Texas Tech in his home town—and reduction of the voting age to eighteen. He also worked to improve the state's water supplies, especially for thirsty West Texas, and endorsed a minimum wage.

Smith won a second term over Republican Paul Eggers in 1970 in a race that witnessed the fall of Ralph Yarborough to Houston businessman Lloyd Bentsen, a moderate Democrat. Eggers' 47 percent of the vote indicated growing strength among Republicans, and Yarborough's loss similarly indicated the growing strength of conservatives within the Democratic party.

Shortly into Smith's second term, Texans were shaken by the disclosure of the "Sharpstown" scandal. Speaker Mutscher and two of his aides were accused by the Federal Securities and Exchange Commission of participating in a scheme to

Governor William Clements, the first Republican governor of Texas since Reconstruction.

let Houston banker Frank Sharp evade regulations by the use of new state laws. Mutscher and others, including Smith, profited significantly from stock purchases which were manipulated by Sharp to insure a profit as a payoff. When SEC investigators tried to interview Smith, he entered an Austin hospital, according to critics to avoid the interrogation. When the scandal was finally unraveled, Smith was saved because he had vetoed the legislation Mutscher was accused of passing for Sharp's benefit. Mutscher and his two aides were later convicted and removed from office; much of the credit for opposing Mutscher went to the efforts of a determined group of Representatives, some liberal, some conservative, and many in between, called the "Dirty Thirty."

Perhaps the most significant member of this group was Frances "Sissy" Farenthold, who ran against Smith in 1972 for the governorship. Other Democratic candidates included Dolph Briscoe and Ben Barnes. Smith and Barnes were both tainted by the scandals of the previous administration, although not made legally culpable in the Sharpstown prosecutions, and "Sissy" was too liberal and perhaps too feminine for Texas voters. Texans had accepted "Ma" Ferguson as a stand-in for Jim Ferguson, but Mrs. Farenthold would have been her own governor. So Texans turned to the quiet Dolph Briscoe.

Briscoe served a two-year term, then won election to the state's first four-year term in 1974 after a constitutional amendment increased the terms of several state offices. "No New Taxes" became his constant theme, although this translated into "No New" or sometimes "No Continued State Services." Many liberals claimed that Briscoe, who was often absent from the capitol, was the only man in the state who made Smith seem active and articulate. However, Briscoe did not please Republicans either: Henry Grover ran him the closest race that any Republican had run since the 1890s. If the new La Raza Unida candidate, Ramsey Muniz, had received more that six percent of the vote, Grover might have been the first Republican governor since Davis. Instead, that distinction fell to William Clements in 1978.

The Briscoe administration did witness an attempt to revise the state constitution, the longest and most amended in the nation. Led by Speaker Price Daniel, Jr., the legislature formed itself as a constitutional convention in January 1974, then argued for five months and spent well over a million dollars, finally producing an eleven article constitution that they refused even to submit to the electorate. It contained many items inappropriate to a constitution, and resembled, as one said, a camel assembled by a committee that was trying to put together a horse. In 1975 eight proposed amendments encompassing most of the attempted revision were submitted to the people's vote and all eight were defeated.

The success of the Republicans at the national level in 1972 paralleled the growth of the party in Texas. The Watergate fiasco of President Nixon and the loss of Gerald R. Ford to Jimmie Earle Carter in 1976 could not stop them. In 1978, William Clements, president of an oil field equipment corporation named SEDCO, defeated longtime Republican stalwart Ray Hutchinson in the party primary and went on to defeat Attorney General John Hill, who had won the Democratic primary over Briscoe. Disgruntled conservative Democrats, led by the Briscoe family, deserted their party to support Clements who spent over $7 million, largely on a media campaign to gain name recognition. He hammered home the line that Texans were tired of liberalism at the national and state levels, tired of regulations that interferred with business, and especially tired of Democrats.

Clements was aided by a light turnout at the polls, by a letdown among Hill's workers, especially in large cities, and by a general acceptance of his hard-hitting, direct, plain-spoken statements. Hill did not lose the election — Clements won it — and the Republican cause benefited as members of the party entered the legislature, the congress, and many local offices on the rising crest of a wave that elected Ronald Reagan and adopted-Texan George Bush to the presidency and vice-presidency in 1980. And Clements helped deliver Texas into their electoral column.

Clement's control of the state, and especially of the legislature, became as complete as any of his recent predecessors', including Connally's. Connally lost some of his luster in Texas by joining the Nixon cabinet, renouncing the Democratic party, and above all by losing early in the Republican primaries in 1980.

Clements made good on his pledge to the voters to provide a business climate for the state, and gained popular support for his tough stand against rulings by Federal District Judge William Wayne Justice concerning prison conditions and schooling for alien children. But his tough remarks were abrasive to many, and his policy of appointing as many Republicans as possible to state offices, even though many were as conservative as Clements, offended Democrats, who were accustomed to dominating such selections.

Many Texans felt that Clements would win a second term, but in 1982 he fell to the Democratic challenger, Attorney General Mark White. White, who had survived a primary fight against Railroad Commissioner Buddy Temple and Land Commissioner Bob Armstrong, defeated Clements in an election which surprised everyone except White. Utility regulation emerged as the major issue of the campaign, but more than anything else the Democratic Party got back together to oust the state's only Republican governor since redemption. Led by Agriculture Commissioner candidate Jim Hightower and State Treasurer candidate Ann Richards, with the more conservative Mark White heading the ticket, the Democrats managed to pull together for the first time in decades in a state-wide election.

The Sixty-eighth legislature convened in early January, 1983, with many problems to solve, including rising unemployment in a state which Clements had boasted was recession-proof, the need for a comprehensive water plan, reduced state revenues, rising utility and service costs, and uncertainty about the future. A fire in the Senate wing apartment of Lieutenant Governor William P. Hobby, Jr., cost one life and did damage which required millions of dollars to repair, with needed modernization for the capitol. Texans, and their legislature, had just cause to feel apprehensive about the future, but perhaps they should not do so. After all, one capitol burned down and a better one replaced it. Recessions, wars, strife, all visited Texas before, too. But the land remains, always, and so do the people. With such resources, how can Texas or Texans fail to endure?

Johnson Space Center, Houston.

13

Texas Today

Texas. Land. The two words seem to have had the same meaning for so long. Then the people came, and the rivers became political boundaries and transportation arteries, and needed bridging; Texas skies rumbled with sonic booms and glistened with reflected sunlight on aluminum mechanical birds, and sometimes glowed in hues of red and orange from top soil loosened by plows, blowing in the wind. Great cities grew from the stimulus of cattle, crops, and oil, and the words of men on deeds and documents made the land and its produce private and precious, and Texas no longer was only land. Then, although the land remained—drier and scarcer in places from plowing and planting and pumping, and cut into parcels by ribbons of asphalt and barbed wire, and salted with schemes of dreamers and watered with the sweat of laborers—then Texas became people.

For over four centuries invaders changed the land and created a state, a state of the Union and a state of condition and a state of mind. From beginnings with only a few Indians 450 years ago, Texans numbered 14,228,383 on Census Day, April 1, 1980, and will grow to more than 16 million before long. It seems that most Texans operate cars on Houston or Dallas freeways on any given afternoon. The 1980 population total is just over 3 million greater than the previous census figure, representing a 27 percent increase, with a density of 54.3 persons per square mile, an increase from 24.9 persons fifty years ago and 6.1 persons per square mile a century ago.

Texas' population growth between the last two censuses

San Antonio skyline showing Tower of the Americas.

— Courtesy San Antonio Convention and Visitors Bureau

exceeded the national average of 11 percent, with only California growing at a faster pace. Moreover, the population growth is spread more evenly now over the entire state; 210 counties reported gains in 1980, despite the fact that the most significant growth occurred in counties with the largest cities. Harris County increased by 668,000 persons, Dallas County by 229,000, and Bexar, Tarrant, Travis, El Paso, and Hidalgo each had increases exceeding 100,000 persons. Harris County alone accounted for 22 percent of the state's population increase. A total of 11,389,384 persons, greater than the state's total population only ten years ago, lived in the twenty-six designated urban areas and comprised better than 80 percent of all Texans in 1980. Houston ranked fifth among the nation's cities, Dallas ranked seventh, and San Antonio was eleventh. For the first time in four decades, though, the rural areas also reported increases.

Other demographic changes included continued increases in female preponderence, with females outnumbering men by 232,000. Texans have also become older: the median age of all Texans jumped from 18.7 years in 1900 to 28.2 years in 1980. The number of Texans younger than fifteen years increased only 6 percent in the last decade, while persons over sixty-five increased by 38 percent; one of every ten Texans is in the older group. The population is cosmopolitan, representing nearly every ethnic background in the world. Among the major groups, Anglos, or all whites excluding Hispanics, comprise 66 percent, Hispanics 21 percent, and blacks 12 percent. Texas ranks third among the nation's states in black population and second in the number of Hispanics.

Texas' twenty-six Standard Metropolitan Statistical Areas constitute the largest number for any state. The Houston area SMSA enjoyed a 29.2 percent growth in the last decade and closed the gap between the Bayou City metropolitan area and the data of the state leader, the Fort Worth-Dallas SMSA. The Dallas city growth rate was much lower at only 7 percent, but Metroplex suburban areas of Arlington and Garland increased by 77.5 percent and 70.5 percent, respectively.

This phenomenal population growth is aided by some natural increase of births over deaths, but it is due mostly to a massive "frost-belt" out-migration to "Sun-belt" states, especially during the recent years of economic reversal in the automobile and steel industries. Whole industries, such as Ameri-

Dallas skyline and convention center.

Casa Manana, "Theatre in the Round," Fort Worth.

can Airlines, have relocated their central offices from New York to Dallas, or from Chicago to Houston, seeking the better business climate they perceive in Texas. Texas has labor, right-to-work legal provisions, adequte if dwindling water supplies, and a boomer spirit long gone from many other markets.

Even if the state's oil production has declined to one billion barrels per year, the industry still employes over 400,000 persons in a direct way to produce, refine, and distribute petroleum; its spirit dominates the optimistic business attitude so prevalent in Texas' two major cities as well as in a host of lesser urban clusters. No one can remember a time when some massive, downtown building was not under construction in either Houston or Dallas, sights long gone from most eastern and northern cities.

Texans still go to church, although recreational activities on hundreds of lakes and the seashore lure many to a weekend worship of nature. "Blue laws" prohibit the sale of forty-two classes of items on Sunday, but not beer. Baptists, with nearly 2 million church members, lead in numbers, followed closely by the Roman Catholics and United Methodists, and trailed by members of the Churches of Christ, the Presbyterians, the Protestant Episcopalians, and the Lutherans and a host of other saints who total at least half the state's population.

Schools are adequate but not exceptional: teacher pay still lags behind that of two-thirds of the other states, and per capita expenditures for scholastics generate pride among some Texans if it edges out Arkansas and Mississippi, hardly the natural competitors for the nation's third largest and richest state. Texas has over 150 institutions of higher education, including universities, colleges, community colleges and vocational centers. These range from the 45,000-plus student body of the University of Texas at Austin to denominational colleges of fewer than 1,000 students.

Texans, like other Americans, are joiners. Fewer of them now enroll in the historic male lodges — the Freemasons, the Odd Fellows, or the Woodmen — but Rotary, Kiwanis, Lions, Optimists, Business and Professional Women, Pilot, and dozens of other clubs, many with auxiliary and juvenile counterparts, count millions of Texans in their numbers. Professional and business associations, which have some social functions, double as lobbies in legislative years. Veterans' groups ranging from the American Legion to the Veterans of World War I gather to remember and promote the causes and government benefits. Hundreds of associations and societies testify to Texans' desire for "in-group" status, including genealogists, numismatists, philatelists, history buffs, and cattlemen, to name five of hundreds that meet monthly, yearly, or anytime, to associate with their own kind.

Modern Texas can best be viewed in its parts rather than the whole, for gone are the days when sweeping generalities could accurately portray so vast a population so fragmented by different origins. Bob Akres, former editor of *The Beaumont Enterprise,* wrote a daily column called "Waiting for a Train," meaning the musings of his mind as he waited for one of the omnipresent freight trains which criss-crossed his town on five separate lines. Victor Fain does the same now in *The Daily Sentinel* with a column called "Dots and Dashes"; Hubert Mewhinney, Lynn Ashby, Paul Crume, and Felix McKnight have provided the same service for Houston and Dallas readers.

So let us be done with statistics and go back to the land and the real people who live on it, to see that Texas is . . . the National Aeronautics and Space Administration headquartered near Houston, which has mesmerized millions the world over by directing the flights of Mercury, Gemini, Apollo, and the shuttle and proud that the first word spoken on the moon was "Houston . . ."; Texas is . . . Neiman's, every Texan's favorite store, both for what it is and for what he imagines it to be, for most Texans can't afford to do much of their basic shopping there but still enjoy strolling through and wishing; Texas is . . . oil, drilled for, pumped, refined, and occasionally spilled, as when the Pemex well gushed into the green Gulf of Mexico and fouled Texas beaches; Texas is . . . the awesome spread of Dallas-Fort Worth Airport, DFW on the claim check, that looks like many terminals from the air and mystifies with an efficiency that is as good as most of the nation's other and much smaller terminals.

Texas is . . . *Texas Monthly* and the *Texas Observer*, one slick and one pulp and both twitting the pompous, one full of ads and one nearly devoid of them, but both eagerly awaited and devoured by the faithful; Texas is . . . country music from Bob Wills and his western swing to Ernest Tubb's monotone so reflective of grass-roots Texans, to Gilley's and the mechanical bull and longnecks, and to Willie and Waylon and Luckenbach. Although some of the "country" folks look more like the hippies of the 1960s than the star-spangled Nashville country singers, they drew Texans into the Armadillo World Headquarters in Austin while it functioned and to the Rio Palm Isle in Longview and hundreds of other watering holes from honky-tonks to class gigs.

Texas is . . . flying high in the sky with American out of Dallas, or with Texas International, long since shedding its TTA (Tree Top Airline to the wags), to fly the world, as Continental or with Southwestern, which sells Love in hotpants.

Texas is . . . classical performers such as Van Cliburn, who practiced in Kilgore until appreciated in Moscow, and the less classical but — many think — still classic Janis Joplin, who wailed in Port Arthur long before she wooed urban microphones with Southern Comfort and a cracked voice; Texas is . . . Madalyn Murray O'Hair, high priestess of atheism, attempting to debate Rev. W. A. Criswell, pastor of Dallas' First Baptist Church, the largest of his denomination, and neither making much headway with the beliefs of the other; Texas is . . . rock-and-roll, 1950s variety, when a Rolling Stone still gathered no moss, with Buddy Holley of Lubbock still learning the value of bass strings and J. P. Richardson of Beaumont, who masqueraded as the "Big Bopper," until premature death silenced both talents; Texas is . . . The Galleria in Houston or NorthPark in Dallas or just plain ole' Joske's in San Antonio, shopping in covered surroundings and hearing fifteen languages from other shoppers.

Texas is . . . perhaps most of all to many, FOOTBALL, including the over twenty professional players that have been produced in Beaumont with many of them sharing a common grandparent; it is football from the Southwest Conference, to the Lone Star Conference, to the Houston "Earlers" (as some have called Bud Adams' team in the Bayou City after the incomparable Earl Campbell of Tyler), to America's Team, the one with the prettiest cheerleaders, the smartest coach, the cagiest scouting and drafting system, the shrewdest general manager, and the quietest owner, a team of Cowboys made of Landry, Brandt, Schramn, and Murchison, and forty-five practically interchangeable parts that have made the NFL playoffs

Music and dance performances on the River Walk, San Antonio.

— Courtesy San Antonio Convention and Visitor's Bureau

The Rose Garden at Tyler.

Major League Football comes to Texas. The Houston Oilers in action.

— Courtesy the Houston Chamber of Commerce

annually as long as even Howard Cosell can remember; Texas is . . . Don Meredith, pride of Mount Vernon, having the temerity to sing on national television most Monday nights during the fall season; Texas is . . . the Astros, namers of a new synthetic turf and the Eighth Wonder of the World, but never quite able to get past the Dodgers, and it's the Rangers who wish they could get as far as the Astros; Texas is . . . The Mavericks and the Rockets and the Spurs and even the Toronado, some throwing and some kicking a round ball.

Texas is . . . wetbacks — now more politely called undocumented workers — flooding into East Texas as well as the rest of the state to take jobs others will not do; Texas is . . . women meeting in a world conference in Houston to denounce male chauvinism or meeting on Main Street and waiting for their men to open their car door; Texas is . . . Porferio Salinas painting a field of bluebonnets, or Jose Cisneros drawing a conquistador; Texas is . . . "snowbirds" flocking to the warmer climate and new jobs, swelling the cities, and changing Michigan license plates for stickers made in Texas and turning in their one-way U-Haul trailers; Texas is . . . the Aggie joke, our version of ethnic humor without the ethnic butt, just Aggies, who work just as well (Did you hear about the WATTS number for an Aggie joke? Just dial AGGIE IQ - then watch your pigeon try to find the Q on Ma Bell's magic wheel).

Texas is . . . still the Alamo, shrine of Texas' past, the only defeat ever turned into a magnificent victory by retelling the story, standing in the shadow of the Tower of the Americas, Governor Connally's monument in San Antonio, and Reunion Tower in Dallas, a monument named for a socialist experiment in the most unlikely place in the world; Texas is . . . "Dallas" and J. R. and all the rest of the hot-blooded Ewing clan which helps confirm what much of the rest of the country has thought about Texans for a hundred years and what Texans have thought about themselves even longer, for in their souls, many recognize a little of J. R. or Sue Ellen in their friends.

Texas is . . . the Tall Oaks such as Sam Rayburn, Albert Thomas, Olin Teague, Wright Patman, and Barbara Jordan, and a few who might make it — Jim Wright and Jake Pickle — and the Tallest of Them All, Lyndon Baines Johnson, the Texas Conservative-national Liberal who ended up with both sides against him, who always omitted the "d" in Pedernales, but who knew the Potomac's ways when it came to people, who pressed the flesh with the best and the worst, working for himself, working for others, and remembering an under-nourished Mexican student in San Marcos when he declared War on Poverty in Washington City thirty-odd years later.

Texas is . . . well . . . Texas IS. Texas cannot be boxed, gift wrapped, microwaved, or dehydrated. Texas was, is, and will be, too big and too diverse for all the invaders from Paleo-Americans to Spaniards to Anglos to Michiganers to completely change. Like the face of the moon its NASA-based astronauts visited, it is pitted from the impact of numberless hordes. All have changed Texas, altered it, left some mark of their passing. But Texas survives, it endures, and if it never quite achieves its potential, because of self-denial more than anything else, Texas always IS.

Visitors Center at the Lyndon B. Johnson State Park in the Texas Hill Country.
— Courtesy Texas Tourist Development Agency

The Battleship Texas at permanent anchor near the San Jacinto Battleground near Houston.
— Courtesy Texas Tourist Development Agency

INDEX